THE BOOKS THAT
DEFINE IRELAND

THE BOOKS THAT DEFINE IRELAND

BRYAN FANNING AND TOM GARVIN

MERRION

First published in 2014 by Merrion
an imprint of Irish Academic Press

8 Chapel Lane
Sallins
Co. Kildare

© 2014 Bryan Fanning and Tom Garvin

British Library Cataloguing in Publication Data
An entry can be found on request

978-1-908928-44-3 (cloth)
978-1-908928-52-8 (paper)
978-1-908928-45-0 (e-book)

Library of Congress Cataloging in Publication Data.
An entry can be found on request

Printed in Ireland by SPRINT-print Ltd

Contents

1

Irish Arguments

Londoner Dr Samuel Johnson famously remarked that the Irish were a fair people: they never spoke well of each other. This was echoed by Dubliner George Bernard Shaw's remark, 'If an Irishman were roasting on a spit, one could always find another one to turn it.' Whatever the fairness of these adages, it is the case that the Irish seem to be addicted to long and occasionally endless argument, without being quite aware that the arguments have long ceased to be new; they are rediscovered as if for the first time in generation after generation. Much of this long conversation has been heavily infested by the *argumentum ad hominem*. Examples of such long-running arguments have been: the question of who is and who is not Irish? Could a viable Irish nation consist only of the Protestants loyal to the Crown? (This question changed over time to a more dangerous one: Geoffrey Keating's 1634 question as to whether Protestants had any place at all in the Irish nation.) Should Ireland stay in union with Britain or have recourse to foreign aid from a great power of some sort outside these islands? Should Ireland be freed by constitutional action or through revolutionary insurrection?

Should the Irish speak English, Irish or both? Should Ireland be ruled as a unit, or as two states? Who should rule Ireland: an upper caste or aristocracy of a particular religion, a clerisy of priests, or those individuals elected by the general population from among themselves? Should Ireland have a king, and if so, should that king be Stuart or Hanoverian? If not, should it be a republic, and what kind of republic should it be? Should the Irish be encouraged to get rich, or should they live in frugal comfort combined with a virtuous poverty? Should the Irish be prevented from losing their innocence, or allowed to see the world's seamy side freely? Should the Irish be given that dangerous thing, an education, or should they be kept in a useful ignorance? Should they be educated or just trained? Should Irish sexuality be controlled and repressed by the Church or the State? Or the question posed by Jonathan Swift: Must the miserable condition of Ireland and the corruption of Ireland's government always be mentioned in the same breath?

This book is by way of an experiment, for which neither author can find a convincing precedent in this country. Each of us trawled through the historical and social literature of the island of the last three centuries to come up with books which seemed to have had an impact on Irish opinion, have defined or best exemplified long-running debates, or have been under-appreciated in terms of their significance. An example of the latter is Brian Merriman's 1780 Irish-language poem *The Midnight Court*, which satirises the reluctance of Irish men to get married early. This poem crops up over the centuries and several times in the book in discussions of social class, cultural revival and issues of sexuality.

Both of us are historically-minded social scientists, one in political science and the other in social policy. Neither of us are graduate students of literary criticism, and our selection inevitably will reflect that fact. Some might argue that in the much-tilled field of Irish Studies, not having such a qualification is a distinct advantage. The few works of fiction we include are chosen for the social and political arguments they provoked at the time of publication or later rather than for their place in some or other canon of Irish literature. The twenty-nine chapters each deal with one or two books which symbolise or clearly state a point of view that is shared by many and disagreed with by many others at the time of writing and commonly for many years afterwards. Other works that address the same issue are dealt with as well. In all, over fifty books scattered over three centuries are touched on or discussed at length.

Geoffrey Keating's 1634 appeal for the creation of a united Irish Catholic nation has echoed down the centuries. He couples that plea with a wonderful and half-mythological account of the allegedly world-famous rise of the Gaelic nation in Ireland since the time of Patrick. A few decades later, William Molyneux made an argument in favour of parliamentary autonomy for a *Protestant* Irish nation at the end of the seventeenth century, a few years after Aughrim's Great Disaster of 1691 which resulted in the expulsion from Ireland of the Catholic ruling class and the taking of the entire island by a new property-owning class of Protestant faith. Swift's mordant satire on the corruption and tyranny of British rule in Ireland a generation later concludes that the Irish might as well eat their own young; they would be better off if they did. His *Modest Proposal* (1729) and his pamphlets of the same decade have found an Irish audience in every generation since. The Catholic Church reorganised itself after the great defeat of the Jacobite cause with priests trained in Europe and with penny catechisms that enabled its doctrines to be widely taught in the eighteenth century, despite a hostile government in London and Dublin. Wolfe Tone, the famous rebel leader of the bloody 1798 rising, reveals a very whiggish political vision of a free Ireland where only the well-to-do of all religions had the franchise. Presumably he would have approved of Daniel O'Connell's acceptance of the disenfranchisement of the Forty-Shilling Freeholders in 1829 in return for Catholic Emancipation. O'Connell understood that in an open-vote election, poor men did not have a truly free vote. In his *Jail Journal* (1861) and other writings John Mitchel influentially denounced O'Connell's constitutionalism and his championing of English liberalism.

A prominent debate on the possible cultural and political sources of Irish poverty and backwardness was started at the beginning of the twentieth century by two well-known protagonists, Horace Plunkett and Father Michael O'Riordan; Protestant squaring off against Catholic as usual in what became a notorious and fascinating duel. James Connolly's *Labour in Irish History* (1910) owed as much to Mitchel as to Karl Marx. Connolly championed the same romantic nationalists – Tone, Mitchel and Fintan Lalor – that Patrick Pearse also included in his 'new testament' of Irish nationalism. The themes of many of Canon Sheehan's novels, including his last, *The Graves at Kilmorna* (1913), were the search for virtue and holiness in a fallen world and heroic martyrdom in the sacred cause of the Irish nation. Patrick Pearse's world view appears in many ways to echo the views of this forgotten bestseller-writing priest.

Daniel Corkery's *The Hidden Ireland* (1924), arguing for an Irish cultural revival based on the Gaelic tradition of Munster in the eighteenth century, became almost official dogma after 1924, and led to impassioned debate among Irish writers and academics for decades afterwards, including Sean O'Faoláin and Frank O'Connor, Corkery's rebellious students. P.S. O'Hegarty's *Victory of Sinn Fein* of the same year was possibly the first eye-witness account of the tragic treaty split in the Sinn Fein leadership with descriptions of the personalities of the leaders of both sides. His argument has been wrangled over ever since, often by protagonists who have never heard of his book.

The non-fiction fruits of the romantic 'Celtic Twilight' included a remarkable series of autobiographical works in Irish (*The Islandman*, *Twenty Years A-Growing*) which emanated from the Great Blasket Island in the 1920s and 1930s. The community was dying and knew it; the islanders wished to be remembered as they had been in their prime. In *Guests of the Nation* (1931) O'Connor established himself as the foremost Irish short story writer of his generation, signalling his rejection of violence in pursuit of political goals and tacitly rejecting Corkery's worldview. In 1938, O'Faoláin's *King of the Beggars* rehabilitated the Great Dan after two generations of Mitchelite vilification. Flann O'Brien's satiric works of 1939–1945 (*At Swim-two-Birds, An Béal Bocht, The Third Policeman*) echoed the Blasket school to great comic effect and also satirised the Gaelic revival's often absurd posturings.

Fr James Kavanagh's manual of social ethics of 1954 set out the official familial and Thomistic line espoused by the Catholic Church in Ireland at that time. It depicted Church dominance of public morality, education and even sociology as part of a God-given natural order. In the same year, Paul Blanshard's *The Irish and Catholic Power* set out a damning critique of the effects of such power upon Irish society. Blanshard's polemic was unpalatable even to liberal Catholics, a much intimidated and rather small group of people at that time. However, Blanshard's critique of Church authoritarianism and of a public morality obsessed with sex yet soft on financial dishonesty prefigured later debates.

Michael Sheehy's *Divided We Stand* of 1955 started a debate about the partition of Ireland that is also still going on, and was echoed and expanded by Conor Cruise O'Brien in his *States of Ireland* of 1972. It was raised again from a very different point of view by A.T.Q. Stewart's *The Narrow Ground* of 1977, a book that has had a deep influence behind the scenes on late twentieth-century Irish political thought. Both O'Brien and Stewart challenged anti-partitionist perspectives that had predominated in the twenty-six counties for three-quarters of a century after independence. These are exemplified here by Todd Andrews's 1979 memoir and its sequel, among other things a behind-the-scenes account of how a single generation of post-revolutionary republican Catholic leaders under de Valera ran the country for several decades until they became a gerontocracy.

Philip Larkin famously wrote in his poem *Annus Mirabilis* that 'Sexual Intercourse Began/ In Nineteen Sixty-Three/ (which was rather late for me) – /Between the end of the Chatterley ban/ And the Beatles' first LP'. If Larkin had been Irish he might have instead bookended the arrival of sex as a topic for public argument as occurring between the publication of Edna O'Brien's *The Country Girls* (1960) and John McGahern's *The Dark* (1965). O'Brien owed and acknowledged a two-century-old literary debt to fellow East Clare writer Brian Merriman in *The Country Girls*. McGahern's *The Dark* depicted child sexual abuse, the savage beating of young children and the troubled sexuality of a priest; themes that struggled for attention for a few more decades before official Ireland professed to be shocked and set up its tribunals of inquiry. *The Dark* was, of course, banned and its author was fired from his teaching job by the Catholic Church.

Many of the big Irish arguments of recent decades have, yet again, concerned unfinished business with the past. The gradual healing of the scars left on the Irish imagination by the catastrophe of 1845–47 made Cecil Woodham-Smith's seminal *The Great Hunger* (1962) very well timed. By the 1960s, the Irish could read about the Famine relatively calmly and see it as being at least in part a natural disaster. Nell McCafferty's excoriating exposé of Irish official attitudes toward sexuality, *A Woman to Blame* (1985), marked the beginning of a reckoning with the authoritarian consequences of Catholic public morality. Noel Browne's autobiographical account of the Mother and Child crisis of 1951 was part of this new Zeitgeist. It had a huge impact in 1986, and was for years the record-holder for Irish book sales. Fintan O'Toole's 1995 study of the conspiracy between the leaders of Fianna Fáil and the crooks who ran so much of the Irish beef export trade concluded prophetically that not only had the Catholic Church lost all credibility in Ireland, but also that this unhappy fate had been shared by Fianna Fáil. Four years later Mary Raftery and Eoin O'Sullivan's *Suffer the Little Children*, in company with many other horrendous memoirs and studies, lifted the lid on the Irish Catholic Gulag for children and emphasised how authoritarianism and the lack of institutional accountability buttressed each other in the making of both clerical and political corruption scandals. The latter got its first major academic study in 2012 in the form of Elaine Byrne's *Political Corruption in Ireland*, complementing recent work by O'Toole and many others.

Finally, a word on how this book was written. As social scientists, we have argued about the merits of these books and many others for many years. Our debates sent us back to reread the books examined in this volume and many others besides. Overlapping interests in the social and political condition of Ireland gave us common ground and grounds for argument. Each of the chapters that follows has been designated an individual author. Often we agreed but sometimes agreed to disagree. How else could a book by two authors about Irish arguments come into being?

2

Geoffrey Keating, *The History of Ireland/Foras
Feasa ar Éirinn* (1634)

Geoffrey Keating was born in South Tipperary, south-west of Mallow, around 1580, of 'Old English' (*Sean-Ghaill*) or Anglo-Norman stock. He presumably grew up well aware of the near-genocide that had occurred in Desmond (South Munster) some decades before his birth, and knew also of the Nine Years War that was going on in Ulster in the last decade of Elizabeth's reign. Not much is known of his personality or private life other than what is offered the reader by his written work. As Bernadette Cunningham remarks in her wonderful study *The World of Geoffrey Keating*, 'The real Geoffrey Keating is more elusive than Shakespeare. No manuscript in his hand has been identified and none of his contemporaries mentions having met him.'[1] He seems to have come from a comfortable landed family in the barony of Iffa and Offa and was educated at a local school of poetry specialising in Irish and Latin manuscripts. He studied theology in France (Rheims and Bordeaux) as was the custom for Catholic seminarians of that time and later was ordained to the priesthood. He returned to Ireland around 1610. He died no later than 1644.[2]

Writing extensively in Irish, his first work was *Eochair-Sgiath an Aifrinn* (The Key Shield of the Mass), a defence of the Catholic Mass. He became well known in the south of Ireland as a preacher, and eventually published the background material to his sermons as *Trí Bior-Ghaoithe an Bháis* (The Three Spears of Death) around 1631. However, he is best remembered for his four-volume history of Ireland, *Foras Feasa ar Éirinn* (Compendium of Knowledge about Ireland) published in 1634 (hereafter referred to as *FFE*). This work continues to be valued not only for being a compendium of Irish history, pseudo-history and mythology but also for being the first major historical work to be written in modern Irish. It is still quite accessible to anyone reasonably familiar with the modern version of the language and able to deal with the old spelling which was to be replaced eventually by a more streamlined official standard in the 1950s.[3] Keating was evidently competent in Old and Middle Irish as well as Latin and his book became the major conduit by which versions of old tales and the common mediaeval version of the history of the Irish race was passed on to an increasingly literate and English-speaking country.

Inevitably, *FFE* was appropriated for political purposes unimagined by Keating in his historical era, and was to become material for unionist and nationalist self-justifications in the eighteenth century and after. Keating was commonly titled 'the Irish Herodotus'. Herodotus was, of course, the early fifth-century Greek writer who was famous for his extraordinary blending of myth, unverifiable if entertaining anecdotes and genuine historical information. However, Herodotus was traditionally known to the Greeks not only as being the Father of History but also as the Father of Lies. It was the Greek historian's fate to be contrasted tacitly with the evidence-based scientific approach represented by his successor Thucydides in his extraordinary eye-witness analysis of the Peloponnesian War (432–404 BC). This is not to suggest that Keating was the Irish equivalent of either Greek figure because he had a healthy scepticism about many of the accounts and fables which he presented to the reader combined with an unquestioning acceptance of writings which he held to be divine Revelation. To be fair, he tended to distance himself from the more outlandish anecdotes and narratives which the traditional lore offered him.

An ambivalent contemporary recommendation of Keating to the historian Luke Wadding by a Church of Ireland bishop (John Roche) displayed scepticism of Popish pleadings:

> One Doctor Keating laboureth much in compiling Irish notes towards a history in Irish. The man is very studious, and yet I fear that if his work ever come to light it will need an amendment of ill-warranted narrations; he could help you to many curiosities of which you can make better use than himself. I have no interest in the man, for I never saw him, for he dwelleth in Munster.[4]

In the early seventeenth century, Catholicism in Ireland was a reluctantly tolerated religion, keeping its head down and defending itself in whispers rather than in bellicose sermons. Corish describes it accurately as becoming increasingly 'hidden' in the period between 1700 and 1800.[5] The Flight of the Earls and the beginning of the Ulster plantations in the first decade of the seventeenth century symbolised the slow approach of a new, putatively Protestant order in Ireland. Keating's book, which is a claim for the essentially authentic character of a *Catholic* Irish nation going back to the fifth century and with links to a semi-imaginary but very noble pagan prehistory, was, by the standards of the time and place, unusually self-assertive. The complete breakdown of the Catholic and Jacobite cause lay two generations in the future, after Aughrim's Great Disaster of 1691.

FFE begins with a long and polemical introduction (*díonbhrollach*) which denounces various English, Welsh and Anglo-Irish (Palesman) historical writers who, in Keating's view, betrayed their noble academic calling by libelling the Irish, an ancient and noble people who had been the founders of a great and early civilisation on the island of Ireland, later extended to North Britain in the form of the Kingdom of Scotland or, in Irish, Alba ('Albion', or the Gaels' share of Great Britain, Albion being the White Island as seen from France). The argument was that the Irish were learned and that their monks had reintroduced learning and writing into western Europe, including Britain, after the barbarisation of the continent in the aftermath of the fall of the Western Empire in the fifth century. Not only were the ancient Irish very learned, they were also brave, and they had at one stage allegedly invaded Britain under a King Dáithí and got as far as the Alps before going home in triumph, their king having unfortunately got himself killed. Almost certainly, this is a mediaeval fable. The first paragraph of the book sets out his purpose clearly:

Whosoever proposes to trace and follow up the ancient history and origin of any country ought to determine on setting down plainly the method which reveals most clearly the truth of the state of the country, and the condition of the people who inhabit it: and forasmuch as I have undertaken to investigate the groundwork of Irish historical knowledge, I have thought at the outset of deploring some part of her affliction and of her unequal contest; especially the unfairness which continues to be practised on her inhabitants, alike the old foreigners who are in possession more than four hundred years from the Norman invasion down, as well as the native Irish who have had possession during almost three thousand years. For there is no historian of all those who have written on Ireland from that epoch that has not continuously sought to cast reproach and blame both on the old foreign settlers and on the native Irish.[6]

These allegedly malicious and uninformed writers are accused by Keating of not acknowledging the favourable characteristics of Irish people: their evident bravery, their religious piety, their generosity to the church, their ancient respect for learning and, unlike some of their twentieth-century descendants, their humane treatment of orphans. The writers are accused of ignoring the extraordinary hospitality of the Irish shown to foreigners in their midst and of paying no attention to the literary assemblies of the Irish, institutions unique in Europe. They concentrate on the poor and marginalised among the Irish, thus dismissing the great and the good among the gentry of Ireland; unlike other nations, the Irish are to be characterised by these mainly English or Welsh writers by the features of the deprived and depraved rather than by the virtues of the noble and high-born among them. Keating again demonstrates to his own satisfaction the valour of the Irish by pointing to the great wall the Romans felt forced to build against the allied tribes of the Irish and their Gaelic-speaking colonists in North Britain, the Scots, who were in turn allied with the non-Gaelic Picts. Strabo, an ancient writer, imagined that the Irish were cannibals, but there is only one instance of cannibalism mentioned in the Irish annals, and this was seen as so abnormal as to get special mention.[7] Camden claimed there were no bees in Ireland, a ridiculous proposition remarks Keating, easily refuted by casual observation. Here there may be some echo through mistranslation of the well-known fact that there were, and still are, no snakes in the island. St Patrick is traditionally supposed to have banished snakes from Ireland. Giraldus Cambrensis has a celebrated book chapter, one sentence long, which is entitled 'Snakes in Ireland'. The sentence announces that there are no snakes in Ireland.

Cambrensis, who wrote a celebrated and comically hostile anatomy of Ireland, comes in for special mention by Keating. 'Gerald of Wales' alleged that Ireland paid tribute to King Arthur of Caerleon, an absurd story, refuted by Cambrensis himself later in his own work, when he observes that 'From the first, Ireland has remained free from the invasion of any foreign nation.' Even the Romans decided not to meddle with the Irish, and Ireland was a refuge for many who wished to flee from tyrannical Roman rule. This seems to be a remote echo of Agricola's characterisation (in Tacitus' *Agricola*) of a first-century independent Ireland living in a notorious freedom and being a provocation to rebellious elements among the British tribes in the time of the Western Empire. Keating twits Spenser's fraudulent attempts to interpret surnames which are evidently Gaelic or gaelicised Viking as being in reality derived from ordinary English surnames. Here he is attacking a common English and Scottish tendency to describe the Irish as degenerate English and Scots, rather than constituting an historically distinct cultural entity. He rebukes Palesman historian Richard Stanihurst for his apparent hatred of his own countrymen, presumably an emotion often fuelled in invaders by mingled subconscious guilt and fear of vengeance being wreaked on the English lands in the Pale of Dublin by a revived and vengeful Gaelic Ireland. That alternative Ireland was seen as roosting in the hills of Wicklow and looking down hungrily on the fair pastures of Dublin.

> From the worthlessness of the testimony Stanihurst gives concerning the Irish, I consider he should be rejected as a witness, because it was purposely at the instigation of a party who were hostile to the Irish that he wrote contemptuously of them; and, I think, that hatred of the Irish must be the first dug he drew after his first going into England to study, and that it lay as a weight on his stomach till, having returned to Ireland, he ejected it by his writing. I deem it no small token of the aversion he had for the Irish, that he finds fault with the colonists of the English province [in Ireland] for that they did not banish the Gaelic [language] from the country at the time when they routed the people who were dwelling in the land before them. He also

says, however excellent the Gaelic language may be, that whoever smacks thereof, would likewise savour of the ill manners of the folk whose language it is. What is to be understood from this, but that Stanihurst had so great a hatred for the Irish, that he deemed it an evil that it was a Christian-like conquest the Gaill had achieved over Ireland and the Gael, and not a pagan conquest.[8]

Here can be seen a major theme of *FFE*. The Norman incursion into Ireland in 1169 and afterwards is seen as a benign event, one which laid the foundation for a joint Hiberno-English nation in Ireland, united in loyalty to the Catholic faith and acceptant of the union with England under the (Catholic) crown of England, seen as the legitimate successor to the High-Kings of Ireland. There seems to be a tacit paralleling of the 1169 event with the legendary Milesian incursion of a millennium earlier, seen as equally benign. This Christian conquest by the Normans is unconvincingly described as peaceful and involving settling mainly on unoccupied land. It is explicitly contrasted with 'pagan' invasions by the English which happened later, after the death of King John in 1215 and which did indeed involve the illegitimate stealing of the lands and properties of the Gaelic nobility and gentry by incomers. It also involved criminal assault on the sacred lands of the Church by these hypocritical marauders, pretending to be civilising the Irish and bringing them back into the fold of a true and civil Christianity:

> The Irish were at length enraged by these unsupportable [thirteenth century] oppressions, for when they observed that the English, instead of propagating the religion of Christ, and reforming the rugged manners of the people, had nothing in view but plunder and booty, and that churches and monasteries were not exempt from their covetous and sacrilegious

attempts, they formed a design to free themselves from such merciless auxiliaries, and to drive them out of the island. For this purpose the principle of the Irish nobility applied themselves to O'Connor Maoinmuighe, king of Conacht, and offered to raise him to the sovereignty of the island, if he would but assist to expel these foreigners, and restore liberty to his country. The first who made these proposals to the king of Conacht was Daniel O'Bryen, king of Limerick, who was followed in the same generous design by Roger, son of Dunsleibhe, king of Ulster, Daniel Mac Carty, king of Desmond, Maolseachluin Beag, king of Meath, and by O'Rourke, king of O'Broin and O'Conmaine. But before any resolutions were formed upon this scheme, O'Connor, king of Conacht was unfortunately killed by an accident …'[9]

This kind of denunciation particularly applied to the recent transfer of lands from Catholic to Protestant hands, a process he saw already happening in the early seventeenth century. Obviously, he did not live to see the wholesale transfer of nearly the entire island of Ireland and the expulsion of its entire Catholic ruling class that occurred later in the seventeenth century and early eighteenth, but his words were prescient. Furthermore, they helped to delegitimise the seventeenth-century land grab and keep the memory of it fresh in Irish people's minds for over two centuries.

Keating had mediaeval standards of evidence. There is a wonderful attempt in the book to explain how it was that so much was known about the history of Ireland before the deluge since presumably everyone in Ireland was drowned, like nearly everything on the planet. He does distance himself from the account he gives, suggesting somewhat desperately that perhaps, being pagans, the scribes were informed by demons, or perhaps it was all written down in stone somewhere. Elsewhere he suggests that a few people survived despite not being on the Ark.[10] He also mentions tentatively the legend of Tuan mac Cairell but does not relate it. Tuan, a son of a sixth-century king of Ulster, was represented in the mythology as a very long-lived antediluvian shape-changer who survived the inundation by turning into a fish which is later caught, fed to a princess to whom he is reborn and eventually grows up to tell the tale of Parthelon and company from personal memory.[11]

The main body of the book is a classic example of mediaeval macro-history. The Old Testament is accepted unquestioningly as an historical account, derived from Revelation, of the history of mankind since Adam and Eve, seen as living some six millennia earlier, and separated from us by the great deluge that flooded the entire planet some five thousand years previously. The Irish are claimed to be descended mainly from Scythia, seen as the source of the population of ancient Palestine and Judea, with a later admixture coming from Spain into Ireland led by Galamh, or *Míl Easpáine*, *Miles Hispaniae* or Soldier of Spain. Oddly enough, modern DNA testing confirms the existence of North Spanish ancestry among the modern population of Ireland, most of the Irish being now seen as descended from near Eastern migrants through Europe to these Islands. Possibly the prehistoric Spanish immigrants were blown in on ships by the prevailing westerly winds. Alternatively, it has been suggested speculatively by modern Celtic scholars that the Milesian legend echoes a faint memory of Roman *foederati* or barbarian allied troops coming into Ireland with Roman soldiering experience to set themselves up for life somewhere far away from the continent's wars.

Besides the Bible, a major source of the book is the *Lebor Gabala* (*Leabhar Ghabhála* or Book of Invasions), a mythical history of Ireland put together between the sixth and twelfth centuries. It was designed in part to devise a fictional noble ancestry for the O'Neill dynasty so as to strengthen its claims to the High-Kingship of Ireland. Other sources included *Acallam na Senórach*

(Conversations of the Ancients), *Cogadh Gael re Gallaibh* (The Wars of the Irish and the Vikings), Cambrensis' *Expugnatio Hiberniae* (Conquest of Ireland), *Flaithusa Eireann* (Regnal Lists of Ireland) and *Saltair Chaisil* (Psalter of Cashel) together with an impressive list of manuscript books in Irish, English and Latin held at that time in various monasteries and great houses around Ireland. The narrative includes a boiled-down version of the narrative of the *Táin Bó Chualnge* (Cattle Raid of Cooley) with its legendary war by the Men of Ireland on the men of Ulster and the heroic defence of Ulster by the solar hero Cú Chulain ('The Hound of Culain'). It also covers the colonisation of western Scotland, and an almost endless listing of raids, battles, duels between champions and, eventually, the coming of Patrick in the fifth century, seen as the crucial event in Irish history. This rather contrasts with the modern nationalist view, which tends to see the Viking and Norman invasions as the crucial and disastrous main set of events. Keating argues for an Irish identity which includes all Christians loyal to the Roman faith and which explicitly excludes the recent *Nua-Ghaill* who happen to be mainly Protestant and therefore imperfectly Christian and almost pagan. They are also, of course, rather low-class folk.

The book circulated far and wide in manuscript in the seventeenth century, and was translated in full or in summary several times into English in its first two centuries.[12] However, it was only at the beginning of the twentieth century that the full Irish and English texts were published in parallel translation. English-language versions were available by the early eighteenth century, most conspicuously represented by Dermod O'Connor's *Keating's General History of Ireland*, first published in 1723, reprinted many times and read widely by the emergent nationalist movement's adherents in the nineteenth century with James Duffy's Dublin reprints being much favoured. John O'Mahony, the famous Fenian leader, also tried his hand at a translation, published in New York in 1857.

FFE was used as a source by many later historical and pseudo-historical works, in particular by Roderick O'Flaherty's *Ogygia*, a

17

moderate and respectful history of Ireland, derived in great part from Keating. It dealt with events down to the eleventh century and was published originally in Latin in 1685. The book celebrates the long and learned intellectual tradition of the Celtic Irish, seen as one of the most ancient nations of the earth and one of the most distinguished. Hely's English translation of *Ogygia* appeared in the early eighteenth century, and it was reprinted many times.[13] Like *FFE*, it became grist to the nationalists' mill in the following centuries.

Brendan Bradshaw, in a brilliant essay, has described Keating's book as being, in effect, a rallying cry to a nascent Irish Catholic nation by providing it with an origin myth of benign and peaceful incursions into Ireland later betrayed by an illegitimate stealing of the land and polity of Ireland in Keating's own century.[14] It could be counter-argued that Keating was also the innocent legitimator of a definition of the Irish nation that excluded all non-Catholics from potential membership of that nation. Certainly, as Marc Caball has argued, he was Irish Catholicism's leading intellectual, historian and poet of the seventeenth century.[15] His poetry is still remembered, the most well-known being perhaps Patrick Pearse's favourite, *A Bhean lán de Stuaim* (O woman of great subtlety).

Right up to the present, Keating's best-known book has lived on, partly because it was the first major book to be 'published' in the modern Irish language and partly because it is a genuine source for mediaeval Irish writing, most of which is linguistically inaccessible to most modern Irish readers and some of which is no longer extant, having not survived the wars and destruction of the seventeenth-century 'Taking of Ireland' or the burning out of the Great Houses and their libraries by the anti-Treaty IRA in 1922–23. It was a standard text for undergraduates taking Irish language courses in Irish universities throughout the twentieth century. Keating's influence has been extraordinarily persistent and wide. Eamon de Valera, for example, used Keating as late as 1947 as a source of abuse of his political opponents. Referring specifically to Oliver Flanagan, he compared the deputy to a mud-loving insect documented by Keating.[16] To an unknowable extent, *FFE* has been the direct or indirect source of a kind of folklore that was once familiar to most Irish children. For better or worse, that particular folklore has now faded out. Much of the pseudo-history of traditionalist outfits like the IRA is directly or indirectly inspired by Geoffrey Keating.

TG

Notes

1 Bernadette Cunningham, *The World of Geoffrey Keating* (Dublin: Four Courts, 2000), p.xiii.

2 Bernadette Cunningham, 'Keating, Geoffrey', *Dictionary of Irish Biography* (Cambridge and Dublin: Cambridge University Press and Royal Irish Academy, 2009), vol. 5, pp.42–4.

3 Geoffrey Keating/Seathrún Céitinn, *The History of Ireland/Foras Feasa ar Éirinn*, translation by David Comyn and Patrick S. Dineen (London: The Irish Texts Society, David Nutt, 4 vols, 1902–1914), written MS circa 1634.

4 Patrick J. Corish, *The Catholic Community in the Seventeenth and Eighteenth Centuries* (Dublin: Helicon, 1981), p.41.

5 Ibid., pp.2–3.

6 See Keating, *The History of Ireland/Foras Feasa ar Éirinn*, trans. David Comyn, vol. I, p.3. The two populations are normally referred to by Keating as *Sean-Ghaill* and *Gaeil*. The spelling has been modernised.

7 Ibid., pp.10–11.

8 Ibid., pp.36–7.

9 Dermod O'Connor, *Keating's General History of Ireland: Translated from the original Irish, with many curious amendments taken from the Psalters of Tara and Cashel & c.* (Dublin: James Duffy, 1865), p.545.

10 See Keating, *The History of Ireland / Foras Feasa ar Éirinn*, pp.151–5.

11 Cf. for example Robin Flower, *The Irish Tradition* [1947] (Dublin: Lilliput, 1994), pp.14–15.

12 See Raymond Gillespie, *Reading Ireland* (Manchester: University Press, 2005), p.14 for MS distribution of *FFE*.

13 See Cunningham, *The World of Geoffrey Keating*, pp.204–5. My own edition of O'Flaherty (Hely's translation) dates from 1793, and my O'Connor version of *FFE* is James Duffy, undated but probably 1860s.

14 Brendan Bradshaw, 'Reading Seathrún Céitinn's Foras Feasa ar Éirinn', in Pádraig O Riain (ed.), *Geoffrey Keating's Foras Feasa ar Éirinn: Reassessments* (Dublin: Irish Texts Society, 1986), pp.1–18.

15 Marc Caball, 'Patriotism, Culture and Identity: the Poetry of Keating', in Pádraig O Riain (ed.), *Geoffrey Keating's Foras Feasa ar Éirinn: Reassessments* (London: 1986), pp.19–39.

16 Elaine A. Byrne, *Political Corruption in Ireland 1922–2010*, (Manchester: Manchester University Press, 2012), p.56.

3

William Molyneux, *The Case of Ireland's being bound by Acts of Parliament in England, Stated* (1698)

'Spirit of Swift, Spirit of Molyneux,' Henry Grattan famously declared, 'Your genius has prevailed! Ireland is now a nation!' He was referring to the establishment in 1782 of the independent Irish Ascendency Parliament that lasted until the Act of Union in 1801. Jonathan Swift is remembered, as he was in Grattan's time, as the presiding genius of eighteenth-century Ireland. William Molyneux (1656–1658), no less important in Grattan's eyes, has since been forgotten. Molyneux was toasted by Grattan for his 1698 pamphlet, *The Case of Ireland's being bound by Acts of Parliament in England, Stated*, which made a constitutional case for the re-establishment of an autonomous Irish Parliament, something Ireland did not have since the enactment of Poynings' Law in 1492.[1] The specific case for Irish parliamentary autonomy advanced by Molyneux was built upon ideas that really only entered the domain of mainstream political argument several decades later. During the eighteenth century *The Case of Ireland* came to be cited by Swift, Charles Lucas, Grattan and even Wolfe Tone. Rising interest in Molyneux over time and the trajectory of Protestant patriotic politics coincided with the rising influence of Locke, particularly in America, whose own case for independence from England came to influence late eighteenth-century politics in Ireland.

In 1682, through Molyneux's influence, Locke's *Essay on Human Understanding* became part of the curriculum at Trinity College Dublin. However, it was not until the late 1770s that it came to be joined by his *Two Treatises on Government*. During the first half of the eighteenth century Locke could be claimed as the father of Irish philosophy. Locke framed philosophical and theological questions that variously preoccupied Bishop Berkeley and Edmund Burke. In 1724, in his fourth Drapier letter, Swift cited Locke and Molyneux as dangerous authors, 'who talk of Liberty as a blessing to which the whole race of Mankind hath an Original Title; whereof nothing but unlawful force can divest them.'[2] Swift and some other Irish writers presumed a familiarity among their readers with Locke. Perhaps they envisaged them as having come across *The Essay on Human Understanding* at Trinity. Locke had come to be cited as an authority on education in Ireland. However, it was not until the 1770s that the *Two Treatises* become his best-known work.

Molyneux was a natural philosopher who engaged in scientific experimentation and contributed to philosophical debates. In 1683, at the age of twenty-five, he became a founding member of the Dublin Philosophical Society, established upon the empirical principles of the Royal Society. His studies of optics were highly regarded by Robert Boyle amongst others. By profession he was a lawyer and a surveyor but he had also inherited estates in Armagh, Limerick and Kildare. He held a number of posts on government commissions. Before the war between William of Orange and King James II he was the surveyor-general of fortifications and buildings and was responsible for the design of Dublin Castle. During the war he fled with his family to Chester in England and returned to Dublin after the Battle of the Boyne. Many other Protestant Irish with the means to do so did likewise.

Molyneux's aim in charting this constitutional history was to build a case for Irish parliamentary autonomy. He drew upon the Lockean principle of rule by consent as well as upon precedent. That Ireland should be bound by Acts of Parliament made in England, was against reason and the common rights of all mankind:

> All Men are by Nature in a State of Equality, in respect of Jurisdiction or Dominion. This I take to be a Principle in itself so evident, that it stands in need of little Proof. It is not to be conceived, that Creatures of the same Species and Rank, promiscuously born to all the same Advantages of Nature, and the Use of the same Faculties, should be subordinate and subject one to another; these to this or that of the same Kind. On this Equality in Nature is founded that Right which all Men claim of being free from all Subjection to positive Laws, until by their own Consent they give up their Freedom, by entering into civil Societies for the common Benefit of all the Members thereof. And on this Consent depends the Obligation of all human Laws; insomuch that without it, by the unanimous Opinion of all Jurists, no Sanctions are of any Force.

Molyneux's innovation was to extend the principle of rule by consent to nations, a term he used repeatedly in cases where Locke had referred only to individual men. He argued that the principle of consent was breached when laws made in the English Parliament were applied to Ireland. This went against the Common Laws of England that were in force in both England and Ireland. The Irish were not represented in the English parliament but had its laws applied to them.

Even though Locke eventually came to be canonised as the great Whig theorist of the 1688 Glorious Revolution, only a handful of English acquaintances or correspondents are known to have mentioned the *Two Treatises* with Locke's approval. Thanks to Molyneux he gained public identification as a major political authority in Ireland before he did so in England even though he was intellectually influential amongst the emerging Whigs during his own lifetime. By the mid-eighteenth century *The Two Treatises* loomed large in Whig histories of the Glorious Revolution; notably in the writings of David Hume. By the end of the eighteenth century Locke emerged as the most frequently cited authority in Irish pamphlet literature generated by the debate preceding the Act of Union. These took from Locke what Molyneux did, refutations of the notion that claims based on conquest conveyed power over the descendants of the conquered and assertions of the principle of rule by consent.

Following the original 1698 edition *The Case of Ireland* was reprinted in 1706, 1719, 1720 and 1725. After a twenty-four year gap it was again republished in 1749. A further four editions were published between 1770 and 1782. The foreword to the 1770 edition explained that *The Case of Ireland* was first published at a time when William of Orange had rescued Irish Protestants from the 'bigotry of the deluded followers' of James II. It restated Molyneux's sense of grievance at having been driven temporarily abroad as part of a history of Protestant anxiety and grievance:

> ... the Protestant Families had been stripped of their Properties, and forced to seek Refuge in this Country; they were received with Humanity, by many particular Persons, and Money was raised by private Subscription for their Relief; their Lands had been wasted, their Houses burned, and the whole Island thrown back, as to matter of Improvement, at least a Century; all this did the Irish suffer in the Cause of Liberty ...

The oppressed Irish so described were Protestant Irish descended 'from Ancestors, who brought with them the Manners, Customs, Laws, and Constitution of England'. They 'saw their Independence as a Kingdom, unjustly violated, their Trade wantonly restrained, and Mr Molyneux's modest dispassionate irrefragable Proof of the Rights and Liberties of his native Country, profanely burned by the Hands of the common Hangman'. The 1770 foreword argued that inadequate parliamentary autonomy had brought to pass constitutional dangers foreseen by Molyneux. A weakened monarchy and the absence of Irish parliamentary autonomy had rendered the interests of Ireland a pawn on the chessboard of English parliamentary politics:

> An English Minister would move Heaven and Earth to corrupt a Majority in the House of Commons, and contrary to that Golden Rule of Politicks, which prefers the greater Part to the smaller, he would, in order to secure a single Member, the Circumstances of whose Estate may render it convenient to destroy the entire Trade of Ireland, readily Sacrifice so respectable a Part of the British Empire: To cut off the left Arm, in order to save a little Finger of the Right Hand from Amputation, would be strange in Surgery. Ireland has many unhappy Peculiarities in her political Situation, the chief of which seems to be, that she is a Kingdom without a King, for the Minister with an obsequious British Privy Council, has assumed the Power of putting a Negative upon the most salutary Laws; the Man who is not well acquainted with the Interest of Ireland, must surely be incapable of advising his Majesty concerning such Interest.

The 1770 foreword distinguished the Irish, meaning the Protestant patriot Irish, from 'the wild ferocious Natives of Ireland'. This was not a phrase ever used by Molyneux himself though it was congruent with his obvious indifference to their existence and to his Lockean rationale for not considering their entitlement to rule by consent. However, the late eighteenth century witnessed new readings of Locke that did. At a 1791 celebration of Bastille Day in Belfast, Molyneux was the sole Irishman other than Grattan to be toasted.

In April 1782 Grattan secured the Irish Parliament that Molyneux wished for. In May that year the London Parliament rescinded Poynings' Law and passed various other Acts that gave independence to Irish judges subject to the Irish House of Lords. In his April 1782 speech that divined the Spirit of Molyneux at work, Grattan optimistically summarised the new political settlement:

> I rejoice that the people are a party to this treaty, because they are bound to preserve it. There is not a man of forty shillings freehold that is not associated in this our claim of right, and bound to die in its defence; cities, counties, associations, Protestants and Catholics; it seems as if the people had joined in one great national sacrament; a flame has descended from heaven on the intellect of Ireland, plays round her head, and encompasses her understanding with a consecrated glory.[3]

While Catholics did secure some important freedoms within the 1782 settlement, the revitalised Parliament came to be defined by the Penal Laws and a Protestant patriot mindset proposed by Molyneux at the end of the previous century. It took a mere eighteen years for Grattan's Parliament to fall asunder.

BF

Notes

1   William Molyneux, *The Case of Ireland's being bound by Acts of Parliament in England, Stated* (facsimile, Online Library of Liberty, 1698).

2   Jonathan Swift, *The Drapier's Letters and Other Works, 1714–1725*, in H. Davis (ed.), *The Works of Jonathan Swift, vol. X* (Oxford: Basil Blackwell, 1966), p.88.

3. Henry Grattan, 16 April 1782, Irish House of Commons.

4

Jonathan Swift, *A Modest Proposal* (1729)

A Modest Proposal for Preventing the Children of poor People in Ireland from being a Burden to their Parents or Country, and for making them beneficial to the Publick, to give its full title, proposed that the babies of the impoverished poor, a vast proportion of the population as a whole, 'destined to turn thieves for want of work, or leave their dear native country to fight for the Pretender in Spain, or to sell themselves to the Barbados' could be made into useful members of the community, if reared as a luxury dish for the tables of persons of quality or fortune. At one year old, Swift proposed, babies could be rendered plump and fat for the good table. Swift computed the gaps between the rich and poor that made his modest proposal financially feasible. He assessed the charge of nursing a beggar's child (he included all cottagers, labourers and four-fifths of the farmers in this category) to be about two shillings per annum. A gentleman would, he assured, pay ten shillings for the carcass of a good fat child, leaving the mother with eight shillings net profit and fit for work until she produced her next child. The market would be seasonally glutted by babies born nine months after the end of Lent. This he attributed to a Lenten diet that included fish, popular in Catholic countries. Swift lampooned the conclusions that could be drawn from the marshalling of facts. 'Empiricks' and Royal Dublin Society scientists with faith in progress were always in his crosshairs. *A Modest Proposal* invoked statistics, weights and measures to propose a mad panacea for Ireland's problems.[1]

A year before the publication of *A Modest Proposal* in the third of his Intelligencer Papers, Swift sprang to the defence of John Gay's *Beggar's Opera* which had been dismissed in a sermon by a fellow Divine as containing merely a low kind of humour. Swift accepted that some things were too serious, solemn, or sacred to be ridiculed but abuses of them certainly were not. It was wrong perhaps to mock religion, politics or law but corruptions in these made proper topics for satire. He argued that *The Beggar's Opera* would probably do more good than a thousand such sermons. His defence of Gay identified two reasons for writing satire. The less noble was for the private satisfaction of the author. The other was to write it in a public spirit, to prompt men of genius and virtue to mend the world as far as they were able. Swift argued that *The Beggar's Opera* had such a moral purpose. It placed vices of all kinds in the strongest and most odious light and thereby, did eminent service to both religion and morality.

A Modest Proposal appeared at the tail end of a decade during which Swift wrote a number of anonymous pamphlets on the condition of Ireland. The first major one, *A Proposal for the Universal Use of Irish Manufacture,* was published in 1720.[2] This exhorted its Irish readers to burn everything that came from England except its people and its coal. It was partly inspired by the distress of the 1,700 or so weavers living in the vicinity of St Patrick's cathedral over whom Swift presided as Dean and magistrate when the export of Irish woollens to England was prohibited. Swift set up a loan fund of £500 to help them fund the purchase of looms and tools which many weavers had pawned off to avoid starvation.

Swift came to present himself as a patriotic Protestant Irishman loyal to the King, but like William Molyneux he argued for parity with, rather than subservience to, England. In his fourth Drapier letter in 1724 he ranked Molyneux and John Locke amongst the dangerous authors who regarded 'Liberty as a blessing to which the whole Race of Mankind hath an Original Title.' The Irish ought to be constitutionally 'free' under a limited Monarchy. But the disabilities of Ireland had everything to do with the Monarchy. His 1724 *Letter to Shopkeepers, Tradesmen and Farmers and Common-People in Ireland* opposed a scheme for minting Irish copper halfpence and farthings which came about because of the need to fund a pension for a mistress of the King. Wolverhampton entrepreneur William Wood got the contract to mint coins to the face value of £100,800 for £10,000. The King signed his approval in July 1722 and the Irish Revenue Commissioners had objected strenuously to the Treasury in London some two years before Swift joined the fray as Drapier. Ireland had not been permitted to mint currency since Tudor times, and sometimes the circulation of money was poor. Wood's scheme was perceived by the Irish Establishment as the wanton mismanagement of Irish affairs by Englishmen and as a test of strength between officials in Dublin and London. The scheme unravelled. The London government under Walpole proposed some concessions, a smaller issue of coins with more copper in them than proposed by Wood. But the compromises were politically unsuccessful. Wood lost his patent and was recompensed. For Swift the underlining problem was one of attitudes to the Irish with whom he, born in Dublin to English parents, sided. As put in a 1724 open letter to Lord Chancellor Middleton from the Drapier:

> As to Ireland, they know little more than they do about
> Mexico, further than is a country subject to the king of
> England, full of bogs, inhabited by wild Irish Papists,
> who are kept in awe by mercenary troops sent from

thence. And their general opinion is, that it were better for England if this whole island were sunk into the sea; for they have a tradition that, every forty years there must be a rebellion in Ireland. I have seen the grossest suppositions pass upon them; that the wild Irish were taken in toils, but that, in some time, they would grow so tame as to eat out your hands. I have been asked by hundreds, and particularly by my neighbours, your tenants at Pepper-harrow, whether I had come from Ireland by seas. And upon the arrival of an Irishman to a country town, I have known crowds coming about him, and wondering to see him look so much better than themselves.

But like Molyneux, Swift's focus was on the rights of the Protestant Irish. Papists and peasants only figured in his pamphlets as objects of concern when 'British natives' like himself were disparaged alongside them in the same breath. In the same year in which *A Modest Proposal* was published, Swift wrote despairingly about the consequences of the constitutional disabilities under which the Protestant Irish laboured. In the unpublished bitter *Answer to Several Letters from Unknown Hands* (1729) he argued that the 'British Natives' of Ireland were emigrating out of despair of things getting better in their own country. Three reforms were needed, he argued, to cure the misgovernment of Ireland.[3] 'First, a Liberty of Trade, Secondly, a Share of preferments in all kinds to the British Natives, and Thirdly, a return of those absentees, who take away almost one half of the Kingdom's Revenues.' He made no plea to rescind the penal laws against the Catholic majority.

Prudent laws, Swift first argued in *A Proposal for the Universal Use of Irish Manufacture*, encouraged industrious cultivation in England but in Ireland landlords were 'everywhere, by *penal* clauses, absolutely prohibiting their tenants from ploughing'. As a result it was cheaper to import corn from England. Swift lambasted country landlords (and landed clerics by implication) who 'by unmeasurable *screwing* and *racking* their tenants all over the kingdom have already reduced a miserable *people* to a *worse condition* than *peasants* in France, or the *vassals* in Germany and Poland'. In various 1729 writings he disparaged the modest proposals of others for schemes for improvement that, for all that these might work in other countries, ignored the fundamental barriers to the economic improvement of Ireland:

> There is hardly a scheme proposed for improving the trade of this kingdom, which doth not manifestly shew the stupidity and ignorance of the proposer: and I laugh with contempt at those weak wise heads, which proceed upon general maxims, or advise us to follow the Examples of Holland or England. These Empiricks talk by rote, without understanding of the Constitution of the Kingdom; as if a physician knowing that Exercise contributed much to health should prescribe to his Patient under a severe fit of gout, to walk ten miles every morning.[4]

Another 1729 unpublished essay, *The Truth of Some Maxims in State and Government examined with reference to Ireland* – his most coherent analysis of the political context of Irish social and economic problems – summed up how trade barriers imposed by England, patronage on matters such as charters to mint coinage and an absentee landlord system that promoted rack-renting, made maxims for improving land and industry ineffectual in Ireland. Such maxims presumed that the people of Ireland enjoyed natural rights in common with the rest of mankind who had entered into civil society. And as for the maxim 'that people are the riches of a nation', this clearly did not hold in the Irish case. With little of the satire of *A Modest Proposal*, Swift declared:

But, in our present situation, at least five children in six who are born lie in dead weight upon us for the want of employment. And a skilful computer assured me, that above one half of the souls in the kingdom supported themselves by begging and thievery, whereof two thirds would be able to get their bread in any other country on earth. Trade is the only incident to labour: where that fails, the poorer native must either beg, steal, or starve, or be forced to quit his country. This has made me often wish, for some years past, that, instead of discouraging our people from seeking foreign soil, the public would pay for transporting all our unnecessary mortals, whether Papists or Protestants, to America, as drawbacks are sometimes allowed where a nation is over-stocked. I confess myself to be touched with a very sensible pleasure, when I hear of a mortality in any country parish or village, where the wretches are forced to pay for a filthy cabin and two ridges of potatoes treble the worth, brought up to steal or beg, for want of work, to whom death would be the best thing to be wished of, on account of both themselves and the public.[5]

Swift's grim unpublished assertion that the Irish poor might be better off dead was reworked as satire in *A Modest Proposal*. But he disagreed with the unnamed 'skilful computer' in an undated sermon, *Causes of the Wretched Condition of Ireland*, that must have been written around the same time as *A Modest Proposal*:

It is a very melancholy reflection, that such a country as ours, which is capable of producing all things necessary, and most things convenient for life, sufficient for the support of four times the number of its inhabitants, should yet lie under the heaviest load of misery and want, our streets crowded with beggars, so many of our lower sort of tradesmen, labourers, and artificers, not able to find clothes and food for their families.[6]

The opening paragraph of this sermon seems to be subverted in the opening paragraph of *A Modest Proposal*. It begins almost the same way ('It is a melancholy object to those …') but instead of workers unable to provide for themselves we are told about female beggars followed by their children in rags, destined to become thieves or sell themselves to Barbados. *A Modest Proposal* was close in content and argument but often only slightly more sardonic in tone than the bitter unpublished writings, serious polemics and sermons he wrote during the 1720s on the condition of Ireland. Across these, the same voice, the same arguments and the same obsessions are readily discernible. As such *A Modest Proposal* cannot be understood in isolation.

In *The Battle of the Books* (1704) Swift described satire 'as a sort of glass wherein beholders do generally observe everybody's face but their own', which was the chief reason why so few were offended by it. *A Modest Proposal* was not just the palatable and humorous expression of Swift's frustration but a satire on the impossibility of schemes of improvement proposed by others and a mirror held up to his own face that mocked the Protestant patriot case for economic autonomy and constitutional reform he earnestly advanced. For making this case he came to be celebrated by subsequent generations of patriots and nationalists as varied as Henry Grattan, Wolfe Tone, Thomas Davis and John Mitchel. In 1847, Mitchel edited a pamphlet on behalf of the Irish Confederation entitled *Irish Political Economy* that republished Swift's *A Proposal for the Universal Use of Irish Manufacture* and pressed it into the service of a new separatist ideal.

Swift viewed himself as exiled from England and as having to cast his lot with the Irish. The manner in which he did so and the genius with which he expressed his own and Ireland's predicaments canonised him for generations as a model patriot and as the architect of Anglo-Irish identity. But Swift's relationship with Ireland remained ambivalent. As put in a 1727 poem, written at the port of Holyhead, awaiting passage to the land of his birth:

> Remove me from this land of slaves,
> Where all are fools and all are knaves,
> Where every knave and fool is bought,
> Yet kindly sells himself for nought…

BF

Notes

1   Jonathan Swift, *A Modest Proposal for Preventing the Children of poor People in Ireland from being a Burden to their Parents or Country, and for making them beneficial to the Publick* (Dublin, 1729).

2   Jonathan Swift, *A Proposal for the Universal Use of Irish Manufacture in Cloaths and Furniture of Houses, &c. Utterly Rejecting and Renouncing Every Thing wearable that comes from England* (Dublin, 1720).

3   Jonathan Swift, *An Answer to Several Letters sent to me from Unknown Hands* (Dublin, 1729).

4   Jonathan Swift, *Answer to Several Letters from Unknown Persons* (1729) (first published, London: William Johnston, 1765).

5   Jonathan Swift, *A Sermon on the Causes of the Wretched Conditions of Ireland* in *The Sermons of Rev Dr Jonathan Swift* (Glasgow: Urie, 1763).

6   Jonathan Swift, *The Truth of Some Maxims in State and Government examined with reference to Ireland* (Dublin, 1729).

5

Long before the invention of PowerPoint and frequently asked questions on websites, Catholics were instructed in their faith by means of question and answer booklets setting out Church doctrine. The standard reference for pre-Vatican II catechesis (religious instruction given in advance of baptism or confirmation) was the Catechism of the Council of Trent, 1566, also known as the Roman Catechism. This emerged in response to catechisms devised by Lutherans. Printing had made the Reformation possible by making Scripture available to literate laypeople. Protestantism emphasised the primacy of the Bible and its unmediated study by the faithful, Catholicism the primacy of doctrinal interpretations of Scripture by the priesthood. In the centuries since, the Reformation printed Catechisms tailored in different editions for children and the general population; these so-called Penny Catechisms were far more influential than the Bible in shaping Irish Catholicism.

The Penny Catechisms were derived from longer ones designed for the education of priests. An early Irish example, *The Catholic Christian Doctrine for the use of pastors and Catechesis in order to instruct Children and Illiterate Persons,* attributed to Rev. F.W. Devereux of the Diocese of Ferns, drew on the text of the Douay Catechism, published in Rheims in France in 1648, the town where the standard Catholic English-language Bible was first printed. Both answered similarly a question about how children, the old, blind people and the lame would be represented on Judgement Day. All would be restored as if they had reached the perfect age of thirty-three years, because that was reportedly the age at which the saviour died.

One authored during the 1770s by James Butler, Archbishop of Cashel, remained in print into the twentieth century. A 1922 Butler catechism published in Waterford was described on the front cover as 'Revised, Enlarged, Approved and Recommended by the Four R.C. Archbishops of Ireland.' The earliest full-length catechism to be published in both English and Irish was composed by Andrew Dunleavy (or Donleavy) in the early 1740s. Dunleavy was Director of the Irish College at the time. He had grown up in Sligo under the Penal Laws but escaped to France in 1710 to study for the priesthood. His catechism appeared in both Irish (Gaelic) and English: *The Catechism of Christian Doctrine by way of Question and Answer Drawn Chiefly From The Express Word of God and Other Pure Sources.* It was published in its third edition for the Royal Catholic College of St Patrick, Maynooth in 1848 after which it was adopted by a number of dioceses. An early edition was accompanied by a 1741 testimonial to its excellence by Michael O'Gara, Archbishop of Tuam. A near-copy of the Dunleavy Catechism attributed to Michael O'Reilly, who became Archbishop of Armagh in 1749, remained in use in Derry well into the twentieth century. [1]

Dunleavy set out his text in both languages on facing pages and the 1848 Maynooth edition included an appendix that explained the spelling, typeface and pronunciation of the Gaelic alphabet. It also reproduced Dunleavy's original 1742 foreword which argued that children's catechisms were inadequate for the spiritual education of lay adults. Dunleavy explained that his work had been prompted by the great scarcity of full catechisms in Ireland. Unlike many other catechisms which began with the question, 'Who made the world?' Dunleavy's first question was, 'What is the Catechism?' He defined it as 'a plain and intelligible explanation of the Articles of the Christian Faith necessary for salvation; and of other points belonging to the service of God'.

Unlike subsequent abbreviated Penny Catechisms, Dunleavy cited specific passages from Scripture in support of answers to questions. And again, unlike later ones, responses to some questions took the form of scholastic disputations and discussions of social norms. For example, what became a simple question later on whether to fast on the Sabbath opened up into a discussion of fasting as mandated by the 'Jewish Church' and 'the modern Churches of England and Holland'. Dunleavy recommended restricting the faithful to one midday meal during periods of fasting with further moderate consumption permitted at night or at the end of a long day. He exempted sick people, weakly older people, young people under twenty-one years of age, women big with child and people who undertook hard labour. In Dunleavy then, doctrine, custom and practice were not presented as one and the same.

Many catechisms from other English-speaking countries also circulated in Ireland. A collection of these is to be found on the shelves of the Central Catholic Library in Dublin. Moral instruction in the shorter versions aimed at children and the uneducated poor tended to be stern and forcefully put. For example, the *Abridgement of Christian Doctrine for the Lower Classes* (1906) by Thomas Byrne, Bishop of Nashville, declared in response to a question on mortal sin that one such sin would merit hell. But in Byrne's longer *Abridgement of Christian Doctrine for the Higher Classes* (1906) no such simple question was posed. Instead the emphasis was on how those in mortal sin may be deprived of the sacraments. What, Byrne asked, ought a Christian to do if a Bible should be offered him by a Protestant? He 'ought to indignantly spurn it, because it is forbidden by the Church; and, if he should have accepted it without adverting to what it was, he should at once pitch it into the fire, or fetch it to his Pastor'.

Penny Catechisms offered a mechanism for standardising the means by which doctrine was to be taught to children and full-length catechisms were preferred for the instruction of the educated classes to Bible study. An appendix on the history of Catholic religious education in a 1943 *Religious Knowledge Course for Primary Schools*, published by the Archdiocese of Glasgow, explained that the teaching of the Bible seemed 'unrelated to the scheme of religious knowledge; it leads nowhere. And yet, being God's Revelation to man, the Bible is largely the source of dogma.' It argued against teaching 'Bible history' ('perversions of historical truth that do so much to warp the outlook of Catholic children') declaring that 'we, as Christians, have little interest in the history of the Jewish race'. The Old Testament afforded stories showing the beauty of virtue and the punishment of sin and contained much that might be worked into the body of doctrine. The New Testament stood on a different plane, it dealt with divine reality. Antipathy towards the use of the Bible for religious instruction was doctrinal and pedagogical even though it commonly appeared sectarian.[2]

In Ireland during the 1820s religious education became extremely politicised. The Kildare Place Association (named for the Dublin address from which the scheme was run) funded a system of state-funded Protestant schools, which were accused by Catholics of engaging in aggressive proselytising. Such schools co-existed uneasily with a larger and rapidly expanding unfunded system of Catholic schools in a context where Catholics were highly mobilised and where Catholic Emancipation was imminent. In opposition to the Kildare Place Society, Catholic prelates and influential laymen established the *Irish National Society for Promoting the Education for the Poor* in 1821 to articulate Catholic grievances and to propose alternatives. In January 1826 the Irish

Catholic Bishop drew up resolutions, backed by the Catholic Association, supporting a 'Mixed Education' school system. Their proposals endorsed the admission of Protestants and Catholics into the same schools 'provided sufficient care be taken to protect the religion of the Roman Catholic children and furnish them with adequate means of religious instruction'. A Royal Commission had been established in 1824 to examine how existing schools worked and to come up with a viable alternative system.

A form issued by the Royal Commission to all parish priests and ministers in Ireland during the summer of 1824 asked these to enumerate every book and printed paper of every description, which was or had been taught or in any way used, either for amusement or instruction, within School during the previous six months. In cases where Scriptures were used, respondents were asked to state whether it was the Bible at large or the New Testament alone; whether the translation used was that of the Established Church (the King James Bible) or the Catholic Douay Version. 1824 returns from Catholic schools, as analysed by Rev. Martin Brenan, then Professor of Education at St Patrick's College Maynooth, were published as *Schools of Kildare and Leighlin* in 1935. Catholic religious instruction comprised, according to Brenan, 'systematic grounding in the truths of faith as set forth in the catechism, as well as acquaintance with the recognised authorities on the ascetical and spiritual life'. The Commissioners took inventories of the content of parish libraries, reporting that these held between 89 and 280 religious books. The parish priest of Dunleckny wrote a letter to the Commissioners expressing his hope that, having examined his books and Catechisms, they were satisfied as to 'the falsehood of the many charges brought by persons of other religions against the Catholic Clergy, and particularly that of their anxiety to keep the people in ignorance'.[3]

In 1826 in the Diocese of Kildare and Leighlin just under 37,000 Catholic children were able to attend school, about half the total. The Commission identified the existence of many small private pay schools, the so-called 'Hedge' schools, in each parish. Reports collated by the Royal Commission gave tantalising glimpses of how such Hedge Schools were established and run. Fr Edward Earl the local parish priest described one such school in Killkeaskin:

> Margaret Cooly. Opened School Herself. Roman Catholic; is 80 years or more; teaches Reading and Sewing; was taught in Dublin. Salary about £3 per year; rates 1.s.8d. per quarter. Has no fixed school-house; lives in an out-office at Killkeaskin where she teaches. Books – Primer, Reading Made Easy, Spelling Book, Butler's Catechism.

Another better-off school, where the teacher Patrick Moore charged a shilling more per pupil per quarter, described a schoolroom built of lime and stone and thatched with straw, part of a house 14 feet in length with more than 50 pupils, with seats belonging to the Church. Moore had formal qualifications and a better library that, unusually, included both Protestant and Catholic texts. As listed by Fr Earl:

> Books – Primer, Reading Made Easy, Child's New Play Thing, Universal Spelling Book, The Deserted Child, Travels at Home, Gough's and Voster's Arithmetic, 4 Protestant Testaments, 1 Douay Testament, all New Testaments, Butler's Catechism, The Church Catechism. The master said he bought the Douay Testament to compare it with the Protestant Testament; I told him to send it home; he did so. The Protestant Testaments were all given originally by the Protestant Ministers.

In ordering Moore to get rid of his Douay Bible, Fr Earl was doing no more than what Catholic clergy had done for centuries, insisting that the interpretation of Scripture was not the business of laypeople.

The Royal Commission's 1826 proposals required that the master of each school in which the majority of pupils profess the Roman Catholic faith, 'be a Roman Catholic and that, in schools in which the Roman Catholic children form only a minority, a permanent Roman Catholic assistant be employed'. These proposals were worked into a bill by Thomas Wyse, a Catholic Association MP. This bill was subsequently reworked by E.G. Stanley, the chief Secretary for Ireland in consultation with Lord Grey's Whig government. A petition on educational reform from the Irish Catholic Hierarchy was presented to both Houses of Parliament in 1830.

The Catholic Church initially supported the system but became increasingly ambivalent to it over time. Presbyterians clamoured for a return of the old system. In 1832 the Synod of Ulster raised the cry of 'the bible unabridged and unmutilated' and held back from the board's schools. The appearance of neutrality was crucial in managing demands for control from both sides. Under the leadership of the Catholic Archbishop of Dublin Daniel Murray and his Church of Ireland equivalent Richard Whately, the compromise brokered in 1830 survived for two decades. Some Catholic leaders, notably Archbishop McHale of Tuam, campaigned for a system of Catholic denominational schools and stepped up their demands over time. In 1839, to counter such demands, Murray requested that a legate be sent from Rome to evaluate the system. An evaluation was conducted the following year by the future Catholic Archbishop of Dublin Paul Cullen who concluded at the time that the schools 'could not have been more Catholic than they are'.[4] Even before the Devotional Revolution and the cementing of Catholic power usually attributed to Cullen, the widespread use of catechisms by lay teachers helped make this possible.

BF

Notes

1   Michael Tynan, *Catholic Instruction in Ireland 1720–1950* (Dublin: Four Courts Press, 1985).

2   Various catechisms in the holdings of the Catholic Library in Dublin are cited.

3   Rev. Martin Brenan, *Schools of Kildare and Leighlin 1775–1835* (Dublin: MH Gill and Sons, 1935).

4   Peadar McSuibhne, *Paul Cullen and his Contemporaries*, vol. 4, (Kildare, *Leinster Leader*, 1974), p.8.

6

William Theobald Wolfe Tone (ed.),
The Autobiography of Wolfe Tone (1826)

The stature of Wolfe Tone (1763–1798) in the canon of Irish nationalism owes much to the posthumous publication of his autobiographical writings and diaries almost two decades after his death. A few of Tone's pamphlets had an immediate impact during his life, particularly *An Argument on Behalf of the Catholics of Ireland*, published in 1791. After his death Tone's reputation was overshadowed by those of other contemporaries, notably Lord Edward Fitzgerald. It was not until the 1840s, with impatience with Daniel O'Connell's constitutionalism running high amongst Young Ireland nationalists, that Tone was first canonised as the great patriot of 1798. Patrick Pearse declared Tone's *Autobiography* to be the first Gospel of the New Testament of Irish nationalism more than a century after Tone's death. Tone's grave became the topic of a ballad by Thomas Davis (*Bodenstown Churchyard*) and was described as the holiest place in Ireland by Pearse at an oration there in June 1913. Since then Sinn Fein and the IRA have held annual commemorations of Pearse's performance at Tone's graveside. During the period of the Northern Ireland conflict, a folk group named The Wolfe Tones did well with albums such as *Rifles of the IRA* (1969). That The Wolfe Tones went on to record an album titled *A Tribute to Padraig Pearse* illustrated perhaps not just Pearse's hold on the Irish Republican imagination but also exemplified the extent to which romantic nationalists like him had successfully co-opted the real Wolfe Tone.

The first edition of the *Autobiography* edited out some passages of Tone's journal. It included a memoir by Tone's son and editor William, detailing his service as a cavalryman in the Napoleonic wars, and another memoir by Tone's widow Martha, recounting how after his death in 1798 she engineered an interview with Napoleon in order to secure French citizenship for her son.[1] An 1883 edition of Tone's *Autobiography* edited by Barry O'Brien was republished several times. This also excluded the passages censored by William. In 1888 a French edition was published as *Mémoires Secrets de Wolfe Tone*; a portrait of Tone still hangs in the foyer of the French ambassador's residence in Dublin. A 1937 abridged edition by Sean O'Faoláin restored the censored passages. These included Tone's account of his early amours, expressions of his contempt for his brother-in-law ('a most egregious coxcomb'), quarrels with his wife's family (over prospective inheritances), and various scornful remarks about America. Tone lived there briefly in 1795 but couldn't stand the place or its uncouth people. A definitive edition of the *Autobiography* was published in 1998, edited by Thomas Bartlett.[2] This kept to the structure of the 1826 edition but included the excised passages, Tone's correspondence and also reinstated political writings that had been excluded from various earlier abridged editions.

Tone was an Irish patriot for just the final eight years of his 35 year-long life. His political views were the product of his class, religion and, in particular, his life experiences. Tone had a lust for life and craved personal advancement. He sought the latter first in the service of the British Empire and when rebuffed he made common cause with his fellow Irishmen against England. It is not simplistic to understand much of his autobiography as an account of his efforts to find his place in the world. He was hardly the pious ideological martyr that Pearse represented him as. But then Pearse did not have access to the unexpurgated version of his memoir. Here, in one of the passages removed by his son William, Tone describes his infatuation with Eliza, wife of Humanity Dick Martin:

> After one or two fugitive passions about the beginning of the year 1783 I fell in love with a woman who made me miserable for more than two years. She was the wife of Richard Martin of Galway, a member of Parliament, and a man of considerable fortune in that county. Martin was passionately fond of acting and had fitted up a theatre in which he had several dramatic representations. Mrs. Martin, independent of a thousand other attractions, was one of the first actresses I ever saw, and as I lived in the house with her, and being myself somewhat of an actor, was daily thrown into particular situations with her, both in rehearsals and on the stage, and as I had an imagination easily warmed, without one grain of discretion to regulate it, I very soon became in love to a degree almost inconceivable. I have never, never met in history, poetry, or romance a description that comes near what I actually suffered on her account. For two years our acquaintance continued, in which time I made three visits to her house of four or five months each. As I was utterly unable, and indeed unwilling, to conceal my passion from her, she very soon detected me, and as I preserved, as well as felt, the profoundest respect for her, she supposed she might amuse herself innocently in observing the progress of this terrible passion in the mind of an interesting young man of twenty; but this is an experiment no woman ought to make.

His two-year relationship with Eliza was chaste. Tone came to regret not taking his chance to bed her when he found out, some years later, that she had eloped to Paris with another lover. Although he suffered severely from this passion he also reaped much benefit. The desire to render himself agreeable to a highly cultivated woman induced him 'to attend to a thousand little things' so that after the first transports of rage and grief at losing her had subsided, he considered himself on the whole considerably improved.

In 1785 he met his future wife. She was fifteen years of age and living on Grafton Street in the house of her grandfather, a rich old clergyman by the name of Fanning. Tone soon contrived to be introduced to Martha's family and soon afterwards the couple eloped. They then returned to live with her parents, amicably for a short while, acrimoniously after that. In 1787 Tone left Martha and their daughter with her family and moved to London to complete his legal studies, seek his fortune and, as he intimated in another passage supressed by William, to sow his wild oats:

At the age of four and twenty, with a tolerable figure and address, in an idle and luxurious Capital, it will not be supposed I was without adventures with the fair sex. The Englishmen neglect their wives exceedingly in many essential circumstances. I was totally disengaged and did not fail to profit, as far as I could, by their neglect, and English women are not naturally cruel. I formed, in consequence, several delightful connections in London, and as I was extremely discreet, I have the satisfaction to think that not one of those to whom I had the good fortune to render myself agreeable ever suffered the slightest blemish in her reputation on my account. I cherish, yet, with affection the memory of one charming woman to whom I was extremely attached, and I am sure she still remembers me with a mutual regard.

In a foreshadowing of his later efforts to convince the French government that it was in its interest to invade Ireland, he proposed an English colony in one of Cook's newly discovered islands in the South Sea on a military plan, 'in order to put a bridle on Spain in time of peace, and to annoy her grievously in that quarter in time of war'. He spent three months researching his scheme and delivered it by hand to the porter in Downing Street for the attention of the Prime Minister Mr Pitt. It was, he recalled, his first essay in politics. Tone, keen to make his fortune, also made a botched effort to enlist with the East India Company. Still smarting from these failed endeavours he was rescued by an advance of £500 on his wife's inheritance from her grandfather. This allowed him to return to Ireland in 1789, finish his legal studies and enlist as a barrister on the Leinster circuit. He had little interest in a legal career and his ambitions soon turned to politics. He initially hoped to be taken up as a parliamentary candidate by the Whigs but by 1790 under the influence of Sir Laurence Parsons, an MP in the Irish House of Commons, he found his vocation as an Irish patriot:

> I made speedily what was to me a great discovery, though I might have found it in Swift and Molyneux, that the influence of England was the Radical vice of our Government, and consequently that Ireland would never be either free, prosperous, or happy, until she was independent, and that independence was unattainable whilst the connection with England existed.

His political views evolved rapidly. These, as documented in two widely-read pamphlets, *Spanish War!* (1790) and *An Argument on Behalf of the Catholics of Ireland* (1791), propelled him to the centre stage of the United Irishmen and in April 1792 he replaced Edmund Burke's hapless son Richard as the parliamentary agent of the Catholic Association. These were summarised as follows by

William's preface to the *Autobiography*:

The fact is though he preferred in theory a republican form of government, his main object was to procure the independence of his country under a liberal administration, whatever might be its form or name. His tastes and habits were rather aristocratical for the society with which he was sometimes obliged to mingle. I believe that, in reading these memoirs, many people will be surprised at (and some perhaps will blame) the moderation of his views. The persecutions of the government drove him much further than he proposed at first.

Spanish War! recalled but inverted the adventurer spirit with which he canvassed Pitt's support for a South Seas colony to block Spanish trade. The London parliament could ask the king to declare war on Spain, but it could not, Tone insisted, do so on behalf of Ireland, which had its own separate and independent legislature. *Spanish War!* in the spirit of Swift's Drapier letters, argued that Irish trade and prosperity would be, as ever before, undermined by England's self-interest. *Spanish War!* identified some £113,543 of Irish exports (mostly linen, wheat, pork and butter) to Spain in 1789 against imports of £138,001 (including sugar cane, brandy and wine). In a *volte-face* from his submission to Pitt, he declared that peace with Spain was in Ireland's interest and that Ireland would in no way benefit from any victory over Spain over trade routes:

Ireland has *no quarrel*, but, on the contrary, a very beneficial intercourse with Spain, which she is required to renounce to her infinite present detriment; she is called on, likewise, to squander her wealth and shed her blood in this English East Indian quarrel.

The man who tried in vain to enlist in the East India Company less than two years previously was no longer contented to be 'the subaltern instrument' of artful and ambitious England. As long as the good of the Empire was defined as the good of England, Ireland would suffer. If England's warships were built in Irish harbours, if Ireland had its own navy, army, flag and colonies, only then would Ireland have a legitimate interest in England's war.

Tone was a constitutional patriot before he became a rebel. Like other Protestant patriots he was preoccupied with Ireland's lesser status compared to England. The aim of his *Argument on Behalf of Catholics*, he recalled in his autobiography, was to assert the independence of his country, to unite the whole people of Ireland and to 'substitute the common name of Irishman in place of the denominations of Protestant, Catholic'. The pamphlet was addressed to Protestant Dissenters rather than to members of the Established Church or to Catholics:

> The Protestants I despaired of from the outset for obvious reasons. Already in possession by an unjust monopoly of the whole power and patronage of the country, it was not to be supposed they would ever concur in measures the certain tendency of which must be to lessen their influence as a party, how much so ever the nation might gain. To the Catholics I thought it unnecessary to address myself, because, that as no change could make their political situation worse, I reckoned upon their support to a certainty; besides, they had already begun to manifest a strong sense of their wrongs and oppressions; and, finally, I well knew that, however it might be disguised or suppressed, there existed in the breast of every Irish Catholic an inextirpable abhorrence of the English name and power. There remained only the Dissenters, whom I knew to be patriotic and enlightened; however, the recent

events at Belfast had showed me that all prejudice was not yet entirely removed from their minds. I sat down accordingly, and wrote a pamphlet addressed to the Dissenters, and which I entitled, *An Argument on behalf of the Catholics of Ireland*, the object of which was to convince them that they and the Catholics had but one common interest and one common enemy; that the depression and slavery of Ireland was produced and perpetuated by the divisions existing between them, and that, consequently, to assert the independence of their country, and their own individual liberties, it was necessary to forget all former feuds, to consolidate the entire strength of the whole nation, and to form for the future but; one people. These principles I supported by the best arguments which suggested themselves to me, and particularly by demonstrating that the cause of the failure of all former efforts, and more especially of the Volunteer Convention in 1783, was the unjust neglect of the claims of their Catholic brethren.

An Argument on Behalf of Catholics opened with an account of Ireland and its people that is echoed in how Ireland continues to represent itself. Ireland was 'blessed with a temperate sky and fruitful soil', 'abounding with all the material for unlimited commerce', 'filled by 4,000,000 of an ingenious and gallant people', 'posted right in the track between Europe and America, within 50 miles of England, 300 of France', yet, as he argued in *Spanish War!*, 'with all these great advantages unheard of and unknown, without pride, or power, or name; without ambassadors, army or navy; nor of half the consequence in the empire she has the honour to make a part, with the single county of York, or the loyal and well regulated town of Birmingham!' The choice facing the Protestant Irish was to preside over a stunted and inglorious country ('unknown and unheard of in Europe, the prey of England, the laughing stock of the knaves who plunder us') or to exert their power constitutionally to procure a complete and radical emancipation of their country, 'by a reform in the representation of the people'. This new element to his political philosophy was his insistence of the need for solidarity with Catholics.

Tone's proposal for dealing with the political fallout of Catholic Emancipation was to enfranchise such Catholics who had a freehold of £10 per year and to strike off 'the wretched tribe of forty shilling freeholders' whose votes were as much the property of their landlords as the sheep or the bullocks which they brand with their names. Doing so, would purge in one stroke, 'the gross and feculent mass which contaminates the Protestant interest, and restore their natural weight to the sound and respectable part of the Catholic community, without throwing into their hands so much power as might enable them to dictate the law'.

An Argument on Behalf of Catholics addressed hackneyed Protestant fears of what would happen if Catholics were emancipated. There was, he argued, no threat of Rome rule (the Pope was being burned in effigy in Catholic France), or of a Catholic monarch (the Pretender to the throne was dead, Jacobitism was finished); he also dismissed the argument that if Catholics got the upper hand they would ally against England with France.

His solidarity with Catholics was, at this stage, mostly intellectual. How, he asked, could the Dissenters ground their title to liberty in Thomas Paine's *The Rights of Man* whilst riveting the fetters of the wretched Roman Catholics? As explained by his son William in the foreword to the first edition of the *Autobiography*:

> When he first wrote his pamphlet in favour of Catholics he was not acquainted with a single individual of that religion, so complete at that period was the distinction in society between the several sects. In a few months he was a prime mover of their councils and accomplished the union between them and the dissenters of the North.

His diaries for late-1791 record a drink-fuelled debate (one of many) with a fellow Protestant who argued that for all protestations of good wishes towards Roman Catholics, thirty-nine out of forty Protestants would be found, whenever the question came forward, to be hostile to the liberation of the Roman Catholics.

The first volume of the *Autobiography* covered the period prior to his departure to the United States. The second volume of the diaries, written from France, depicts his involvement in three French efforts to invade Ireland between 1796 and 1798 and the articulation of his political aspirations for Ireland. An 18 July 1796 entry recorded a conversation with his French government liaison General Henri Clarke (whose father was an Irishman) about what kind of government might be installed in Ireland. Clarke favoured some kind of monarchy. 'Where on God's earth', Tone replied, 'would we go look for a King?' There was no obvious candidate amongst the Irish nobility and he could not see, in any case, the Irish people spilling their blood for any monarch. 'Maybe, after all,' Clarke suggested, 'you will choose one of your own leaders; who knows but it may be yourself?' Tone replied that he had neither the desire nor the talents to aspire so high. He then outlined his own hopes and fears for an Irish revolution:

> I summed up all by telling him that, as to religion, my belief was we should content ourselves with pulling down the Establishment without setting up any other; that we would have no State religion, but let every sect pay their own clergy voluntarily; and that, as to royalty and aristocracy, they were both odious in Ireland to that degree, that I apprehended much more a general massacre of the gentry, and a distribution of the entire of their property, than the establishment of any form of government that would perpetuate their influence; that I hoped this massacre would not happen, and that I, for one, would do all that lay in

my power to prevent it, because I did not like to spill the blood, even of the guilty; at the same time, that the pride, cruelty, and oppression of the Irish aristocracy were so great, that I apprehended every excess from the just resentment of the people.

Tone went to sea with a French fleet three times between December 1796 and August 1798. Each attempt to land in Ireland ended in failure due to bad weather, poor leadership or poor seamanship. On Christmas Day 1796, contemplating failure, he recorded in his diary that if captured, the best he could expect was to be shot or killed in action. Perhaps there would be trial for the sake of striking terror into others, and then perhaps a hanging or disembowelling, which he wouldn't mind as long as he was dead first. During a sea battle in August 1798 during which Tone turned down an opportunity to be safely evacuated, he was captured, court-marshalled and sentenced to death. He cheated the hangman by cutting his own throat. Whether he meant to take his life or defer his execution is unclear.

In March 1797 Tone recorded a conversation with Thomas Paine in Paris where he described the shattered state of Edmund Burke's mind following the death of his son Richard. Paine retorted that it was the *Rights of Man* that had broken Burke's heart and that the death of his son gave him an excuse to develop the chagrin which had preyed upon him since. Tone recorded that he was sure that *The Rights of Man* had tormented Burke exceedingly, but that he had seen himself the workings of a father's grief on his own spirit and that Paine had no children. Two of Tone's three children were to die of illness in France. Tone's *Autobiography* is very much the story of his family by his family. All three memoirs, his own and equally well-crafted ones by his son William and his wife Martha, capture a life that cannot be reduced to any single political end.

BF

Notes

1   William Theobald Wolfe Tone (ed.), *The Autobiography of Wolfe Tone* (Washington: Gales & Seaton, 1826).

2   Thomas Bartlett (ed.), *The Autobiography of Wolfe Tone* (Dublin: Lilliput Press, 1998).

7

John Mitchel, *The Jail Journal* (1861)

John Mitchel (1815–1875) wrote two hugely influential books. The focus here is upon the better-known *Jail Journal*, described by Patrick Pearse as the final gospel of the new testament of Irish nationalism.[1] It opens dramatically on 27 May 1848 with his imprisonment and sentencing to fourteen-years' transportation. His readers learn why he is being transported, through a series of flashbacks and asides, meditations on books Mitchel reads as he is shipped first to Barbados, then to Cape Town and on to Van Diemen's Land and also through the observations he records of his journey. The *Jail Diaries* document a dramatic escape to New York in 1853. There he set up *The Citizen*, an anti-British and pro-slavery periodical in which he first serialised his *Jail Journal* between January and August 1854. Irishmen in America, he wrote in the first issue of *The Citizen*, could not endure the thought of accepting the defeat which had driven them from the land of their fathers and which had made Ireland an object of pity and contempt to the world. The *Jail Journal* first emerged alongside polemics against the British Empire, the economic and social ideas that Mitchel believed were integral to its success and caused the devastation of Ireland and alongside strident defence of the Southern slave-owning social order that he believed was the only hold-out against the triumph of such ideas in America.

Mitchel's other influential book *The Last Conquest of Ireland (perhaps)* also began life in serial form, this time in *The Southern Citizen* which was established in 1857 after he left New York in disgust for Knoxville, Tennessee. The *Last Conquest* depicted the Famine as the culmination of a process of colonisation whereby Ireland would in future be dominated by the liberal political economy and liberal ideologies that had built the British Empire.[2] It offered a powerful polemic that in many respects resembled Friedrich Engels' *The Condition of the Working Class*. Both were very influenced by the anti-laissez-faire writings of Thomas Carlyle. Whereas Engels described the lives of the Irish poor in urban slums, Mitchel depicted their deaths as due to malign neglect, justified by laissez-faire doctrines at home. Mitchel influentially undermined the reputation of Daniel O'Connell as Liberator, blaming him for this liberal tyranny insofar as O'Connell was the only Irish leader able to do anything about it. Pro-slavery Mitchel attacked O'Connell's preoccupation with Abolitionism, seeing it as a manifestation of the sham philanthropy of a British model of liberalism that had killed hundreds of thousands through famine in Ireland. Mitchel had little political influence during his life but his analysis of the Famine and his anti-liberal anti-colonialism became standard interpretations among the early twentieth-century nationalists who rejected Home Rule. Pearse was drawn instinctively to his revolutionary spirit. Griffith admired Mitchel's contrariness, insisting in his 1913 foreword to a reprint of the *Jail Journal* that no excuses were needed for an Irish nationalist declining to hold the Negro his peer in right. James Connolly admired his critique of British colonialism but quietly sidestepped Mitchel's intense antipathy towards any form of socialism.

The *Jail Journal* was Mitchel's best and best-known book. It is much more than a polemic. He emphasises the decency and kindness of the prison wardens and governors, navy officers and marines he encounters. He never appears to exaggerate any hardships he experienced. Ideas and arguments that are stridently emphasised in his journalism and in his later book *The Last Conquest*, crop up as shifts in register. Mitchel the journalist and Mitchel the author of *The Last Conquest* wrote like a man possessed by great passions and greater hatreds. The Mitchel revealed in the *Jail Journal* was self-possessed. The reader learns of his beliefs and opinions but is invited to judge these against his character. Like all great political memoirs, from Julius Caesar's to Barack Obama's, Mitchel created himself as he wished others to see him. Near the end he describes how the book was written:

> After all, this 'Journal' of mine is not, strictly speaking, a Journal at all; though, for convenience, it is occasionally dated. In truth and fact, it is written long after its ostensible dates. All these reflections, inferences, and predictions: I give exactly as I wrote them down at the time. I stand to them all; though I know that many will say subsequent events have belied them.

Seemingly the *Jail Journal* polished his original notes but did not introduce things he could not have known at the time, either because he was incommunicado or on the other side of the world from the things he was writing about. Because he was a prisoner much of what he wrote about was his own mental states, though the account of his escape reads like a 'Boys' Own' adventure novel.

Page one begins with a striking account of his removal from a Dublin court on 29 May 1848 to a ship that will take him to Spike Island in Cork, the staging post for a journey he knew not where:

> I had returned to my cell and taken leave of my wife

and two poor boys. A few minutes after they had left
me a gaoler came in with a suit of coarse grey clothes
in his hand. 'You are to put on these,' said he, 'directly.'
I put them on directly. A voice then shouted from the
foot of the stairs, 'Let him be removed in his own
clothes'; so I was ordered to change again, which I did.
I asked to what place I was to be removed. 'Can't tell,'
said the man. 'Make haste.' There was a travelling bag
of mine in the cell, containing a change of clothes; and
I asked whether I might take it with me. 'No; make
haste.' 'I am ready, then'; and I followed him down
the stairs.

At Dublin's North Wall he is escorted to a steam frigate which he
learns is to bring him to the Spike Island prison in Cork. Captain
Hall, the first of many friendly gaolers, conducts him to his cabin,
orders his fetters to be removed and calls for sherry and water.
Mitchel asks Hall if he is the author of a book recounting a visit
to China which, it turns out, Hall indeed is. Both men discuss two
books by another Captain Hall, that both had happened to read.
'Your mind,' his companion comments, 'has been running upon
revolutions.' Mitchel: 'Yes, very much – almost exclusively.' The
Captain: 'Ah, sir, dangerous things, these revolutions!' Mitchel:
'You may well say that.'

Mitchel then turns on its head the impression of sangfroid that
he just conveyed. 'No doubt he thought me an amazingly cool
character, but God knoweth the heart. There was a huge lump in
my throat all the time of this bald chat.' As he converses amicably
to Hall he thinks of what might be going on in his desolate house
at Charlemont Bridge in Dublin that evening, of his family, his five
little children, 'none of them old enough to understand the cruel
blow that has fallen on them this day' and, above all, his wife. Later
in the same chapter, now on Spike Island, Mitchel again reveals the
gulf between his outer composure and inner sense of despair. Once

alone in his cell he cries for half an hour. Weeks later, in a relatively comfortable cabin in the prison hulk anchored off Bermuda he contemplates suicide but lists the reasons he must live. It would be an admission that he was unable to bear the consequences of his actions, a dying declaration that England's brute power could not be resisted. It would send his children scandalised to their graves and he hoped to do them some good yet before he died.

Still en route to Spike Island he explains why he did what he did and at such personal cost. In his *United Irishman* he had called for revolution, compelled the government to arrest him and forced it to make a 'martyr' of him. Through his arrest, trial and transportation, he had, he hoped, shamed the country out of what O'Connell called the politics of 'moral force'. There was a chance of his countrymen seeing that the one and only remedy to Ireland's grievances – to famine, emigration, political and legal corruption – was at 'the edge of the sword'. He had made sure, 'for the thing is not going to stop here', that the breach between the Irish people and the Carthaginian government would be made henceforth wider and deeper than ever. Throughout the *Jail Journals* Mitchel referred to England as Carthage, a reference no nineteenth-century schoolboy would have missed to Cato's relentlessly repeated declaration *Delenda est Carthago* ('Carthage must be destroyed').

He followed an account of his motives with portraits of his fellow would-be revolutionaries. He described William Smith O'Brien as bold and high-minded, but capricious, unaccountable, and intractable; also, he was an aristocrat who could not see that his fellow aristocrats were not Irish, but the irreconcilable enemies of Ireland. On 18 October he learns of the 'poor extemporised abortion of a rising in Tipperary' headed by Smith O'Brien on 29 July. On the little information available to him Mitchel considered it to have been ill-judged because it was so badly organised and because it had so little apparent support.

His captors, the Governor of Spike Island and the officers of *The Scourge*, the war steamer that conveys him to Bermuda, give him books to read and much of what he writes is triggered by his reading. He thanks God for Shakespeare. He reads Richard Henry Dana's *Two Years Before the Mast*, 'a pleasant, rough kind of book, but with something too much hauling of ropes and handing of sails in it'. Dana had shipped himself as a common sailor on board a Boston ship bound to California, on a two-year trading voyage, and subjected himself to short rations and the insolence of a brutal captain; and all because he had heard the sea was good for weak eyes. Mitchel had weak eyes also but pondered the contrast with his own case. He received none of the rough treatment that Dana described but he also considered himself a freer man than Dana who went on to become a successful lawyer in Boston, and therefore, perhaps, more a prisoner, drudge, and slave now than ever. He wishes to experience a thoroughgoing storm but also confesses to not being able to keep his food down during a mild one. He thinks *The Scourge* a fine ship and finds its officers good-humoured and generous. He is determined not to write another trite travelogue of the kind written by any young lady sailing to India for a husband, by a missionary or by a literary naval officer.

In a remarkable passage he sets down an inner dialogue between his Ego and a devil's advocate Doppelganger. Why such a fiery zeal for the French Republic, his Ego is asked, given its indifference to Republicanism or the welfare of the human race in the abstract? Was this vehemence born 'of pure hatred to England and a diseased longing for blood and carnage?' Was it a hatred of the millions of honest people who lived in England minding their own business? Would it destroy an economy that kept millions in employment through investment and trade?

Mitchel's Ego retorts that the Anglo-Saxon race worships only money and believes that the world was created, is sustained, and governed, and will be saved by the only one true, immutable and Almighty Pound Sterling. France mints the circulating medium of ideals and sets up poorer nations with capital in that stamp. A true friend of the British nation would declare himself the bitterest enemy of its government and institutions but also one of those content with the economic status quo, including those amongst 'the fed classes' of Ireland who declared that the country was doing reasonably well when it was instead an exploited part of a bankrupt realm with its 'hollow credit system', 'trading on what it knows to be fictitious capital', living in terror of a coming crash, held together by 'yellow chapless skulls of Skibbereen' and 'the ghosts of starved Hindoos in dusky millions':

> *Doppelganger.* - Surely these sore evils are not incurable - by wise administration, by enlightened legislation: the ghosts and skeletons are not an essential part of the picture; not necessary to the main action of the piece.

> *The Ego.* - Absolutely necessary - nay, becoming more and more necessary every hour. To uphold the stability of the grand central fraud, British policy must drain the blood and suck the marrow of all the nations it can fasten its desperate claws upon: and by the very nature of a bankrupt concern sustaining itself on false credit, its exertions must grow more desperate, its exactions more ruthless day by day, until the mighty smash come. The great British Thing cannot now do without any one of the usual sources of plunder.

But was its downfall worth the real horrors of war? Yes, insisted the Ego given the horrors of peaceful and constitutional famine. Because the Irish had been taught peaceful agitation in their slavery, they had been swept by a plague of hunger worse than many years of bloody fighting. The Ego in his dialogue admitted 'bloody dreams of carnage', a grisly frame of mind, a 'high-blazing transcendent fury,' a vehement thirst for vengeance and prescribed 'copious blood-letting upon strictly therapeutical principles':

The vengeance I seek is the righting of my country's wrong, which includes my own. Ireland, indeed, needs vengeance; but this is public vengeance - public justice. Herein England is truly a great public criminal. England! all England, operating through her Government: through all her organised and effectual public opinion, press, platform, pulpit, parliament, has done, is doing, and means to do, grievous wrong to Ireland. She must be punished; that punishment will, as I believe, come upon her by and through Ireland.

But vengeance for what? Mitchel depicts the Famine as England's greatest crime but there is antipathy towards its passive victims. Towards the end of the *Jail Journal* he records a conversation with an American who compares the position of Cuba under Spanish rule to that of Ireland under English rule. They find many similarities except 'in the matter of patience and perseverance in starvation. *There*, the Irish are unmatched amongst the white inhabitants of the earth. *No* people will lie down and die of hunger by myriads and millions, save only the natives of that gem of the sea.'

Many of his fellow convicts are Irish. In Bermuda he considers that many deserve their punishments and wants nothing to do with them. He times his exercise on the jetty so that he does not have to encounter them. After a bout of chronic asthma he is shipped to Cape Town to complete his sentence there along with nearly 200 'famine-struck' Irish prisoners. Most of these do not have a word of English and have been shattered by hunger and hardship. He is far removed from their part of the ship but hears their mournful singing. He imagines that in poor frail huts, on many an Irish hillside, their fathers and mothers dwell in poverty and fruitless labour. He sees them grieving for their lost children, with a mourning that will know no comfort till they are in their graves. But these were stock images.

On the same voyage he defends the slave trade while claiming that the high numbers that die in transit to America ('thrown overboard all alive, to avoid the forfeiture of the ships') do so because of British 'piracy'. The disruption of the slave trade, he insisted, suited British interests and had nothing to do with 'conscience, or Christianity, or any of the fine things they pretend in Parliament'. The real aims, he insisted, were to protect the planters of Jamaica and Barbados from competition and to accustom the eyes of all who sail the seas to the sight of the English flag domineering over everything it meets, like a bully, as it is.

The colony in Cape Town refused to allow Mitchel and his fellow convicts to come ashore, an action in defiance of the British Empire that Mitchel applauded. He drank fine Cape wines and looked forward to the future of an independent Republic of South Africa. The colony's boycott of the ship and its complement did not apply to Mitchel. The ship was eventually rerouted to Van Diemen's Land where the sentences of all were commuted. Mitchel was released on parole, acquired a two hundred-acre farm worked by convicts and was reunited with his family and also with other men of 1848 including Smith O'Brien. Mitchel's daring escape in 1853 was funded by the Irish Directory in New York who sent an agent to organise it. Mitchel walked into a police station with a gun in his pocket and announced that he was revoking his parole. He went into hiding and a month or so later, disguised as a priest, he boarded a ship for San Francisco.

Reunited yet again with his family he travelled to New York with plans for further sedition. His paper *The Citizen* preached against the Empire and the liberal political economy that was its engine. Slavery had to be defended because Abolitionism was the ideological jewel of the system of ideas he argued had devastated Ireland and killed or exiled millions of its people. In September 1854, in *The Citizen* where the *Jail Journal* was first serialised, he argued that the slave trade with Africa should be reopened; the 'ignorant and brutal negroes' would enjoy 'comparative happiness and dignity' as plantation hands. Mitchel arrived in New York when it was in the throes of anti-Catholic, anti-immigrant and Abolitionist agitation. Within a few years he left New York for Knoxville, Tennessee. During the American Civil War two of his sons died fighting for the Confederacy, the third was wounded and lost an arm. Mitchel enlisted as a stretcher-bearer and was imprisoned for a time after the war. Mitchel, the reactionary revolutionary who declared war on the nineteenth-century ideals of economic and social progress, has had considerable and often underappreciated influence on the revolutionary nationalism of early twentieth-century Ireland.

BF

Notes

1   John Mitchel, *Jail Journal* [1861] (Dublin: Gill and Son, 1913; foreword by Arthur Griffith).

2   John Mitchel, *The Last Conquest of Ireland (Perhaps)* [1873] (Dublin: University College Dublin Press, 2005).

8

Horace Plunkett, *Ireland in the New Century* 1904 and Michael
O'Riordan, *Catholicity and Progress in Ireland* (1905)

In 1904–05 Max Weber published in the form of two journal
articles his famous long essay, *Die protestantische Ethik und der
Geist des Kapitalismus*, later to be translated into English by Talcott
Parsons in 1930 as *The Protestant Ethic and the Spirit of Capitalism*.
Apparently as a complete coincidence, the ideas advanced by the
German thinker were also aired almost simultaneously by two Irish
writers, Horace Plunkett and Michael O'Riordan, almost certainly
because such ideas were virtually intellectual commonplaces
at the time: the central notion was that there is a connection
between certain varieties of the Christian religion and the pursuit
of capitalist material objectives. Weber argued that there was a
close sociological connection between certain ascetic varieties of
Protestantism and the rise of capitalism. The belief that work, rather
than being the curse of Adam, was actually spiritually fulfilling,
was itself a main inspiration of capitalist accumulation rather than
any old-fashioned and simple greed for gold (*auri sacra fames*).
This asceticism, associated in mediaeval Catholicism mainly with
monasticism (*laborare et orare*), in the hands of Protestant reformers

became forced into everyday life in an essentially unprecedented
and unique way, peculiar to Europe and the West and hitherto
unknown to mankind.[1] This asceticism was particularly to be
associated with Pietism and Calvinism rather than Lutheranism,
'the Puritan's serious attention to this world, his acceptance of his
life in this world as a task, could not possibly have come from the
pen of a mediaeval writer'.[2]

Horace Plunkett (1854–1932) was of aristocratic Protestant
unionist stock and was educated in Eton and Oxford. He
latched on early to the idea of cooperative organisation for Irish
farmers, a class which had recently been created by the effective
expropriation of the Irish aristocratic landowners and constituted
a half-million smallholders and middle-sized 'ranchers' on the
island of Ireland. For health reasons he spent a good deal of time
doing some 'real' ranching in Wyoming and was struck by the
huge challenge American efficiency in farming would pose in the
near future for small farmers in Ireland and in Europe generally.
From 1891 on he tried stubbornly to spread the practical ideas of
cooperative farming in Ireland, despite much resistance from local
vested interests. He was also a believer in education and scientific
innovation as keys to the progress of Irish agriculture. His unionist
politics weakened him and rendered him untrustworthy in the
minds of some nationalists, and he was forced out of parliamentary
politics in 1907. His 1904 book, *Ireland in the New Century*, didn't
help his political career, as his uncomplimentary views on Irish
character and the alleged hostility of Catholicism to industrialism
became widely touted against him.[3]

Plunkett's book coincides with the Weberian piece, but the ideas
in both were 'in the air' and even commonplace in the intellectual
world of the late nineteenth century. Plunkett focuses on Irish
character in a way that is still fascinating a century later. A key
idea he focuses on first of all is the Irish attitude to 'home'. He
claims that in his time there was 'a singular and significant void
in the Irish conception of home'.[4] He would not have noticed it, he

67

remarked, had it not been pointed out as a source of hindrance to social and economic development:

> It is not the physical environment and comfort of an orderly home that enchain and attract minds still dominated, more or less unconsciously, by the associations and common interests of the primitive clan, but rather the sense of human neighbourhood and kinship which the individual finds in the community. Indeed the Irish peasant scarcely seems to have a home in the sense in which an Englishman understands the word. If he love the place of his habitation he does not endeavour to improve or to adorn it, or to make it in any sense a reflection of his own mind and taste. He treats life as if he were a mere sojourner upon earth whose true home is somewhere else, a fact often attributed to his intense faith in the unseen, but which I regard as not merely due to this cause, but also, and in a large measure, as the natural outcome of historical conditions ... What the Irishman is really attached to in Ireland is not a home but a social order. The pleasant amenities, the courtesies, the leisureliness, the associations of religion, and the familiar faces of the neighbours, whose ways and minds are like his and very unlike those of any other people; these are the things to which he clings in Ireland and which he remembers in exile.[5]

This attitude toward home and community explains much of the history of the Irish in America. They gravitated naturally to the cities, and set up ghetto communities that echoed their ancestral villages or rural townlands back home. He tells the reader an anecdote of a daughter of a small farmer in Galway who, by her age brought up the rear of a 'long-tailed' family, was offered a comfortable home on a farm thirty miles away. She chose instead to go to New York 'because it is nearer'.[6] She preferred to be with her relatives and friends in America in a tenement building rather than be elsewhere in Galway with 'strangers' who were unrelated to her. Anyone who knows modern Ireland will recognise this trait immediately, and the immobility of labour to which it is closely connected. One's own extended family 'out foreign' is closer than non-family parts of Ireland.

A second somewhat crippling trait of the Irish mind according to Plunkett was its obsession with politics. Irish people had an almost magical faith in political nationalism. Home Rule would make some miraculous transformation of Irish realities immediately possible. A certain millennial style of thought had long been common in Ireland, going back to the days of Whiteboyism and the prophecies of Malachy, Colmcille and various other mainly fictional worthies whose scribblings impressed mightily some of the peasantry. The moral to be drawn by Irish political leaders was that one of the worst legacies of centuries of misgovernment was the almost unconscious belief that law-making by a friendly and locally elected legislature could 'provide an escape from the physical and mental toil imposed through our first parents upon all nations for all time'.[7] Irish people were very politically adept and well-informed about their leaders, but there was a 'follow-the-leader' syndrome in Irish political culture by which the leader had a heroic character ascribed to him by the voters; commonly the leader was regarded as a kind of mysterious and benign genius. Parnell and O'Connell are the obvious examples here, but the cults of Lord Edward Fitzgerald or Wolfe Tone presumably occurred to Plunkett as well. The Irish had an extraordinary ability to organise themselves for mass politics, but very little ability to reason politically and separate out policies which made practical sense from those which were really visionary rhetoric. In our own time the exaggerated cults of such genuinely able, but commonly heroised, men as Michael Collins, Seán Lemass or Eamon de Valera make Plunkett's insight seem prophetic:

> O'Connell's great work in freeing Roman Catholic Ireland from the domination of the Protestant oligarchy showed the people the power of combination, but his methods can hardly be said to have fostered political thought. The efforts in this direction of men like Gavan Duffy, Davis and Lucas were neutralised by the Famine, the after effects of which also did much to thwart Butt's attempts to develop serious public opinion amongst a people whose political education had been so long delayed. The prospect of any early fruition of such efforts vanished with the revolutionary agrarian propaganda, and independent thinking – so necessary in the modern democratic state – never replaced the old leader-following habit which continued until the climax was reached under Parnell.[8]

The Irish had the right man, so what did the principles matter? Plunkett argues that in political life the Irish had very great physical courage, but little real moral bravery: an unwillingness to stand out from the crowd and dissent in a way that might be useful but unpopular. The Irish thus had a fixed belief that aggressive agitation was the best way to force a British government to concede reform.

The third feature of the Irish was, of course, their religiosity. Religion was, Plunkett observed, more dominant an element in daily life than in any other country he could think of, and ministers of religion had extraordinary authority; an authority willingly accepted and obeyed normally by the vast majority of the population. This situation is one which the clergy did not themselves create, and they were as much a product of historical forces as were their congregations. If the British were to make religious toleration a mainstay of their polity, Catholicism and its basic claim to control the education of the children of the faithful would have to be respected and accepted by a tolerant and enlightened government. The Irish were divided, he argued, into two 'sections', Catholics and Protestants. Protestantism was centred on Ulster and its industrial towns, whereas Catholicism tended to be associated with farming in the other three provinces of Ireland. Bigotry existed on both sides, although most Irish people were able to live and let live quite happily. Protestantism was associated with relative wealth and absence of a lassitude in regard to work, the latter being commonly a feature of Catholics. In a famous quotation Plunkett remarks:

> Roman Catholicism strikes an outsider as being in some of its tendencies non-economic, if not actually anti-economic. These tendencies have, of course, much fuller play when they act on a people whose education has (through no fault of their own) been retarded or stunted. ... I am simply adverting to what has appeared to me, in the course of my experience in Ireland, to be a defect in the industrial character of Roman Catholics which, however caused, seems to me to have been intensified by their religion. The reliance of that religion on authority, its repression of individuality, and its complete shifting of what I may call the moral centre of gravity to a future existence – to mention no other characteristics – appear to me to be calculated, unless supplemented by other influences, to check the qualities of initiative and self-reliance, especially among a people whose lack of education unfits them for resisting the influence of what may present itself to such minds as a kind of fatalism with resignation as its supreme virtue.[9]

Plunkett conceded that Catholicism had often intervened

benignly in economic life, and he instanced in particular the creation of craft guilds in mediaeval times and the suppression of slavery. However, since the Reformation, Catholic countries had remained poorer, more agrarian and less advanced generally than Protestant countries. Exceptions existed to this general pattern he admitted, notably in Belgium, northern France, parts of Germany, Austria and northern Italy. He further admitted that Catholics in Ireland were for centuries deprived of any opportunity to engage in economic activity of an advanced capitalist nature. Further, the abnormally great power of the Catholic clergy had not been abused as it might well have been. Catholic toleration of Protestants in their midst was impressive, he readily conceded.

However, the clergy had been far too eager to use the donations of their willing faithful on huge and expensive churches, clearly in reaction to the impoverished little side-street 'mass houses' or caves in mountainsides where they had been forced to observe their sacred rites in the eighteenth century. Furthermore, in a poor country with a declining population, the multiplication of prosperous monasteries and convents, involving an enormous annual expenditure, most of it coming out of the pockets of poor people, seemed anomalous, he argued. Many of these organisations did good work in supplying cheap education to the poor and caring for the sick and destitute. Unfortunately, this had commonly the effect of denying to the people instruction by laypeople directly aware of the economic and social worlds in which ordinary people had to live. All this had a noticeable effect on the general character of the Catholic people of the country:

> The impartial observer will, I fear, find amongst the majority of our people a striking lack of self-reliance and moral courage; an entire lack of serious thought on public questions; a listlessness and apathy in regard to economic improvement which amount to a form of fatalism; and, in backward districts, a survival

of superstition, which saps all strength of will and purpose – and all this too amongst a people singularly gifted with good qualities of mind and heart.[10]

This, of course, was the argument which was to enrage many Catholics, whether lay or clerical. A year later, Father Michael O'Riordan was to publish a book-length rebuttal of Plunkett.[11] O'Riordan was the son of a prosperous farmer in Limerick, evidently intelligent and energetic. His education was in the local national school and diocesan seminary, and he spent years in Rome at various third-level institutions and some time in London. The rest of his working life was spent in St Munchin's in Limerick City and he became a well-known propagandist for the Catholic and nationalist causes in Ireland. He later became a conspicuous contributor to *The Catholic Bulletin*, an extremist magazine known to history mainly for specialising in anti-Semitic blood libel stories.

Catholicity and Progress in Ireland is an impassioned investigation into the historical causes of Irish backwardness and lethargy that constitutes a frontal attack on Plunkett's position. Ireland was subjected to legalised looting for two centuries, its land being stolen in the seventeenth century and its people forced by law to pay tithes to a church whose beliefs they did not share. At the same time the Irish people, overwhelmingly Catholic in faith, were prohibited by law from pursuing the kinds of profession or trade that might have made them able to tolerate tithing and other exactions. In the eighteenth century, any Irish export trade to Britain which showed signs of competing successfully against its English equivalent was tariffed or even forbidden to engage in export trade anywhere in the Empire or even planet-wide. He quotes Lecky, a Protestant historian unsympathetic to the Catholic case:

The English, however, were still unsatisfied. The Irish

woollen manufactures had already been excluded by the Navigation Act from the whole Colonial market; they had been virtually excluded from England itself, by duties amounting to prohibition. A law of crushing severity, enacted by the English Parliament in 1699, completed the work and prohibited the Irish from exporting their manufactured wool to any other country whatever. So ended the fairest promise Ireland had ever known of becoming a prosperous and happy country. The ruin was absolute and final.[12]

Many Irish skilled workers, both Protestant and Catholic, were forced by this measure to emigrate to France, Spain or the German states. Their 'simpler, more economically minded' religion did not help the Protestants, who shared the ruin of both communities. Again, the landlords were permitted to increase rents if a tenant tried to improve his holding by extending his cottage or increasing his output. Inevitably, since the fruits of his labour were denied him, he ceased to labour. Such was the obvious historical origin of a certain Irish listlessness. O'Riordan remarks politely that it was a pity that Horace Plunkett, a distinguished and evidently well-meaning man, should have lent his voice to a chorus of denunciation of a people whose condition was so obviously the result of generations of mismanagement, bigotry and class selfishness.[13] An angry passage summarises what seems to have been his gut feeling about the country's wretched history:

The fatalism which [Plunkett] has found among the people was caused by the insurmountable barrier which the law built up between them and all industrial improvement. Even a drowning man strikes out as long as he has hope to reach the shore, but he sinks helplessly to the bottom when all hope is gone. Their fatalism arose not from the inexorable laws of nature,

but from the inexorable laws of man. It is true they
were under the power of three fates. They had their
Clotho, Lachesis and Atropos, in misgovernment, in
landlordism and in Protestantism; their only ray of
hope and spring of happiness came from that Catholic
faith to which their critics trace all their woes.[14]

On top of all this, O'Riordan also remarks acidly that Plunkett had
the temerity to complain when Irish Catholics, confined by law
to shopkeeping and other 'ignoble' trades, at length put together
enough money to replace the churches that had been stolen from
them two centuries earlier. Much of this money actually came from
rich people in Ireland and America, as well as coming from the
pennies of the poor. To condemn them for this admirable attempt at
restitution, O'Riordan felt, was impertinent. A French observer of
an earlier time (Gustave de Beaumont in his *L'Irlande* of 1839, 1863
edition with addendum) had referred in 1863 to that Protestant
mixture of institutionalised exploitation and traditional contempt
toward Catholics in Ireland as a studied 'insolence'. Employment
in the public service in Ireland was subject for some time to what a
later generation would term a glass ceiling. No Catholic needed in
many cases even apply for senior employment in the civil service,
the judiciary, the police, the armed forces or many professions and,
in any case, if actually employed needed not to expect promotion
beyond a humble level. Ireland at the beginning of the twentieth
century was, despite land reform and rationalisation of the
bureaucracy, still governed overwhelmingly by Protestant officials.
Reform was coming, but very slowly and reluctantly. Catholics
emigrated, for obvious reasons. They could exercise their talents
and abilities elsewhere in a way that was effectively forbidden
them in Ireland. No Catholic religious prohibition or disregard
inhibited them outside the Island of Ireland, so why should such
an alleged prohibition or disregard magically disappear once they
left the country? Plunkett seems to have had no real answer to such

questions, reflecting as they did the anger of the Catholic hierarchy and of nationalists in general.[15]

TG

Notes

1   Max Weber, 'Die protestantische Ethik und der Geist des Kapitalismus', *Archiv fuer Sozialwissenschaft und Sozialpolitik*, Vols XX, XXI (1904–05); trans. Talcott Parsons as *The Protestant Ethic and the Spirit of Capitalism* (London: Unwin, 1930).

    See in general, with more emphasis on the problem of usury than on asceticism, R. H. Tawney, *Religion and the Rise of Capitalism* [1926] (London: Murray, 1936).

2   Max Weber, *The Protestant Ethic and the Spirit of Capitalism*, trans. Talcott Parsons (London: Unwin, 1930), p.88.

3   *Dictionary of Irish Biography*, (Cambridge and Dublin: Cambridge University Press and Royal Irish Academy, 2009), Vol. 8, pp.180–82.

4   Horace Plunkett, *Ireland in the New Century* (Port Washington, NY: Kennikat Press, 1970), p.53.

5   Ibid., pp.54–5.

6   Ibid., p.58.

7   Ibid., p.61.

8   Ibid., pp.77–8.

9   Ibid., pp.101–2.

10 Ibid., p.110.

11 M. O'Riordan, *Catholicity and Progress in Ireland* [1905] (London: Kegan Paul, Trench, Trubner and Co., 1906).

12 Ibid., pp.142–3.

13 Ibid., p.359.

14 Ibid., p.258.

15 Patrick Long, *Dictionary of Irish Biography*, Vol. 7, pp.879–80.

9

James Connolly, *Labour in Irish History* (1910)

In *Labour in Irish History* James Connolly (1868–1916) sought to demonstrate the almost total indifference of previous generations of Irish patriots to the sufferings of the ordinary people. He proposed 'to repair the deliberate neglect of the social question' by nationalist historians and to prepare the ground for further analyses of how economic conditions have controlled and dominated Irish history. Connolly's tragedy perhaps was that he died in a revolution that was overwhelmingly nationalist and conservative in character; one that paid lip service only to the principles set out in the 1916 Proclamation that he co-authored, of treating all the children of the nation equally.

Connolly, the child of impoverished emigrant parents, grew up in Edinburgh. He enlisted in the British Army at the age of fourteen and was stationed for most of his seven-year term in Ireland. He returned to Edinburgh to work as a dustman, became a socialist and was sent by Kier Hardie in 1896 at the age of twenty-eight to evangelise the Irish; rather like Saint Patrick, who had also criss-crossed the Irish sea to find his faith and win Ireland for it more than fifteen centuries earlier. Connolly was sent to Dublin to set up an Irish branch of a British Socialist Party but within a month of arriving he went his own way. He founded the Irish Socialist Republican Party (ISRP) and from 1898 edited its newspaper *The Workers' Republic*. There he published early drafts of what would become *Labour in Irish History*.[1] He threw himself into activism and scholarship whilst working variously as a navvy, a cobbler and a printer's assistant.

Much of the analysis and argument in *Labour in Irish History* dates from the immediate period after he returned to Ireland. In his 1897 pamphlet *Erin's Hope: the Ends and the Means* he argued that socialism in Ireland could not be realised without national independence and although the interests of workers were identical all over the world, 'it was also true that each country had better work out its own salvation on the lines most congenial to its own people'.[2] Like Patrick, who repeatedly explained Christianity to the Irish in terms of their own culture and left a Church that consecrated lightly disguised Pagan festivals, Connolly identified Irish antecedents of socialism that could be inserted into the narratives of Irish nationalism.

Connolly's analysis was designed to appeal to the cultural nationalists of the Gaelic Revival who sought to reinstate the Irish Language to its pre-seventeenth-century status. Where cultural nationalists emphasised the destruction of an indigenous Irish culture, Connolly emphasised the social and economic consequences of the post-Reformation conquest of Ireland. As put in the foreword of *Labour in Irish History*:

> If we would understand the national literature of a people, we must study their social and political status, keeping in mind the fact that their writers were a product thereof, and that the children of their brains were conceived and brought forth in certain historical conditions. Ireland, at the same time as she lost her

ancient social system, also lost her language as the vehicle of thought of those who acted as her leaders. As a result of this twofold loss, the nation suffered socially, nationally and intellectually from a prolonged arrested development. During the closing years of the seventeenth century, all the eighteenth, and the greater part of the nineteenth, the Irish people were the lowest helots in Europe, socially and politically. The Irish peasant, reduced from the position of a free clansman owning his tribeland and controlling its administration in common with his fellows, was a mere tenant-at-will subject to eviction, dishonour and outrage at the hands of an irresponsible private proprietor. Politically he was non-existent, legally he held no rights, intellectually he sank under the weight of his social abasement, and surrendered to the downward drag of his poverty.

As part of the intellectual groundwork that culminated in *Labour in Irish History* he published a series of five pamphlets to celebrate (and claim for socialism) the legacy of the 1798 Rebellion. One of these 1798 centenary pamphlets consisted of a section of Wolfe Tone's *An Argument on behalf of the Catholics of Ireland* (1791). An August 1898 editorial in *The Workers' Republic*, headlined 'The Men We Honour' argued that Tone had refused to 'prostitute his genius in the cause of compromise and time serving'.[3] For this he had been crucified in life and idolised in death by Irishmen who, had he been still alive would have repudiated him as a dangerous malcontent. Tone, Connolly argued, grasped that British dominion in Ireland could only be dislodged by a radical revolution in step with the ideals of the French revolution of his day. Modern-day nationalists could only win meaningful freedom for Ireland, he insisted, if they similarly embraced socialist ideals.

Modern Irish history, according to Connolly, started with the close of the Williamite Wars in 1691. The following two centuries of Irish politics came to be largely determined by how different sections of the Irish people regarded the conflict which ended with the surrender of Sarsfield and the garrison of Limerick. Never in all the history of Ireland, he argued, had there been a war in which the people of Ireland had less reason to take one side or another. Connolly viewed the Jacobites – supporters of King James – as little better than traitors for plunging the Irish people into a war on behalf of a foreign tyrant. Jacobite Catholic gentlemen and nobles possessed considerable property to which they had no more right to than any Cromwellian or Williamite adventurer. The lands they held were tribal lands which in former times had belonged to the Irish people. As such, the peasantry, already reduced to the position of mere tenants-at-will, were the rightful owners of the soil, while the Jacobite landowners were either the descendants of men who had obtained their property as the spoils of conquest, or men who had taken sides with the oppressor against their own countrymen and were allowed to retain their property as the fruits of what amounted to treason. Successive waves of Irish patriotism, from the settler nobility who established a Parliament in the time of Henry II to the Ascendency descendants of seventeenth-century planters, represented the interests of Irish landowning classes and not those of the Irish people. As put in chapter five of *Labour in Irish History*:

> At once they became patriots, anxious that Ireland – which, in their phraseology, meant the ruling class in Ireland – should be free from the control of the Parliament of England. Their pamphlets, speeches, and all public pronouncements were devoted to telling the world how much nicer, equitable, and altogether more delectable it would be for the Irish people to be robbed in the interests of a native-born aristocracy than to witness the painful spectacle of that aristocracy being

compelled to divide the plunder with its English rival. Perhaps Swift, Molyneux, or Lucas did not confess even to themselves that such was the basis of their political creed. The human race has at all times shown a proneness to gloss over its basest actions with a multitude of specious pretences, and to cover even its iniquities with the glamour of a false sentimentality. But we are not dealing with appearances but realities, and, in justice to ourselves, we must expose the flimsy sophistry which strives to impart to a sordid, self-seeking struggle the appearance of a patriotic movement.

Connolly also argued that many of the better-off beneficiaries of Catholic Emancipation were also less than credible patriots:

The lower middle class gave to the National cause in the past many unselfish patriots, but, on the whole, while willing and ready enough to please their humble fellow country-men, and to compound with their own conscience by shouting louder than all others their untiring devotion to the cause of freedom, they, as a class, unceasingly strove to divert the public mind upon the lines of constitutional agitation for such reforms as might remove irritating and unnecessary officialism, while leaving untouched the basis of national and economic subjection. This policy enabled them to masquerade as patriots before the unthinking multitude, and at the same time lent greater force to their words when as 'patriot leaders' they cried down any serious revolutionary movement that might demand from them greater proofs of sincerity than could be furnished by the strength of their lungs, or greater sacrifices than would be suitable to their exchequer.

81

Connolly argued that while the Penal Laws made the lives of propertied Catholics more insecure than would otherwise have been the case, their impact on wealthy Catholics had been much overrated. Class interests trumped religious ones and class inequalities undermined solidarity with co-religionists. Like John Mitchel, a strong influence on *Labour in Irish History*, Connolly argued that Daniel O'Connell had betrayed the Irish people. O'Connell had sided with the Whig government at a time when the labouring population of England 'were the most exploited, degraded, and almost dehumanised of all the peoples of Europe'. He had sided with the Irish capitalist and professional classes and worked to quash efforts by Chartists to establish a trade union movement. In further echoes of Mitchel he argued that 'all except a few men had elevated landlord property and capitalist political economy to a fetish to be worshipped, and upon the altar of that fetish Ireland perished'. During the Famine, he claimed, free trade filled the stores of speculating capitalists with corn but left those who had sown and reaped it unfed. Free trade 'unpeopled villages and peopled poorhouses'; it 'consolidated farms and glutted the graveyards with famished corpses'. The language here was Mitchel's but insofar as Mitchel was no socialist, Connolly had to turn elsewhere to find inspiration from the Irish past.

Two chapters in *Labour in Irish History* celebrated nineteenth-century efforts to promote socialist ideas in Ireland. One described the ideas and social experiments of William Thompson, 'a forerunner of Marx', 'a Socialist who did not hesitate to direct attention to the political and social subjection of labour as the worst evil of society; nor to depict, with a merciless fidelity to truth, the disastrous consequences to political freedom of the presence in society of a wealthy class'. Thompson's analyses of labour, capital and surplus value anticipated conclusions drawn by Karl Marx. He argued that political reform should be understood as a means to an end and as inefficient as an end in itself. Connolly located Thompson intellectually as midway between Utopian idealists like Owens and the historical materialism of Marx. Thompson had been 'the first writer to elevate the question of the just distribution of wealth to the supreme position it has since held in English political economy'.

Another chapter described the foundation of a model community in County Clare inspired by Robert Owen's New Lanark. Owen had visited Dublin in 1832 to explain the principles of Socialism at a time, as Connolly put it, 'Socialism was the fad of the rich instead of the faith of the poor.' One of his audience, Arthur Vandeleur, went on to establish a Socialist colony on his estate at Ralahine, County Clare whilst charging its members a hefty rent. It had been envisaged that the cooperative would eventually purchase the land it leased from Vandeleur. However, Vandeleur had a gambling problem and fled in disgrace, unable to pay his debts. In the ensuing bankruptcy proceedings the court refused to recognise the community and in repossessing the estate treated its members as common labourers with no rights to the land they had worked. The failure of Ralahine, Connolly emphasised, was due to the laws of property. If the land had been owned by the people who worked it, it would surely have been viable, he argued.

Labour in Irish History described how, even while the Ralahine experiment was underway, lodges of the secret Ribbon Society:

> ... made midnight raids for arms upon the houses of the gentry, assembled at night in large bodies and ploughed up the grass lands, making them useless for grazing purposes, filled up ditches, terrorised graziers into surrendering their ranches, wounded and killed those who had entered the service of graziers or obnoxious landlords, assassinated agents, and sometimes, in sheer despair, opposed their unarmed bodies to the arms of the military.

Such conflicts, he argued, highlighted the crucial underlying issues that had shaped Irish politics for centuries:

> As we have again and again pointed out, the Irish question is a social question, the whole age-long fight of the Irish people against their oppressors resolves itself, in the last analysis into a fight for the mastery of the means of life, the sources of production, in Ireland. Who would own and control the land? The people or the invaders; and if the invaders, which set of them – the most recent swarm of land-thieves, or the sons of the thieves of a former generation? These were the bottom questions of Irish politics, and all other questions were valued or deprecated in the proportion to which they contributed to serve the interests of some of the factions who had already taken their stand in this fight around property interests. Without this key to the meaning of events, this clue to unravel the actions of 'great men', Irish history is but a welter of unrelated facts, a hopeless chaos of sporadic outbreaks, treacheries, intrigues, massacres, murders, and purposeless warfare.

The final chapter of *Labour in Irish History* was clumsily entitled 'The working class; The inheritors of the Irish ideas of the past – The repository of the hopes of the future.' In it he asserted that Ireland's 1798 Revolution embodied the spirit of the first French Revolution, that Irish society in 1848 (as distinct from the Catholic middle class) 'throbbed in sympathy with the democratic and social upheavals on the Continent of Europe and England' and that the Fenians of 1867 also reflected 'the same coincidence of militant class feeling and revolutionary nationalism'. His unrealised hope was for a twentieth-century nationalist rebellion in tune with the radical socialist ideals he espoused. Many of his heroes – Tone,

Michel and Fintan Lalor – were also those of Pearse, who described their writings as the new testament of Irish nationalism.

BF

Notes

1 James Connolly, *Labour in Irish History* [1910]. All citations from James Connolly, *Collected Works: Volume One* (Dublin: New Books, 1987).

2 James Connolly, 'Erin's Hope: The Ends and the Means' [Dublin 1897], in Owen Dudley Edwards and Bernard Ransom (eds), *Selected Political Writings* (New York: Grove, 1974), pp.187–8.

3 James Connolly, *Worker's Republic*, 13 August 1898.

10

Canon Patrick A. Sheehan, *The Graves at Kilmorna* (1913)

In Canon Sheehan's last completed novel *The Graves at Kilmorna*, set in Tipperary and Cork in the years around the Fenian rising of 1867, Halpin, a Fenian village schoolmaster, sees that the growing materialism of modern Ireland can only be countered by heroic self-sacrifice and violence. The country is becoming indifferent to everything but 'bread and cheese' and needs 'blood-letting a little'. The Fenian rebels are not so much soldiers as 'preachers, prophets and martyrs'. Their message is to be not principally in words but rather in the form of heroic acts.[1]

The hero, Myles Cogan, does time in solitary for rebellion against the Crown and returns to Ireland from prison in time to see the country in the middle of the Land War of 1879–81. Amid the greed for land, there is no room for Fenian idealism, and Cogan dreams of an Ireland preserved from the materialism of other nations. An honest man, he cannot be a successful businessman in this degenerate modern world; his rivals outstrip him by means which the writer gives us to understand are unfair and dishonest. Cogan sees that democracy brings with it cultural and moral decay; democracy will inevitably lead to socialism, uniformity and cosmopolitanism. In his despair, he is comforted by a visionary monk who prophesies that Ireland will become industrialised and prosperous in the future and will inevitably undergo moral degeneracy in the process; the beloved land will be polluted by industry. Eventually the Irish will become disgusted with themselves and will revert to the ancient Irish anti-materialist and monastic ideal admired by people like Geoffrey Keating in the early seventeenth century. Myles stands for election and is killed by a stone thrown by a drunken activist while on the hustings.[2] The book was never out of print in Ireland and Irish-America for half a century after Sheehan's death in 1913. As late as the 1950s, it was serialised for children on Radio Éireann. As an early biographer remarked, 'There were not a few who held that *The Graves at Kilmorna* was the bible of Sinn Fein.'[3]

Patrick Sheehan was born in Mallow, County Cork, in 1852. His parents died in 1863–64, leaving him an orphan and the ward of the parish priest of St Mary's; he was surrounded by the world of priests all his life. His best friend as a child was William O'Brien, later to become a well-known nationalist politician who urged a conciliatory line toward unionists in the 1900s. As priest and patriot together, or perhaps as two bright and energetic Corkmen, Sheehan and O'Brien became life-long allies. Sheehan was to become a secular priest, having his vocation awakened by encountering a young seminarian from Maynooth and experiencing an adolescent feeling of hero worship. He was fascinated by the glamorous cloak and general costume of the young man. He was a dreamy boy, much given to reading but alert to the political life around him, particularly the growing popularity of Fenian insurrectionism.[4] He was ordained in 1875 and spent some time in parishes in England and various parts of Cork, before becoming parish priest of Doneraile, County Cork, in 1895. He became a canon in 1903 and died ten years later in 1913. Sheehan made quite a reputation for himself in his later years as an essayist and novelist, writing tales of Irish Catholic and rural life of a kind that appealed to the popular taste of a newly educated and literate Irish Catholic and English-speaking public. He started writing in earnest around 1888.[5] Between 1895 and 1913, he published ten novels and several works of religious and philosophical thought.

Several prominent themes run through his writings. One is a fervent Catholic piety, often mixed with a horror of the emerging urban, secular English-language world that he saw around him; a world of scepticism and secularism that had triumphed in England and which he saw as threatening his beloved Catholic Ireland. Another theme is an equally fervent Irish nationalism, sometimes taking the form of a sympathy for, if not always agreement with, the passions that lay behind the romantic nationalism of the Fenian movement, later normally referred to as the Irish Republican Brotherhood or IRB.[6] A further theme was a firm belief in the duty of the Catholic priests of Ireland to lead the Catholic people, not just as spiritual guides, but in effect as political and social leaders of the community. A last major feature of his writing was a wish to reconcile the chronic divide between landlord and tenant, typically by means of achieving the religious conversion of the former.

Besides his literary activities, Sheehan attempted to put his ideas on leadership into effect, becoming a very successful organiser of his parish in Doneraile. He helped set up little factories and commercial concerns to keep the young of the parish at home, with particular emphasis on discouraging the emigration of young women from the villages to the big towns of Ireland, Britain and America. In this he was something of a forerunner of later priestly leaders, a more recent example being Father James McDyer of Glencolumbkille, County Donegal, who similarly did parish work in England before embarking on his well-known experiment in village-building in his native county during the late 1960s.

Sheehan's first novel, *Geoffrey Austin: Student* was written quite late in his life, in 1895, and published anonymously apparently because of the general distrust of publication that ran through much clerical culture in the Ireland of that time.[7] His fear of censure was not totally unfounded; around the same time, his contemporary, Father Walter McDonald of the Dunboyne Establishment, was to get into hot water with the bishops for publishing a philosophical treatise entitled *Motion*. He was forced to go around Dublin and buy up copies of his own book and burn them because of some fear of possible heresy.[8] While, *Geoffrey Austin* did receive some Catholic hostility, as it seemed to contain an anonymous attack on Catholic education, its sequel, *The Triumph of Failure*, which narrates the further progress of Austin, got a friendlier reception.[9] Unlike McDonald, Sheehan suffered no humiliation and his works became very popular, remaining staple favourites of Irish Catholic readers in the British Isles and the United States for two generations after his death.

Geoffrey Austin is evidently partially autobiographical; the familiar theme of horror at the emergent secular world gripping the mind of its young protagonist, a Catholic student who spends some time in London, very evidently seen as the Great Wen and centre of urban evil. Austin is introduced by a genial German teacher to the wonders of German romantic thought, in particular the writings of Schiller and Novalis. In *The Triumph of Failure*, published five years later, Austin lives in Dublin as a poor man and comes under the influence of Charles Travers, who is leading a religious revival. Travers is destroyed by powerful people using dishonest means, and Travers dies. However, his heroic failure sparks a spiritual awakening in Austin, who eventually becomes a monk. The title of this book became also the title of Ruth Dudley Edwards' classic study of Pearse, the title being suggested by her mother, Sheila Edwards, wife of Professor Robert Dudley Edwards of UCD. Mrs Edwards evidently saw the Sheehan connection. Strangely, there is no further reference to Sheehan or his novel in the book.[10]

Like many other priests in Ireland at the time, Sheehan was appalled at the character of both the popular and the intellectual literature that was being churned out by the London printing presses and was pouring into Ireland. Unlike some extremists in the Gaelic League, he did not propose the killing off of the English language in Ireland and its replacement by Irish, seen as a more Catholic language than English. English was, after all, the language of a highly successful but overwhelmingly Protestant civilisation. Instead he proposed that 'Christian idealism' be tried in Irish English-language literature instead, and that this cultural experiment would be tried in Ireland as a means of counteracting English post-Christian thought. He was not very optimistic about success, and felt that Ireland had suffered a great moral and cultural degradation due to English cultural influence and the coming of popular and democratic modes of thought, styles, songs and reading:

> The literary instinct has died out in Ireland since '48. Our colleges and universities, with one or two exceptions, are dumb. The art of conversation is as dead as the art of embalming. And a certain unspeakable vulgarism has taken the place of all the grace and courtesy, all the dignity and elegance of the last century.[11]

Sheehan was much influenced by German romanticism and linked this perceived decay in culture and manners with the general European tendency to desert Christianity; a trend which he saw as stemming from the French Revolution and ultimately, from the Reformation. Materialism was the motivating power behind this process of 'retreat towards Paganism'. He was willing to see in Irish Catholicism and even in the various reformed versions of Christianity, a potential core of resistance to this apparently diabolical encroachment of modernism and secularism:

> The intense devotion, the sweetness, the delicacy, the elevation of thought, that belong to Catholicity are beginning to pall on a world that is every day becoming more egotistic, more selfish, more sensual. But to all

pure and lofty minds ... in every one of the dissolving creeds that spring from the fatal Reformation, the divine and holy spirit which breathes through the testaments of Christianity, will still appeal [12]

Like many other Irish provincial intellectuals in the period between the Famine and the end of de Valera's isolationism in the 1950s, Sheehan felt isolated, even lonely. Francis MacManus described a similar set of emotions vividly, writing a generation later in an account of Sheehan's correspondence in 1910 with his friend, Oliver Wendell Holmes of the US Supreme Court:

'The great want of my life is lack of intellectual intercourse; and your letters are a stimulus that drives me from the superficialities of daily life into depths of thought where I have no temptation otherwise to plunge ...' ... It was not mere courtesy to his distinguished friend. It was the controlled cry of loneliness in an ageing man who could deal with all the frustrating powers only in the privacy of his study and on paper. 'The infirmities of age are creeping down on myself,' he wrote, 'and I am becoming more home-tied every day, working on and trying to get in as much useful travail as I can before the night falls.' ... The priest-citizen would show, 'that there are no invincible antagonisms amongst the peoples who make up the commonwealth of Ireland, no mutual repugnances that may not be removed by a freer and kindlier intercourse with each other.'[13]

Toward the end of his life, which coincided with the rise of the Gaelic League, the failure of constitutional politics in Ireland and the rise of military volunteering, Sheehan began to see a connection between the ideology of anti-materialism and the cult of violence which was growing stronger in Ireland, much as it was elsewhere in Europe.

Sheehan saw the priests as the main line of defence against materialism and neo-paganism. He also counted heavily on the womenfolk, as Irish women were more virtuous and spiritual than their English sisters. He recounts with evident approval and hope an anecdote of a lady and her two daughters who visit the National Gallery in Dublin, evidently for the first time, 'with that eager look which people assume when they expect something delightful'. However, when they see the classical nude statuary, they seem 'transfixed themselves, so tense are their surprise and horror'. The three rush out of the Gallery 'into the open air'.[14] Sheehan certainly valued innocence, an innocence he seems to have shared; he was apparently unaware that his great friend Holmes was having an affair with the wife of the revered landlord of Doneraile.

The weak point in the Catholic defences, he felt, was a menace within the gates. This was the growth of a new breed of semi-educated young men who, in Ireland as elsewhere, were looking for a place for themselves in the scheme of things and were suffering certain characteristic frustrations. Many of these would become the 'educated unemployed' of the future, he warned, writing in 1903–04. These young men were commonly discriminated against by employers on account of their Catholicism, although Sheehan did not make that specific point about sectarianism in hiring practices; it was difficult for a Catholic to get employment in the banks, the railways or business, and even in the public sector. Various glass ceilings ensured that few Catholics rose beyond subaltern status. Sheehan argued that the young men would not be like their fathers, who accepted clerical restraint; the sons would try to throw these restrictions off. He suggested that their inevitable tendency to complain should be countered by further education and the 'judicious employment' of some of them. The young men (and some of the women) were showing worrying tendencies of paying attention to non-Catholic or even anti-Catholic writers. He saw George Moore as a particularly dangerous influence. In 1903–04 Sheehan urged the student seminarians of Maynooth to ensure that they retained the intellectual leadership of Ireland which they enjoyed; in view of the inevitable anti-clericalism of the laity, the priests would have to retain that intellectual leadership for half a century.[15]

Canon Sheehan's own life experience both as a child and as an older man suggested the theme of what became his best-known and liked book, *My New Curate*, published in 1899.[16] This rather sentimental work portrays the priest as an old man; a benign patriarchal father of his parish who welcomes a young and inexperienced curate parachuted in on him unexpectedly. The young man introduces new practices and increases devotionalism; the young men go to him for confession and political advice. The new curate also tries to improve local industry in the form of fisheries and shirt-making. A strike wrecks the shirt factory and a trawler sinks, leaving the curate legally responsible for the financial losses. However, the village rallies to him, the local landlord converts to Catholicism, a local saint is created, and all ends happily. In a way, the book can be seen as the old Sheehan interviewing, supervising and advising his younger self, being his own father, befriending his admirable but occasionally wayward son; a father he scarcely knew in real life. Old Father Hanrahan ('Old Daddy Dan') reflects on his new curate:

There is nothing human that does not interest me. All the waywardness of humanity provokes a smile; there is no wickedness so great that I cannot pity; no folly that I cannot condone; patient to wait for the unravelling of the skein of life till the great Creator willeth, meanwhile looking at all things *sub specie aeternitatis*, and ever finding new food for humility in the barrenness of my own life. But it has been a singular intellectual revival for me to feel all my old

principles and thoughts shadowing themselves clearer
and clearer on the negatives of memory where the
sunflames of youth imprinted them, and from which,
perhaps, they will be transferred to the tablets that last
for eternity. But here God has been very good unto me
in sending me this young priest to revive the past. We
like to keep our consciousness till we die. I am glad to
have been aroused by so sympathetic a spirit from the
coma of thirty years. It is quite true that he disturbs,
now and again, the comforts of senile lethargy. And
sometimes the old Adam will cry out, and sigh for
the leaden ages, for he is pursuing with invincible
determination his great work of revival in the parish.[17]

Sheehan was an able writer and a good psychologist. Like all
successful psychologists, he understood himself rather well and
could generalise from his own interior experience to other people's.
He was obviously better on priests than laypeople, and far better on
men than he was on women; women he idealised, demonised and
sentimentalised in classic Victorian fashion. How laymen actually
made a living seems to have been something of a mystery to him.
However, he articulated an ethos which was to become extremely
common in the clericalised Ireland of the early twentieth century
and which was not without its attractions. Much of the modern
revulsion from the commercialised life and the cosmopolitanism
of contemporary life is prefigured brilliantly in his writings, as this
Irish nineteenth-century country priest tried to come to terms with
the English and American commercial and democratic world that
was overwhelming the allegedly benign and patriarchal feudalism
that he grew up with and came to idealise. Also there is in the
books the idea of an eternal repetitiveness of a benign process that
should never be interrupted: the Catholic parish as a tiny Platonic
polity, led by its priests, united by love against landlord, policeman,
bailiff and government. The idea is unreal, but not contemptible.
TG

Notes

1   P.A. Sheehan, *The Graves at Kilmorna* [1913] (Dublin: Phoenix, n.d.), pp.66–8.

2   Ibid., pp.268–70, 339–41.

3   M.P. Linehan, *Canon Sheehan of Doneraile* (Dublin: Talbot Press, 1952), p.155. See in general, Ruth Fleischmann, *Catholic Nationalism in the Irish Revival: A Study of Canon Sheehan, 1852–1913*, (London: Macmillan, 1997).

4   Francis MacManus, 'The Fate of Canon Sheehan', *The Bell*, XV, 2 (November 1947), pp.16–26.

5   Ibid., p.24.

6   Herman J. Heuser, *Canon Sheehan of Doneraile* (London: Longmans, Green, 1918), *passim*. Owen McGee, *The IRB* (Dublin: Four Courts, 2005) is the standard work on the IRB.

7   *Geoffrey Austin: Student* [1895] (Dublin: Phoenix n.d.).

8   Walter McDonald, *Some Ethical Questions of Peace and War* [1919] (Dublin: University College Dublin Press, 1998), pp.xi–xv.

9   P.A. Sheehan, *The Triumph of Failure* [1899] (London and Dublin: Burns, Oates and Washbourne, 1945).

10 Ruth Dudley Edwards, *The Triumph of Failure* (Dublin: Irish Academic Press, 1977).

11 P.A. Sheehan, *Literary Life* (Dublin: Phoenix, n.d.). pp.1–34 and *passim*; quote from p.64.

12 P.A. Sheehan, *Under the Cedars and the Stars* (Dublin: Browne and Nolan, 1903), p.292. See in general, W.F.P. Stockley, *Essays in Irish Biography*, (Cork: University Press, 1933), pp.93–130.

13 See MacManus, 'Fate of Canon Sheehan', pp.25–6.

14 See Sheehan, *Under the Cedars and the Stars*, pp.322–3.

15 *Irish Ecclesiastical Record*, 15 (Jan–June 1904), pp.5–26, at 22–3.

16 P.A. Sheehan, *My New Curate* [1899] (Boston, MA: Marlier, Callanan, 1900).

17 Ibid., p.170–1.

11

Desmond Ryan (ed.), *Collected Works of
Padraic H. Pearse: Political Writings and Speeches* (1917)

Patrick Pearse exerted several strains of influence on twentieth-century Ireland. He came to be celebrated as an educationalist but was not an influential one. As the main author of the 1916 Proclamation, he influenced constitutional understandings of Irish nationhood but because of his passionate advocacy of 'blood sacrifice' he has often been portrayed as a dangerous and destabilising influence on the nation state of which he is officially a founding father. His key writings from 1912 to 1916 – pamphlets including 'The Murder Machine' on education, 'Peace and the Gael,' 'The Coming Revolution', 'The Separatist Idea' and 'The Sovereign People' – were first anthologised in 1917 by Desmond Ryan, a former pupil of Pearse's and a teacher at St Enda's, the school founded by Pearse.[1]

'The Murder Machine' that Pearse attacked was 'the English education system in Ireland', a grotesque and wicked system aimed at debasing the Irish. Its machinery, Pearse argued, was a lifeless thing without a soul: 'A machine vast, complicated, with a multitude of far-reaching arms, with many ponderous presses, carrying out mysterious and long-drawn processes of shaping and moulding'. Into it was fed the raw human material of Ireland to be compressed and remoulded. The machine sought to 'grind' the most able for the English civil service and the so-called liberal professions, leaving those who could not be so refashioned bruised and shapeless.

Under the modern system, he argued, the teacher was a mere civil servant. The modern child was coming to regard his teacher as an official paid by the State to render him certain services; services which it was in his interest to avail of, since by doing so he would increase his earning capacity later on. Under such utilitarian conditions the relationship between both was no more sacred than accepting the services of a dentist or a chiropodist. This turned the time-honoured tradition of master and disciple – in which he included the schools of Ancient Greece, Christ and his disciples, the Medieval scholastics, the Munster poets and nineteenth-century hedge schools – on its head. He also extolled the virtues of the Montessori system with its emphasis on the spontaneous efforts of children rather than the dominating will of the teacher. In all his examples of 'best practice' (a term he would have despised) the role of the teacher was to inspire and foster the individual talents of his pupils, whatever these might be. The idea of a compulsory curriculum was anathema. Schools should be free to shape their own programmes and teachers to impart something of their own personalities to their work. The 'Murder Machine' served as a manifesto for St Enda's:

When we were starting St. Enda's I said to my boys: 'We must re-create and perpetuate in Ireland the knightly tradition of Cuchulainn, "better is short life with honour than long life with dishonour"; "I care not though I were to live but one day and one night, if only my fame and my deeds live after me"; the noble tradition of the Fianna, "we, the Fianna, never told a lie, falsehood was never imputed to us"; "strength in our hands, truth on our lips, and cleanness in our hearts"; the Christ-like tradition of Colmcille, "if I die it shall be from the excess of the love I bear the Gael"'.[2]

In 'Peace and the Gael', written in December 1915, Pearse had exulted in the cleansing carnage of the Great War:

The last sixteen months have been the most glorious in the history of Europe. Heroism has come back to the earth. On whatever side the men who rule the peoples have marshalled them, whether with England to uphold her tyranny of the seas, or with Germany to break that tyranny, the people themselves have gone into battle because to each the old voice that speaks out of the soil of a nation has spoken anew. Each fights for the fatherland. It is policy that moves the governments; it is patriotism that stirs the peoples. Belgium defending her soil is heroic, and so is Turkey fighting with her back to Constantinople.

It is good for the world that such things should be done. The old heart of the earth needed to be warmed with the red wine of the battlefields. Such august homage was never offered to God as this, the homage of millions of lives given gladly for love of country.[3]

War, he continued, was a terrible thing but not an evil thing: 'Ireland had not known the exhilaration of war for over a hundred years.' And when war came to Ireland, 'she must welcome the Angel of God'. Winning through it, 'we (or those of us who survive) shall come unto great joy'. Only a war that destroyed the Pax Britannica in Ireland could bequeath to the next generation the Peace of the Gael.

'No', James Connolly replied, 'we do not think that the old

heart of the earth needs to be warmed with the red wine of millions of lives. We think anyone who does is a blithering idiot.'[4] Ryan described Pearse as looking hurt when he read this. Pearse's defence of his lyrical appeals to the sword and his gospel of blood sacrifice was that he sincerely believed in them and was willing to stake his own life on their truth. His political writings from 1912 to 1916 documented his embrace of the ideal of a Christ-like sacrifice for the sake of Irish freedom. There was, Ryan recalled in his 1934 memoir *Remembering Sion,* a disconcerting side to Pearse. No honest portrait could hide 'a Napoleonic complex which expressed itself in a fanatical glorification of war for its own sake, an excess of sentiment which almost intoxicated him both on the platform and in private ventures, a recklessness in action and the narrow outlook of a very respectable Dubliner who has never left his city or family circle for long'. Although his ideal was the sword, he could not, according to Ryan, have cut a loaf of bread to save his life. Nor could he 'for all his lyrics of smoking battlefields bear the sight of human suffering without squirming'.[5]

In 'The Sovereign People', his final testament on the subject of Irish freedom dated 31 March 1916 ('For my part, I have no more to say') Pearse proclaimed a new testament of revolutionary Irish nationalism with four prophets: Theobald Wolfe Tone, Thomas Davis, James Fintan Lalor and John Mitchel. Of these, 'The Sovereign People' most extensively quoted and paraphrased Lalor, in particular, his 1848 essay 'The Rights of Ireland' published in *The Irish Felon,* a newspaper founded to take the place of Mitchel's *The United Irishman* after this was proscribed and Mitchel imprisoned.[6] Much of Pearse's contribution to the 1916 Proclamation of an Irish Republic which he co-authored with Connolly drew on Lalor's writings. This declared the right of the people of Ireland to the ownership of Ireland, a resolve to pursue the happiness and prosperity of the whole nation and, famously, to cherish all children of the nation equally.

Pearse's writings were peppered with sentences beginning 'I assert', 'I insist', or 'I claim'. 'The Sovereign People' insisted upon nationality as a spiritual fact; but nationhood required physical freedom, and physical power. Without such freedom the nation droops, withers and ultimately perhaps dies; only a very steadfast nation, a nation of great spiritual and intellectual strength like Ireland, can live for more than a few generations in its absence, and without it even so stubborn a nation as Ireland would doubtless ultimately perish. Pearse declared that the sovereignty of the Irish nation extended to all the material possessions of the nation, its soil and all its resources, all wealth and all wealth-producing processes within the nation. No individual right to private right to property, he insisted, held sway over the public right of the nation. But the nation was under a moral obligation to exercise its public right so as to secure strictly equal rights and liberties to every man and woman within the nation. It was for the nation to determine to what extent private property might be held by its members, whether the railways and waterways were to be in public ownership or whether all sources of wealth were to be its property. There was nothing divine or sacrosanct in any of these arrangements; they were matters of purely human concern, matters for discussion and adjustment between the members of a nation, matters to be decided upon finally by the nation as a whole; and matters in which the nation as a whole might revise or reverse its decision whenever it seemed good in the common interest to do so. This was the essence of what he meant by national sovereignty. He defined Irish freedom as the exercise of this freedom by all the people:

> The people, if wise, will choose as the makers and
> administrators of their laws men and women actually
> and fully representative of all the men and women
> of the nation, the men and women of no property
> equally with the men and women of property; they

will regard such an accident as the possession of *'property'*, *'capital'*, *'wealth'* in any shape, the possession of what is called *'a stake in the country'*, as conferring no more right to represent the people than would the accident of possessing a red head or the accident of having been born on a Tuesday. And in order that the people may be able to choose as a legislation and as a government men and women really and fully representative of themselves, they will keep the choice actually or virtually in the hands of the whole people; in other words, while, in the exercise of their sovereign rights they may, if they will, delegate the actual choice to somebody among them, i.e., adopt a *'restricted franchise'*, they will, if wise, adopt the widest possible franchise – give a vote to every adult man and woman of sound mind. To restrict the franchise in any respect is to prepare the way for some future usurpation of the rights of the sovereign people. The people, that is, the whole people, must remain sovereign not only in theory, but in fact.[7]

Much of this built word for word on Lalor's 1848 essay although the emphasis on female franchise was an unsurprising addition. Pearse did not prescribe how the Irish people should govern themselves but, like Lalor, was emphatic that self-government required control and ownership of the land and resources of Ireland. As put by Lalor and endorsed by Pearse:

The principle I state, and mean to stand upon, is this: that the entire ownership of Ireland, moral and material, up to the sun and down to the centre, is vested of right in the people of Ireland; that they, and none but they, are the land-owners and law-makers of this island; that all laws are null and void not made by them, and all titles to land invalid not conferred or confirmed by them, and that this full right of ownership may and ought to be asserted by any and all means which God has put in the power of man. In other, if not plainer words, I hold and maintain that the entire soil of a country belongs of right to the entire people of that country, and is the rightful property, not of any one class, but of the nation at large, in full effective possession, to let to whom they will, on whatever tenures, terms, rents, services, and conditions they will; one condition, however, being unavoidable and essential, the condition that the tenant shall bear full, true, and undivided fealty and allegiance to the nation, and the laws of the nation whose lands he holds, and own no allegiance whatsoever to any other prince, power, or people, or any obligation of obedience or respect to their will, orders, or laws. I hold, further, and firmly believe, that the enjoyment by the people of this right of first ownership of the soil is essential to the vigour and vitality of all other rights, to their validity, efficacy, and value; to their secure possession and safe exercise. For let no people deceive themselves, or be deceived by the words, and colours, and phrases, and forms of a mock freedom, by constitutions, and charters, and articles, and franchise. These things are paper and parchment, waste and worthless. Let laws and institutions say what they will, this fact will be stronger than all laws, and prevail against them – the fact that those who own your lands will make your laws, and command your liberties and your lives. But this is tyranny and slavery; tyranny in its widest scope and worst shape; slavery of body and soul, from the cradle to the coffin – slavery with all its horrors, and with none of its physical comforts and security; even as it is in Ireland, where the whole community is made up of tyrants, slaves, and slave-drivers.[8]

Lalor, for Pearse, was the immediate intellectual ancestor of the democratic aspect of Irish nationalism. Davis inspired its spiritual and imaginative elements, the Gaelic League cultural nationalism that was the main vehicle of Pearse's patriotism – in poetry, plays and polemics and as an educationalist – until he abandoned constitutionalism for the gospel according to Mitchel. Mitchel, according to Pearse, was the author of the last 'apocalyptic' testament of Irish nationality: 'the fieriest and the most sublime'. Mitchel 'was of the stuff of which great prophets and ecstatics have been made. He really did converse with God; he did really deliver God's word to man, delivered it fiery-tongued.' Pearse's final article, 'The Sovereign People', his own last testament, offered the following synthesis:

And just as all the four have reached, in different terms, the same gospel, making plain in turn different facets of the same truth, so the movements I have indicated are but facets of a whole, different expressions, and each one a necessary expression, of the august, though denied, truth of Irish Nationhood; nationhood in virtue of an old spiritual tradition of nationality, nationhood involving Separation and Sovereignty, nationhood resting on and guaranteeing the freedom of all the men and women of the nation and placing them in effective possession of the physical conditions necessary to the reality and to the perpetuation of their freedom, nationhood declaring and establishing and defending itself by the good smiting sword. I who have been in and of each of these movements make

here the necessary synthesis, and in the name of all
of them I assert the forgotten truth, and ask all who
accept it to testify to it with me, here in our day and, if
need be, with our blood.[9]

Pearse's political tracts are now most readily found on Sinn Fein
and republican splinter group websites or encountered second-
hand as quoted fragments. They have been the focus of ongoing
scholarly criticism anxious about the potential political influence
of Pearse's emphasis on violence and blood sacrifice. The definitive
essay here has been 'The Canon of Irish History: A Challenge'
by Francis Shaw SJ, published in the Jesuit journal *Studies* at the
height of the Northern Ireland crisis.[10] Shaw was distressed by
Pearse's misappropriation of Christ's sacrifice, his presumption
that nationalism and holiness were identical and by how cheaply
he appeared to hold life. From 'The Coming Revolution' he quoted
Pearse as writing, 'We may make mistakes in the beginning
and shoot the wrong people; but bloodshed is a cleansing and a
sanctifying thing.' Shaw's essay was meant to have been published
in a 1966 issue marking the fiftieth anniversary of the Rising but
was held back as being too controversial. The generation of 1916,
now a gerontocracy, had run the country for decades. Ireland had
yet to find itself, as it did a few years later, under the shadow of a
new generation of gunmen.

BF

Notes

1 Desmond Ryan (ed.), *Collected Works of Padraic H. Pearse: Political Writings
and Speeches* (Phoenix: Dublin and Belfast, 1917).

2 Ibid., p.39.

3 Ibid., p.216.

4 James Connolly, *Workers Republic*, (25 December 1915).

5 Desmond Ryan, *Remembering Sion* (London: Arthur Barker, 1934), p.122.

6   See Pearse in Ryan, *Political Writings and Speeches*, p.350.

7   Ibid., p.342.

8   Ibid., pp.335–6.

9   Ibid., p.371.

10 Francis Shaw SJ, 'The Canon of Irish History: A Challenge', *Studies*, 61, 242 (Summer 1972), p.113.

12

Daniel Corkery, *The Hidden Ireland: A Study of Gaelic Munster in the Eighteenth Century* (1924)

Daniel Corkery (1878–1968) had multiple aims in writing *The Hidden Ireland: A Study of Gaelic Munster in the Eighteenth Century*. His account of the place of poetry in the lives of a downtrodden people sought to rescue the Gaelic revival from pedants within and its enemies without. He wished to recover the memory of a vanished Gaelic civilisation, one that he believed found expression in the poetic culture of ordinary people rather than that of its elites, from the destruction it encountered in the wake of the seventeenth century. This was an Ireland that was hidden not just from the twentieth century but from post seventeenth-century English-speaking historians and travel writers. In doing so he wished to challenge the 'slave mind' legacies of what he termed 'the Ascendency's creed' and its belief that the native Irish were a lesser breed and anything of theirs ('except their land and their gold!') was therefore of little value: 'If they have had a language and a literature it cannot have been anything but a *patois* used by the hillmen amongst themselves; and as for their literature, the less said the better.'[1] In a 1983 article, Seamus Heaney wrote of Corkery's centrality to his own intellectual and poetic formation.

He described how *The Hidden Ireland* had helped to realign his own sense of belonging in the face of the gulf he experienced whilst growing up between the official British culture and the local anthropological one. Corkery's message, for Heaney was succinct; 'We were robbed,' he said. 'We lost what makes us what we are. We had lost the indigenous Gaelic civilisation and he evoked that civilisation with elegiac nostalgia.'[2]

In *The Hidden Ireland* Corkery argued that a noble Munster Gaelic tradition, exemplified in its poetry, managed to survive the ravages of the seventeenth century and the Penal Law era that followed. The eighteenth-century peasant poets, he argued, were the lineal descendants of the old bardic line, the proud possessors of an aristocratic tradition of literature and living proof in their day of an indomitable Irishness. The topic of their poetry was often the reduced circumstances they lived in following the decline of their Gaelic noble patrons. These Gaelic houses, according to Corkery, were in some ways similar to Planter ones yet possessed certain notes of their own; 'freer contact with Europe, a culture over and above that which they shared with their neighbours, a sense of historic continuity, a closeness to the land, to the very pulse of it, that those Planter houses could not even dream about'. Corkery proclaimed the native superiority of the bardic schools to the European type of university where the main study was of the Roman Law – 'the relic of a dead empire' – and the literature of dead languages. By contrast, the history that was taught in the bardic schools was 'that of Ireland, namely the Brehon Law system; the language was that of Ireland, the literature that of Ireland – and through the medium of the native language were all subjects taught'.

To his opponents, most notably Frank O'Connor and Sean O'Faoláin, Corkery's account of the Gaelic past was a misrepresentation that fuelled post-independence isolationism, censorship and puritanism. Corkery, who had trained as a carpenter, had been a father figure, literary mentor and role model to both.

Much of what both wrote about nationalism, censorship and conservatism were reactions against ideas influentially espoused in *The Hidden Ireland*. O'Faoláin argued in *King of the Beggars* that the bardic tradition of the eighteenth century was intensely anti-realistic.[3] Their poetic convention was one of exaggerated effusive praise of patrons, their palaces and the gifts they bestowed. It was never for things like pennies or bacon, which the poets would be lucky to get, but for 'silks, wines, jewels, steeds, cloaks, gold in abundance, silver and arms for heroes'. Later it became one that bewailed the loss of patronage. The cast of these poems, O'Faoláin emphasised, were the bards themselves and the aristocrats they identified with, but 'never once a peasant'. The bards praised by Corkery were, at best, hapless men out of tune with their times. At their worst, they were a craven lot and fantasists to boot. Whilst his people starved in windowless hovels, the poet Aodhagán O'Rahilly fantastically listed over and over, the glories of erstwhile great houses; 'glories in which we do not find one homely detail, a thing we could take for fact, one item to make us feel that we are not been taken by the hand into a complete dream-world'.[4] The literary value of such poetry was not an issue but it had nothing to say about the actual culture within which it was produced:

> It means either that these semi-popular poets had nothing to say to the people that was related to their real political and social condition; or else it means that the people were themselves living in a conventional attitude of mind, asked for and desired no realistic songs, had no wish for a faithful image of their appalling conditions – were, in one word sleep-walking. [5]

The now destitute last official poet of one family cited by Corkery wrote:

My craft being withered with

change of law in Ireland,
O grief that I must henceforth
take to brewing!

Another replied:

O Tadgh, understanding that you
are for the brewing,
I for a space will go skimming the milk.

A good proportion of the verses cited by Corkery contained laments for the reduced living conditions of their authors. He also gave many examples of the kinds of verses such poets had formally been commissioned to write, including a 1698 elegy written by O'Rahilly (to Diarmuid Ó Laoghaire of Killeen near Killarney, who served in a Jacobite regiment) which was structured on the following plan:

1. The terror caused by his death (about 12 lines).

2. The man himself (about 20 lines).

3. Genealogical matter (about 50 lines).

4. His prowess in sport and learning (about 8 lines).

5. The places known to bewail him (about 10 lines).

6. The fairy Women of the Gael bewail him (about 13 lines).

7. The rivers and mountains of Munster weep for him (about 20 lines).

8. The gifts bestowed upon him at birth (about 20 lines).

9. His hospitable house is now desolate (about 20 lines).

10. His people now defenceless; his wife's desolation

(about 16 lines).

11. The women will weep him. All Munster will do so. I myself till death will weep him (8 lines).

12. The *envoi* (20 lines).

In the aftermath of the Williamite conquest such genealogical elegies to Big House Gaelic patrons became redundant. But O'Rahilly was one of the inventors of a new genre, the *aisling* (vision poem), where the *Spéir-bhean* or spirit of Ireland appeared as a majestic and radiant woman to bewail the exile of the Stuart Pretender. In this convention the poet lamented the condition of Ireland rather than his own sorrowful state. Typically the poet fell into a sleep whilst bemoaning the woe that had overtaken the Gael. He then dreamt of a beautiful woman, wondered if she might be Deirdre of the Sorrows or Helen of Troy only to find that she was Erin, waiting for her true consort to return to the throne from exile beyond the seas. For all the limits of this stock scenario Corkery argued that the *aisling*, as known and recited by ill-clad and half-starved peasants, exemplified the lineage of a thousand years of literary culture, and an appreciation of beauty amongst a people discounted by their English-speaking masters as senseless brutes.

In Corkery's pantheon O'Rahilly was the Dante of Munster. He devoted a chapter to the case for excluding Brian Merriman, author of *Cúirt an Mheadhon Oídhche* (*The Midnight Court*) – one of the greatest poems in Irish – from his canon. *The Midnight Court* was a fantastical bawdy satire on peasant society, its priests and its cuckolds; as captured in Frank O'Connor's translation published 21 years after *The Hidden Ireland*, but banned soon after by the Irish censor:

Down with marriage! Tis out of date,
It exhausts the stock and cripples the state.

The priest has failed with whip and blinker,
Now give a chance to Tom the Tinker,
And mix and mash in nature's can
The tinker and the gentleman;
Let lovers in every lane extended,
Follow their whim as God intended,
And in their pleasure bring to birth
The morning glory of the earth.[6]

Corkery excluded Merriman from the hidden Ireland he claimed as the authentic model for Irish-Ireland cultural nationalism. The banning of O'Connor's translation of *The Midnight Court* in 1946 and indeed of twentieth-century writings about rural Ireland such as *The Tailor and Ansty* owed much to the dominance of the nation-building project Corkery championed. In *The Hidden Ireland* he laboured the technical objection that County Clare where Merriman resided should properly be considered part of Connaught. Clare Irish was that of Munster, but County Clare was separated from the rest of the province by the River Shannon. Corkery argued that Merriman's sensibility was modern (definitely a bad thing in his view). Corkery lambasted Merriman's lack of bardic refinement and judged Merriman's much praised opening descriptions of east Clare to be commonplace. As translated by Frank O'Connor this was hardly the case:

When I looked at Lough Graney my heart grew bright,
Ploughed lands and green in the morning light,
Mountains in ranks with crimson borders
Peering about their neighbour's shoulders.[7]

O'Connor, in his foreword to his 1945 translation objected to Corkery's 'sneer' at Merriman. He depicted him instead as an independent intellectual who drew on contemporary English verse to produce an authentic piece of Gaelic literature rooted in the spoken Irish of Clare rather than the sanitised literary Irish extolled by Corkery as exemplifying the true heritage of Gaelic culture. In a telling anecdote, O'Faoláin recalled when he was Corkery's protégé, being allowed to look at a copy of *Ulysses* which Corkery kept in a locked drawer. When *The Hidden Ireland* was published O'Faoláin objected to Corkery's idealisation of uneducated peasant culture as the model for independent Ireland when, in his view, Ireland had its own cosmopolitan European tradition and a place in world literature to build upon.

Corkery stood on the literary culture wing of post-colonial nationalism. *The Hidden Ireland* spoke to the same historiographical claims as did James Connolly's *Labour in Irish History* and various nationalist histories of Ireland preoccupied with the destruction of Gaelic Ireland. The idealisation of pre-seventeenth-century culture as a template for twentieth-century Ireland was taken seriously by nationalists and anti-liberals of different stripes. In the rhetoric of the time this variously meant turning back the clock on the Reformation to achieve a Catholic Restoration as well as cultural de-colonisation by means of a Gaelic Restoration – or both. In this context, cultural nationalists and Catholic conservatives found common cause against the foreign ideas that, from their various perspectives, had subordinated the Irish people to an imported modernity. In its crudest form the conflict was one between isolationists who sought to protect Ireland's authentic culture, however understood, from outside contamination and their intellectual opponents.

BF

Notes

1   Daniel Corkery, *The Hidden Ireland: A Study of Gaelic Munster in the Eighteenth Century* [1970] (Dublin: Gill and Macmillan, 1970).

2   Seamus Heaney, 'Forked Tongues, Ceilís and Incubators', *Fortnight*, 197 (September 1983).

3   Sean O'Faoláin, *King of the Beggars: A Life of Daniel O'Connell, the Irish Liberator* (Dublin: Poolbeg, 1980).

4   Ibid.

5   O'Faoláin, *King of the Beggars*, p.25.

4   Frank O'Connor (trans.), *The Midnight Court by Brian Merriman* [1945] (Dublin: O'Brien Press, 1989).

5   Ibid.

13

P.S. O'Hegarty, *The Victory of Sinn Fein:*
How it Won It and How it Used It (1924)

The Victory of Sinn Fein is one of a select group of extended memoirs
written by people who were close to the centre of things in Irish
separatist politics during the most crucial and activist phase of
the movement between 1913 and 1923.[1] Comparisons might be
drawn with such classics as C.S. Andrews' *Dublin Made Me*, David
Hogan's *The Four Glorious Years* or Ernie O'Malley's *On Another
Man's Wound*.[2] However, these three works were written after a
long interval and from a markedly anti-Treatyite and republican
point of view. For these reasons they have remained better known
to the general public. The O'Malley book is less reliable than
the O'Hegarty book as a memoir; it was written much later and
strives for a pronouncedly romantic literary effect rather than
strict historical accuracy. Again, Andrews was trying to give an
accurate and conscientious account of the events of the period and
an analysis of the mentality of a young IRA volunteer of the time.
However, he wrote a full generation after the events. A comparison
might also be drawn with Ernest Blythe's Irish-language trilogy,
which would merit translation and a much wider readership.

O'Hegarty's book is written from a point of view that is almost completely forgotten. The clearest statement of it that I have come across other than *Victory* is Eimar O'Duffy's fictional but partly autobiographical *The Wasted Island*. Both writers, early members of Sinn Fein, argue passionately in very different ways that most of the violence associated with the independence movement was unnecessary and even self-defeating. O'Hegarty regretfully accepted the inevitability of a defensive 'War of Independence', but argued in *Victory* that violence clearly had no part to play after the Truce of July 1921. After that, negotiation with London and with Belfast should have become intense and without any threat of violence from anybody. He argued also that the Rising of 1916 was sufficient; a protest in arms had been made, and the rest should have been left to the political process.

Whatever about the Anglo-Irish War of 1919–21, the Civil War of 1922–23 was, he claimed, an avoidable disaster, one which killed the spirit of the national movement and cost the country the leadership of Michael Collins and Arthur Griffith. Collins and Griffith were O'Hegarty's heroes; to him, Griffith was the wise leader, always in the background, always trying to subordinate military considerations to the political purposes which he saw as being far more important. At one stage (May 1920), when the IRA proposed some unnamed enormity, he said to O'Hegarty:

> The military mind is the same in every country. Our military men are as bad as the British. They think of nothing but their own particular end, and cannot be brought to consider the political consequences of their proceedings.[3]

Griffith is portrayed as being free from an all-too-common obsession with symbolic forms, and wanting Irish independence under whatever formula was politically possible, even under a Hanoverian monarchy if necessary. Arguments about Free State versus Republic were, to him, pointless. What counted for both Griffith and Collins was the means of state power: control of the army, taxation, customs and the ports. Given these, all else would follow quickly or gradually. O'Hegarty was sympathetic to this view, but unfortunately, not all the leaders saw it that way.

The character sketches of Griffith, Collins and de Valera are vivid, and make you almost feel that you had met them and even been on close terms with some of them. The portrait of Collins is affectionate and evidently drawn from a long familiarity with the man. They had become friends as young fellows in London, both of them working as clerks in Mount Pleasant Post Office in North London in the 1900s. Even now, the hostile treatment of de Valera in O'Hegarty's memoir might give offence to some, much as did Neil Jordan's rather similar take on him in his *Michael Collins* film of 1996. However, many people in the early twenty-first century, if they think of de Valera at all, see him not as the putative wrecker of the treaty settlement of 1922, but rather as the old and wily statesman who kept the country out of the Second World War and, perhaps, outstayed his welcome in the 1950s. He has come to represent a long-vanished past version of Irish society and his behaviour as a relatively young man in 1921–23, devastatingly described by O'Hegarty, has been forgotten or forgiven.

Certainly, de Valera's extraordinary conduct in 1921–22 when he rejected the Treaty sight unseen and foolishly permitted his name to be associated with a ghost presidency of a ghost republic under the actual control of Liam Lynch's rump IRA did untold damage to an emergent Irish political culture. It permitted many to question the constitutional continuity from Griffith's Dail government to Cosgrave's Free State and it provided alibis for many murders afterwards. The legitimacy of the new state was routinely questioned for over a generation afterwards. O'Hegarty believed that Dev's almost reverential reception in America went to his head and encouraged him to overrate his own importance and centrality to the movement. Certainly, after America, de Valera was extraordinarily self-righteous, untrusting and unwilling to have his equals in ability close to his throne. When he returned to Ireland over a year later, he had found that Collins had put himself at the head of an entire underground government and political system. Whenever he felt like it, Collins, a brilliant administrator and an even more able conspirator, could bypass everyone else in the revolutionary apparatus and get his way.

However, de Valera had, in turn, ways of getting round Collins. Ernie Blythe, later Minister for Finance in the Provisional Government, apparently heard Kevin O'Higgins (later Minister for Justice) say sometime in early 1922, 'That crooked Spanish bastard will get the better of that pasty-faced blasphemous fucker from Cork.'[4] De Valera came to fear and even hate Collins and Griffith, seeing them as betrayers of *him*, never mind Ireland. Certainly de Valera can be accused of creating a political culture of complaint, denial and delegitimation of democratic processes. He can also be accused of infantilising Irish political discourse permanently. O'Hegarty takes an even less kind view. Yet, the true problem of the Sinn Fein party was intellectual. It was led by men and women who were not equipped by background and education for the task ahead of it after its electoral victory in 1918. O'Hegarty gives an eye-witness account of Collins and Boland as machine politicians:

The great mistake which Sinn Fein had made was its refusal to look ahead, above all its refusal to face obvious facts and provide for them. When it went to the polls in 1918 for that General Election at which it won its first majority, it selected its candidates purely with an eye to votes. The man who was in prison, or who had been in prison, obviously had the best chance, and neither his ability nor his suitability were considered. Ability, on the contrary, was rather a disqualification, because it tended to make its possessor difficult to handle by a machine, and Sinn Fein was rapidly becoming a machine. I had an illuminating insight into democracy in practice one day in 6 Harcourt Street. Harry Boland, who was then Secretary to Sinn Fein, was sitting at a desk as I entered, and going over a list of names. 'John Brown. We can't have him.' Then 'John Black. I wonder is he safe. I'll ask X.' Then 'John Green. He's all right.' Then he came to another list and he looked at it, and said to me: 'Gavan Duffy. Do you think, P.S., that Gavan Duffy is a good Republican? Do you think we ought to let him go up?'[5]

O'Hegarty persuaded Boland to let Duffy stand for the first Dáil, but independent-minded people were discouraged for reasons of power. The second Dáil of 1921 was, he argues, even less representative than the first: 'a collection of mediocrities in the grip of a machine, and leaving all its thinking to Griffith, Collins and de Valera'.[6] This machine, under different labels, was to dominate Irish electoral politics for two generations.

The Victory of Sinn Fein is a polemic and a period piece, as the author himself conceded even at the time of publication in 1924. The hero worship of Collins and Griffith, the demonisation of de Valera and the unsentimental treatment of the female extremists will strike some minds as over the top and possibly offensive. The women are portrayed as aggressive, naïve and able to intimidate the men into taking political stands which were far more extreme than their private opinions would have prompted them to take. However, his point of view was not looked upon as being eccentric or outlandish at that time; much of what O'Hegarty says would have been accepted by very many people of his generation of both sexes as a common-sense view of things.[7] For that reason, it is a valuable source of IRB and 'Free State' mentality and gives a view of Irish history which the author lived through that is invaluable, illuminating and sometimes surprising. *The Victory of Sinn Fein* was written in a hurry, and is sometimes repetitive; however it is also written with enormous passion, verve and energy; it reads like a thriller. It is also very much an insider story, who was telling the truth as he saw it, however exaggerated or distorted some might take his judgements to have been.

O'Hegarty was quite a prolific writer both before and after writing *Victory* and was an early contributor to the pre-1914 IRB newspaper, *Irish Freedom*, a profoundly liberal and republican-nationalist paper by the standards of the time. He vehemently opposed any attempt to coerce the North into a united Ireland, enunciating a doctrine of Northern consent long before it was popular or profitable, and long before republican propagandising and later Fianna Fáil rhetoric made it anathema among large sections of the Irish public. He would have had contempt for the republican argument that unionist consent to a united Ireland would have been forthcoming were it not for British military might enforcing partition in defiance of the wishes of the vast majority of Irish people. Like many other Irish Republican Brotherhood veterans, he had a curious mixture of radical and conservative views. For example, this otherwise quite enlightened man believed that education beyond the age of fourteen or so was unnecessary and a burden on the nation. Young people should, presumably, educate themselves in public libraries and at the school of hard knocks.

O'Hegarty championed many Irish writers of his time, and saluted with enthusiasm James Joyce's *Ulysses*, published in 1922. He defended Sean O'Casey's *The Plough and the Stars* in the face of howls of nationalist and clerical execration. He wrote short memoirs and character sketches of several other well-known figures of the period. Of his later writings, the most substantial was his highly nationalistic *A History of Ireland under the Union* (1951). Interestingly, his account in the later book of the events dealt with in *The Victory of Sinn Fein* rows back somewhat and is somewhat gentler on the anti-Treatyites, while retaining his central charge against de Valera: that he transformed a difference of opinion over the Treaty into a question of trust and betrayal which then led to a political split and subsequently sowed the seed of the Irish Civil War.[8] The book became quite an Aunt Sally for 'revisionist', mainly liberal or leftist historians from the sixties onward, who commonly argued that it had a tendency to glorify the protagonists of the separatist cause and demonise the British government, particularly its officers in the governance of Ireland. The fashion for portraying British governance in Ireland as unfailingly enlightened and well-intentioned has in turn faded. Nowadays *A History of Ireland Under the Union* is apparently forgotten, along with its critics.

TG

Notes

1 P.S. O'Hegarty, *The Victory of Sinn Fein: How it Won It and How it Used It* (Dublin: Talbot Press, 1924).

2 David Hogan was a pseudonym of Frank Gallagher.

3 See O'Hegarty, *The Victory of Sinn Fein*, p.47. It is likely that the 'enormity' was Cathal Brugha's plan to drive a car bomb into Westminster. Collins apparently remarked that if they wiped out the British cabinet, a far worse cabinet (from the Irish point of view) would replace it.

4 James Matthews, *Voices* (Dublin: Gill and Macmillan, 1983), p.400.

5 See O'Hegarty, *The Victory of Sinn Fein*, pp.75–6.

6 Ibid., p.77.

7 For similar views on the republican women: Batt O'Connor Papers, University College Dublin Archives, (28 December 1921), p.68; Michael Hayes Papers, University College Dublin Archives, p.53, p.303; *Freeman's Journal*, 23 February, 1922. See also, Tom Garvin *1922: the Birth of Irish Democracy* (Dublin: Gill and Macmillan, 1996), pp.97–104. It was objected to vehemently by some feminist historians and calmly accepted by others.

8 See my sketch of O'Hegarty in P.S. O'Hegarty, *The Victory of Sinn Fein* [1924] (Dublin: University College Dublin Press, 1998; introduction by Tom Garvin), pp.vii–xiii.

14

The Blasket Islands are a small archipelago off the coast of the Dingle peninsula in north-west Kerry, itself a rugged county in the south-west of Ireland. The largest island, the Great Blasket, is about three miles from the mainland and about five miles long. The area is one of great natural beauty. The entire Dingle area was, until very recently, completely Irish-speaking, and the inhabitants of the Blaskets were themselves nearly all monoglot Irish speakers until the evacuation of the islands in 1953. Tomás O Criomhthain ('O Crohan') was born in 1856, in the wake of the Great Famine, which had killed a million people and driven another million out of the island of Ireland. The inhabitants of the Blaskets, perhaps two hundred strong at that time, survived the famine mainly by the fact that they subsisted in large part on fishing and hunting rather than on that monocrop that had doomed Ireland, the potato. Seal hunting, rabbit hunting and fishing preserved other communities along the west coast of Ireland during the terrible years of the 1840s, and commonly preserved also the Irish or Gaelic language as the common speech of the people. The Blaskets survived into the modern era as a strange museum of ordinary people who had memories of an almost mediaeval existence; some commentators have used the term 'Neolithic' with some exaggeration. The islands used barter among themselves but were perfectly capable of trading with mainland merchants and foreign fishing boats, exchanging catch for cash or manufactured goods.

However, it is clear that the magical world of Geoffrey Keating would not have been completely alien to them. America was the New Island, and seems sometimes to have been seen as a kind of earthly paradise where their loved ones spoke English, were happy people, lived marvellous lives, wore beautiful clothes and experienced a transfigured existence. Life was hard in the Blaskets, and even the supply of turf fuel on the island was disappearing. Emigration to the United States weakened the community in the early twentieth century, and a change in the migration patterns of fish in the late 1930s made the future of the island community look bleak. Eventually the Irish government had the remnant population of the Great Blasket evacuated in 1953. The inhabitants were resettled on the mainland among an Irish-speaking community near their old island home.

Tomás O Criomhthain was taught to read and write in the English language in the 1860s, but his grasp of that tongue was relatively weak, and he spoke an eloquent and rich version of Irish all his life. As a young man he attempted to write down a recitation of a poem by an older man, using English phonetics to represent the Irish, rather like modern Manx; the impulse to record was always there.[1] At age forty he was taught by Brian O'Kelly of Killarney to read and write properly in Irish which he eventually did excellently. This achievement was to transform his life, turning him into the author of several minor classic works and one major classic book in the Irish language, starting in 1928 with *Island Cross-Talk*, pages from his diary between 1919 and 1923.[2] His major work, published in 1929, was *An tOileánach* (*The Islandman*), which is not just a classic of Gaelic literature, but a significant contribution to world literature in itself.[3] Padraig O Siochfhrada ('An Seabhac') helped with the editing. Tomás never travelled outside Dingle in his life, and those centres of Kerry emigration, Springfield and Holyoke in Massachusetts were as close and as real to him as was Dublin, the putative capital of his country. Ireland began at Dingle, and he lived in a little country of his own mind, comprising the Blaskets and the western end of the Dingle peninsula.

The Islandman was written as a series of letters to O'Kelly, and is a simple autobiography of a highly intelligent and observant man with little formal education and no library to speak of. What he did have was a folkloric memory which reached back in its jumbled way for hundreds of years, mixing actual historical events with mythology: Fionn Mac Cumhail meets Oliver Cromwell, so to speak. The book begins with his childhood, and he remembers clearly being weaned and looking hungrily at his mother's breast when already a walking talking little boy of four or five. His schooling was rather hit and miss, as was commonplace among Irish country people at the time. Learning the basic skills of kitchen gardening, game hunting, trapping and sea fishing were regarded quite naturally as being of greater urgency than book learning. The islanders were proud of their independence, being descended mainly from tenants of estates on the mainland who had found a freedom there that they had not enjoyed before. Technically they were tenants on a large estate that covered much of western Dingle, but physical resistance to rent collectors and their police escorts was the norm. In particular, the womenfolk organised themselves with piles of stones to rain down on would-be invaders of their island fastness. In modern times the naomhóg, or canvas skinned canoe ('currach'), was the main means of transportation by sea and for fishing. However, up to the middle of the nineteenth century the islanders had used larger wooden boats with seine nets for fishing, according to Tomás. Apparently the naomhóg had been partly superseded in the early nineteenth century by the larger boats but came back into its own because of landlord action. Unable to collect rents, the landlord confiscated the island fleet and put it up for sale. The boats were never sold and rotted away in a field near Dingle town, an early example of the use of the people's weapon of boycott. The naomhóg, being of relatively little value, was used by the islanders in part as a way of dodging rent. Generally the islanders paid no rent to anyone. Eventually the Land Acts were to hand the islands over to the inhabitants after the Land War of 1879–1881. Later still the Congested Districts Board reformed land tenure, in a benign attempt to eliminate rundale.

The book is full of youthful escapades and rough humour, but the harsh realities of life on the Great Blasket are never understated. Tomás was to watch several of his own children die, either from the many incurable diseases of the era or from the physical dangers attendant on island life. Death was a commonplace and everyday thing, and commonly seen as a sought-after release from this hard world and a welcome into a better one elsewhere. The post-Famine diet returned to being based on potatoes, with yellow meal standing in for the potatoes during the scarce months of summertime; fish or small game was a necessary and much appreciated supplement. A shipwreck was regarded as a piece of very good fortune, and wood planks from ships were much coveted on the treeless islands. Whiskey and exotic drinks from wrecks were much sought after, as was clothing. Famously, tea was first used on the island as a dye for home-spun clothing. Later the islanders became, like most Irish people, great tea-drinkers. The First World War was a prosperous time from the islanders' point of view, as the shipwrecking rate went up mainly due to the operations of U-boats in the western Atlantic. The ending of the book is justly famed, written as an old man in 1926 awaiting death or perhaps the pension payable at age seventy. He lived long enough to enjoy the money for a decade. He has no complaints, and concludes calmly:

It was a good life in those days. Shilling came on shilling's heels; food was plentiful, and things were cheap. Drink was cheap too. It wasn't thirst for the drink that made us want to go where it was, but only the need to have a merry night after the misery that we knew only too well before. What the drop of drink did to us was to lift up the hearts in us, and we would spend a day and a night ever and again in company together when we got the chance. That's all gone now, and the high heart and the fun are passing from the world. Then we'd take the homeward way together easy and friendly after all our revelry, like the children of one mother, none doing hurt or harm to his fellow.

I have written minutely of much that we did, for it was my wish that somewhere there should be a memorial of it all, and I have done my best to set down the character of the people about me so that some record of us might live after us, for the like of us will never be again.[4]

Fiche Blian ag Fás, or *Twenty Years A-Growing* was written a few years later by Maurice O'Sullivan and was a worthy successor to *An tOileánach.* A much younger man, born in 1904, Maurice spent his childhood in Dingle, and came to the island around 1910. An English-speaker, he learned his Irish on the Great Blasket, and did so very quickly. O'Sullivan describes a similar world, but seems to have had a stronger bent toward mythology and tall tales in general. Unlike Tomás he was eventually to leave the island and travel through the great world of Ireland to the big city of Dublin. Like Tomás, he was befriended and helped by an outside scholar, George Thompson, a well-known academic writer of the time. Surviving film demonstrates that Thompson learned perfect Kerry Irish with a barely detectable English accent. Their first encounter in 1923 is described vividly and amusingly by Maurice:

He was now only forty yards away, a man neither too tall nor too short, with knee-breeches and a shoulder-cloak, his head bare and a shock of dark brown hair gathered straight back on it. I was growing afraid. There was not his like in the Island. Where had he come from and he approaching me now from the top of the hill in the darkening of the day? I leant my back against the bank of the ditch. I drew out my pipe and lit it. Then I turned my gaze to the south-east, thinking no doubt he would pass me by on his way, so that I could take his measure and say I had seen a leprechaun.[5]

Maurice recovered from seeing this apparition. The two men talked to each other. Maurice agreed to teach George Irish, and in return George became a kind of career advisor to the islandman. He persuaded Maurice not to emigrate to America with everyone else, but instead to join the new police force the Dublin government was setting up at the time. It also seems that George persuaded him to write the memoir, which was published soon after *An tOileánach*. It is, of course, *Fiche Blian ag Fás* (*Twenty Years A-Growing*). Thompson, with some help from others, translated it into English, and he seems also to have urged the writing of its still-unpublished sequel, *Fiche Blian ag Bláth* (*Twenty Years A-Flowering*). O'Sullivan did go on to join the Garda Síochána, and eventually resigned from the force and went into farming on the mainland in Galway. There is an entertaining account of his recruitment into the Garda and Thompson's role as a minder of sorts in Dublin in *Twenty Years A-Growing*. He was to have considerable difficulty with the timetabling of the Irish railway system of the time and finding his way around the city.

The mini-renaissance that occurred on the Blaskets between 1880 and 1940 seems to have been derived from a benign encounter between three very different sets of people: the islanders themselves,

Protestant missionaries in the 1830s who made them literate, and the romantic linguistic movements in academia in western Europe in the last decades of the nineteenth century. Thompson and Flower together with Kenneth Jackson were among the half-dozen English academic scholars known to have perfected their Irish on the Island in the first decades of the twentieth century. Eibhlís Ní Shúilleabháin wrote letters to George Chambers of London between 1931 and 1951 in a similar exercise to that of Tomás, who was her father-in-law.[6] Similarly, Peig Sayers was persuaded by Máire Ní Chinnéide to dictate her reminiscences to her son, and her two principle books, *Peig* and *An Old Woman's Reflections*, were both created in the mid-1930s and translated into English much later. From the beginning of the century onward, Irish scholars inspired by the Gaelic League followed the Englishmen to the island, and there was at least one Norwegian (Carl Marstrander) among these new missioners. Strangely, these missioners came at the last moment, as even the islanders themselves knew by around 1930 that their time was limited. Among other things, the supply of turf (peat) as fuel was running out and would be gone within the lifetimes of the younger inhabitants. Too much can be made of this, however; for years the Aran Islands were supplied with turf from the mainland by hooker (turf boat). J.M. Synge's early sojourn on the Aran Islands and his visit to the Great Blasket in 1905 seem also to have operated as an inspiration to the visitors.

Fiche Blian ag Fás contains many strange tales. One involves a traveller ('The Wanderer') from Dingle who visits the Great Blasket. He has been all over the world and relates a supernatural experience, presumably some form of nightmare or hallucination. He walks with a companion towards Springfield. They encounter a man with a big black dog. Then he finds himself alone suddenly in a graveyard in an unfamiliar landscape. A path leads to a castle with bright lights. He encounters various obstacles, but it becomes clear that the castle is inhabited by people whom he has known long ago in this life and who are now dead. They are banqueting.

He wanders farther and finds himself in a laneway only as wide as he is, and bordered by high concrete walls:

> I was walking on and on with no sight of the city of Springfield yet nor with any news of it to be had. ... I heard a bell ringing behind me. Looking back I saw a bicycle coming towards me like the wind. I could not get out of the way. It was impossible. God save my soul, said I, he will split me. He was nearer now, a big lamp of light on the bicycle and no slackening of speed. I looked up at the wall to see if I could climb it. But at that moment the bicycle passed me like a whirlwind. That was the strangest thing of all.[7]

Apparently the bicycle is riderless. He believes himself to be dead and in the next world. He finds himself suddenly in familiar surroundings, his companion from the previous night in danger of death from supernatural causes. People seem to think that the Wanderer is himself to blame for this. All of this seems to be echoed in parody by Flann O'Brien's *The Third Policeman*, written ten years later and involving supernatural policemen, a nameless man who is dead, who realises gradually that he is guilty of murder and having a brief but vivid love affair with a sentient and very charming bicycle. O'Brien used the Blasket writings in various ways, and this appears to be one of the most complete and unacknowledged, probably because his book was published posthumously. As in *The Third Policeman*, not only is there a bicycle, but there are plenty of policemen in O'Sullivan's autobiography. Again, the world view of Tomás is lampooned gently in O'Brien's Irish-language satire, *An Béal Bocht* (*The Poor Mouth*), written in 1941.

Although the Blasket writers did get official recognition, their work was not really a source of the nostalgia expressed by de Valera in his well-known speech on radio on St Patrick's Day 1943 ('The Ireland we have Dreamed of'). As has been pointed out by several commentators, the Ireland Dev was recalling was that of rural Munster in the late nineteenth century, stable and reasonably prosperous in a frugal way. It was more the priest-led village Ireland of Canon Sheehan or the Knocknagow of Charles Kickham and Matt the Thrasher, rather than the semi-pagan, poor but free-wheeling society portrayed by Tomás or Maurice and the other writers. The paradox of the western islands of the Blaskets, of western Connacht and Donegal was that much of their cultural achievement was fostered by foreign academics driven by a romanticisation of western Irish popular culture, but irresistible in a cleaned-up form, purged of its Rabelaisian features, to puritan Irish Catholic nationalists. The 'Playboy' riots of 1907 reflected a real conflict between puritan and romantic currents in Irish society at the time.

TG

Notes

1   Muiris Mac Conghail, *The Blaskets: People and Literature* (Dublin: Country House, 1994), pp.142–3.

2   Tomás O Criomhthain, *Allagar na hInise* (Dublin: An Gum, 1928). *Island Cross-Talk*, trans. Tim Enright (Oxford: Oxford University Press, 1986). Robin Flower, *The Western Island* (Oxford: Oxford University Press, 1944). The latter is an essential introduction to these writers and their community. Muiris Mac Conghail, *The Blaskets: People and Literature* is equally necessary. I am indebted to Muiris for many conversations over many years about this topic.

3   Tomás O Criomhthain, *An tOileánach* (Dublin: Educational Company of Ireland, 1929). Tomás O'Crohan, *The Islandman*, trans. Robin Flower [1937] (Oxford: Oxford University Press, 1979).

4   Tomás O'Crohan, *The Islandman*, trans. Robin Flower (Oxford: Oxford University Press, 1979), pp.243–4.

5   Maurice O'Sullivan, *Twenty Years A-Growing* (Oxford: Oxford University Press, 1953, first published 1933), p.221.

6   Eibhlís Ní Súilleabháin, *Letters From the Great Blasket* (Cork and Dublin: Mercier, n.d.,1978). The Gaelic originals have not been published.

7   See O'Sullivan, *Twenty Years A-Growing*, pp.167–170.

15

Frank O'Connor (1903–1966) was the pen name of Michael O'Donovan, formed by taking his own middle name and his mother's maiden name. *Guests of the Nation* was his first collection of short stories, and he was to become known as Ireland's premier writer of short fiction of his generation.[1] Throughout his life his output was prolific, consisting of dozens of short stories and, towards the end of his life, brilliant translations of Irish-language poetry and studies of Irish cultural history. He grew up in the city of Cork and formed part of an intellectual coterie centred round Daniel Corkery and a group of literary-minded young people, many of whom were students at University College Cork in the second decade of the twentieth century. He had less than a decade of formal education due to the extreme poverty of his family, but as a young man he made it his business to learn from literary figures such as Corkery and his friend and fellow writer, Sean O'Faoláin. Corkery's *magnum opus*, a book-length study of Irish cultural history in the seventeenth and eighteenth century (*The Hidden Ireland*) was the book that both O'Faoláin and O'Connor had to grapple with to arrive at their own very different takes on Irish cultural history.[2] O'Connor participated in the Irish War of Independence and took the anti-Treaty side in the subsequent Irish Civil War, as did O'Faoláin. The stories in *Guests of the Nation* are, then, partly autobiographical and provide a valuable insight into the emotional mentalities of the young men of the time.

The title story, 'Guests of the Nation', has been often claimed to be one of the best Irish short stories of the century, perhaps coming second only to James Joyce's 'The Dead'. It is a story that has often been imitated or echoed, most famously perhaps by Brendan Behan (*An Ghiall, The Hostage*) in the 1950s and Neil Jordan's *The Crying Game* in the 1990s.[3] It is strange that this young anti-Treatyite firebrand was, some years later, to write an admiring (and intriguing) biography of Michael Collins (*The Big Fellow*), despite Collins being the man who signed the Treaty, remarking accurately that he had just signed his own death warrant.

It seems that O'Connor was originally told the anecdote behind 'Guests of the Nation' while in a Free State government prison camp. Another key experience in O'Connor's life was a tragicomic incident in Gormanstown prison camp during and after the Civil War. He had seen hideous things done by Irishmen to other Irishmen, men who had been on the same side against the British a few months earlier. As usual, the captured IRA men duplicated the government's military structures and rules, even though they refused to recognise that government. In their own minds *they* were the 'real' government. As O'Connor often said afterwards, for a while Ireland had two semi-imaginary governments, only one of which could be real in the long run. In *An Only Child*, O'Connor remembered:

> The first incident that revealed to me what the situation was really like was funny enough. A man … had had a disagreement with his hut-leader about the amount of fatigues he had to do, so he refused to do any more.

There was nothing unusual about this of course. In an atmosphere where there was no such thing as privacy and people were always getting on one another's nerves, it was inevitable, and the sensible thing would have been to transfer Murphy to another hut. … Murphy was summoned before a court martial of three senior [IRA] officers, found guilty, and sentenced to more fatigues. Being a man of great character, he refused to do these as well. This might have seemed a complete stalemate, but not to imaginative men. The camp command took over from the enemy a small time-keeper's hut with barred windows to use as a prison, and two prisoners, wearing tricolour armlets to show that they really were policemen and not prisoners like the rest of us, arrested Murphy and locked him up. … I felt the imaginative improvisation could not go farther than that, but it did. Murphy still had a shot in his locker, for he went on hunger strike, not against our [government] gaolers, but his own, and – unlike them when they went on hunger strike soon after – he meant it.

The IRA then called a meeting and denounced Murphy for defying majority rule. O'Connor felt this was a bit thick for men who were in prison for defying majority rule, the vast majority of Irish people being in favour of the Treaty of 1921–22. He was the only vote in favour of Murphy among the entire body of prisoners. Revealingly, he remembered, 'Later in life I realized that it was probably the first time I had ever taken an unpopular stand without allies.'[4]

A growing collective sense of the absurdity of their situation eventually broke a hunger strike ordered long after the main body of the anti-Treatyite armed forces had given up and gone home on de Valera's instructions. The government deliberately let the republican prisoners go home in dribs and drabs, so as to cause no great stir or demonstration. Interestingly, the government also usually let them out under cover of darkness, so that they could slink home unobserved. The young men commonly feared ridicule, particularly on the part of young women. Eventually O'Connor was released. When he got home to Cork, his mother stared at him, burst into tears and said, 'It made a man of you!'[5]

'Guests of the Nation' concerns a group of west Cork IRA men during the Irish War of Independence, or 'the Tan War' as many of its veterans called it. Two English soldiers are captured and held hostage in a remote cottage to be shot if IRA captives in Cork Jail are executed by the British. The Englishmen charm the old lady who owns the cottage and do her chores for her. They play cards with the IRA lads and argue about religion and the possibilities of an afterlife, rather like young people anywhere and anywhen. They become friends. The British in Cork city hang their own prisoners, and the IRA commanding officer announces that the two soldiers are to be shot in retaliation. They meet their fate calmly, and the IRA OC (interestingly named Donovan, almost having O'Connor's real name) shoots them. Donovan is the only one of the young IRA men who really hates the English. The last two sentences in the story are among the best-known passages in Irish storytelling. After the killing:

> Noble says he saw everything ten times the size, as though there were nothing in the whole world but that little patch of bog with the two Englishmen stiffening into it, but with me it was as if the patch of bog where the Englishmen were was a million miles away, and even Noble and the old woman, mumbling behind me, and the birds and the bloody stars were all far away, and I was somehow very small and very lost and lonely like a child astray in the snow. And anything that happened to me afterwards, I never felt the same about again.[6]

O'Connor distanced himself from Corkery in later life, dissenting in particular from the older man's dismissive and rather po-faced hostile judgement of a bawdy eighteenth-century poem, Brian Merriman's *Cúirt an Mheadhon Oídhche*; O'Connor's translation of which was banned in 1946. O'Connor's final confrontation with his old mentor did not occur until after his own death in 1966. *The Backward Look*, his own scholarly assessment of the Gaelic literary tradition, was based on a series of lectures he gave in Trinity College Dublin and was published posthumously.[7] At one point he remarks with a characteristic blunt extravagance, 'Unlike Daniel Corkery, who wrote a very lyrical and wrong-headed book on it, I can see nothing to admire in Irish eighteenth-century poetry.'[8] Elsewhere in the book he describes the much-revered *Táin Bó Cuailgne* as 'a simply appalling text' and essentially a palimpsest of different versions and unconnected tales all thrown together over several hundred years.[9] This is tacitly a snipe at Patrick Pearse's extravagant claims for the old saga half a century earlier, another backward look of a more personal kind.

O'Connor became utterly anti-militarist after the Civil War, and became publicly convinced of the futility and evil of the entire Irish tradition of 'freedom struggle'. Several of the stories in *Guests of the Nation* combine a young man coming of age and realising the pointlessness of the IRA campaigns. In 'September Dawn', for example, during the Civil War two young IRA men evade Free State soldiers and eventually hole up in an old woman's house, where, unexpectedly, the more thoughtful and shyer of the pair finds love. It is a beautifully handled little story.[10] A similar epiphany occurs in '*Soirée Chez Une Belle Jeune Fille*'.[11]

Like many another young man in Ireland over the last hundred years, prison was the nearest he ever got to a university education. Like the very different Seán Lemass or Brendan Behan, incarceration forced him to read rather than engage in unthinking action and derring-do, and induced him to ponder the old question asked by every exasperated Irish parent of a wild and wayward child, 'What in the name of the good God do you think you are trying to do?' In a way, O'Connor's writings contain, among much else, an extended set of answers to that question, a question he is tacitly setting the Irish people and Irish political leaders. As late as the early 1960s, in a lecture on William Butler Yeats, he gives pride of place to an entertaining anecdote recounted by George Russell ('AE') about the great poet:

> As if it weren't enough, Yeats was also a member of a secret society called the Irish Republican Brotherhood. I was very curious to know how he got on with that group, and one night he replied: 'Oh, they were always sentencing one another to death. Once a man arrived at my house from London, raging because he had been sentenced to death by the Dublin branch. I told him not to worry because there was no danger, but that only made him angrier. "Danger?" he said "Do you think I'm afraid of what that crowd might do to me? It's the insult, man; the insult!"'[12]

During the Second World War O'Connor worked in both Ireland and England, desperately trying to earn a living because he was prevented from working on Radio Éireann by John Charles McQuaid, Archbishop of Dublin. This was because he was living in sin, in the phrase of the time, with a woman who was not married to him. McQuaid considered him to be giving a bad example. Many Irish writers, including John McGahern some decades later, were persecuted directly or indirectly by McQuaid. As 'Ben Mayo', O'Connor had a column in the *Sunday Independent*. At one stage a priest came to the hall door and informed O'Connor's girlfriend that Radio Éireann had been forbidden to employ either of them. The priest was challenged to prove it. The following day a one-week contract with Radio Éireann fell through the letter-box.

After the war, despite many rejections, O'Connor began to sell stories regularly to American magazines. The Americans paid very well, and he struck up a warm friendship with Bill Maxwell of the *New Yorker*. Their correspondence survives and has been published. It is, among other things, a practical manual on how to write for magazines, and displays the fruits of a great intellectual friendship. Maxwell used to wonder quietly how O'Connor put up with Ireland at all. Eventually O'Connor married an American girl. By the mid-1950s, his boat had come in and he seems to have achieved some kind of peace and happiness, having escaped financially from his Irish entrapment.

O'Connor used his strong sense of the absurd to ridicule not only the often bizarre antics of Irish republicanism, but the similarly weird anti-intellectual antics of Irish governmental leaders. For example, he loved to harp on the fact that his translation of Brian Merriman's *Cúirt an Mheadhon Oídhche* (*The Midnight Court*) was banned in Ireland for being in general tendency indecent and obscene, while chunks of this marvellous poem in the original language were included in every schoolchild's Irish-language poetry book. The censorship, however, survived O'Connor by one year and a general lifting of the bans was effected in 1967 by Brian Lenihan; Irish censorship was felled not just by O'Connor's public assaults on it but also by the weight of its own absurdity.

Many of O'Connor's short stories were, by the standards of the time and place, relatively sexually explicit. He was preoccupied with the human condition, a condition whose central constituent was loneliness, a loneliness that can be assuaged although not cured by sexual love. This got him into trouble with the censorship people again and again, and fuelled his vitriol against them. He found himself at odds with Irish society in many ways, not least his avoidance of public houses, probably for fear of his father's chronic alcoholism. He quarrelled with Patrick Kavanagh and Brian Nolan (Flann O'Brien), and eventually had a breach even with O'Faoláin. O'Connor and O'Faoláin both wrote books on the short story as an art form, O'Faoláin's *The Short Story* appearing in 1948, O'Connor's *The Lonely Voice* being published in 1962.[13]

O'Faoláin's book contains an admiring commentary on one of O'Connor's stories ('In the Train'). Despite their quarrels and differences, O'Faoláin was grief-stricken at O'Connor's sudden death, as though part of himself had died. Both writers espoused a theory that in Ireland it is almost impossible to write a first-rate novel, as Irish society is unsettled and shifting. In such a shapeless and incoherent society, the short story finds a role for itself more readily. It is not clear even fifty years later whether Irish society has yet achieved any shape or coherence.

TG

Notes

1 Frank O'Connor, *Guests of the Nation* [1931] (Swords: Poolbeg, 1979).

2 Daniel Corkery, *The Hidden Ireland* (Dublin: M.H. Gill & Sons, 1924).

3 James Matthews, *Voices: A Life of Frank O'Connor* (Dublin: Gill and Macmillan, 1983), p.72.

4 Frank O'Connor, *An Only Child* (London: Macmillan, 1958), pp.256–7.

5 Ibid., p.274.

6 See O'Connor, *Guests of the Nation*, p.18.

7 Frank O'Connor, *The Backward Look* (London: Macmillan, 1967).

8 Ibid., p.114. (The book is, of course, *The Hidden Ireland*.)

9 Ibid., pp.30–52.

10 Ibid., pp.46–55.

11 See O'Connor, *Guests of the Nation*, pp.130–44.

12 See O'Connor, *The Backward Look*, pp.165–6.

13 Sean O'Faoláin, *The Short Story* (Cork: Mercier, 1948); Frank O'Connor, *The Lonely Voice* [1962] (Cork: City Council, 2003).

16

Sean O'Faoláin (John Whelan) and Frank O'Connor (Michael O'Donovan) were, like Alexis de Tocqueville and Gustave de Beaumont or Karl Marx and Friedrich Engels, an intellectual partnership of the type that makes it difficult to know, intellectually speaking, where one starts and the other leaves off. The two Corkmen, born within a few years of each other (O'Faoláin in 1900, O'Connor in 1903) worked together and knocked sparks off each other on and off for a generation, before they finally went their separate ways around 1950. O'Faoláin was a policeman's son, and received a third-level education at University College Cork and later, at Harvard under a British Commonwealth scholarship. O'Connor left school while still a child and was almost completely a brilliantly self-educated scholar and storyteller. Some of the ideas in *King of the Beggars* seem to have been originally O'Connor's, in particular the notion that the old aristocratic Gaelic order, so much lamented by the eighteenth-century poets, had been indifferent to, or even inimical to, the interests or general wellbeing of the common Irish people.

King of the Beggars is a powerful polemical argument in favour of Daniel O'Connell as the true founder of the modern Irish political nation, a nation the Irish leader had himself seen clearly as oppressed and profoundly dispirited. The Liberator himself remarked toward the end of his life:

> I never will get half credit enough for carrying Emancipation, because posterity never can believe the species of *animals* with which I had to carry on my warfare with the common enemy.[1]

O'Connell's reputation had, by the 1930s, been fairly consistently darkened by a century-long radical nationalist series of attacks, beginning with John Mitchel in the 1840s and continuing with Fenian and republican critiques in later years. Essentially O'Connell was condemned for his royalism and his acceptance of the continuation of some kind of a union with Great Britain. This acceptance was in the context of a liberated and democratised Ireland faithful to the Crown but enjoying its own representative institutions in the form of a Dublin parliament. He was faulted also by Irish cultural revivalists such as Daniel Corkery or the leaders of the Gaelic League of 1893 for accepting the defeat of Gaelic culture and welcoming the coming of the English language as the everyday language of the people. It is clear that O'Connell had seen this as essential for the mental liberation of the Irish people and their entry into the modern commercialised world of the English-speaking peoples.

O'Faoláin celebrates this O'Connell. He sees O'Connell as far more an authentic representative of the Irish people in his populism, ambivalence, realism and humorous acceptance of the everyday circumstances in which he found himself than was any canting republican ideologue. O'Connell saw the Irish people as degraded, certainly, but as also the human materials out of which might be forged an Irish democracy. He sensed the power that lay in the hands of the masses under the English Constitution if they were only to become aware that in their numbers lay their strength, a strength which could be called upon if they only consented to organise. This forging of an Irish democracy was the task he set himself and was his life's work, argues O'Faoláin. This nation of slaves and beggars was to become a nation of citizens, masters of their government and of their collective destiny. O'Faoláin's O'Connell saw that the Irish Catholic Church and English and Irish liberals of any religion were to be his allies in this task. His enemies were the Irish aristocracy with their corrupt stranglehold on the court system and local government, reinforced by its alliance with the English Tories. His weapons against them were his knowledge of the law and his keen awareness of their contempt for the principles of justice that lay behind the law. His native intelligence and underlying peasant hardness served him well. His public humiliation of judges, plaintiffs and packed juries made him a hero to the ordinary people for whom the law had long been a capricious and dangerous foe. The Irish democracy which O'Connell began to build by turning the law against its aristocratic enemies was to be given its capstone a century later by Michael Collins, who offered an incredulous nation the freedom to achieve freedom in the form of a democratic political order in 1922. An underlying liberalism and a popular capacity for tolerance survived the onset of anti-modernism and isolationism and the consequent imposition of a deeply obscurantist censorship between 1929 and 1967. This spirit of Irish democracy was O'Connell's enduring legacy. O'Faoláin wrote:

> There is but small respect due to the end of the old order of Gaeldom, to that eighteenth-century collection of the *disjecta membra* of an effete traditionalism. There is respect due but to one man. We must respect Dan O'Connell, despite all his faults, all his mean lawyer's tricks, all his ambiguity, all his dishonesty, evasiveness,

snobbery, because he, at least, he alone, had the vision to realise that a democracy could be born out of the rack and ruin of Limerick and 1691, out of the death and decay of antiquity – and it decayed rather than died, for it was rotting before it disappeared, and it stank before it was buried.

He, a Kerry peasant, one of the people, to be acknowledged and entitled *The Man of the People*, took the beggars of Limerick and gave them a kingdom of the mind. All he said to them was that they were not a rabble, and that they could, out of their own collective strength, make themselves into a nation.

With his tall hat cocked on the side of his curly head, his cloak caught up in his fist, a twinkle in his eye, he became King of the Beggars. The dates merge: 1691, and he that came in the middle of the century after, and won out by 1829. The dates merge, for less than one hundred years after he had emancipated his people, this modern Ireland came into being.[2]

This argument is not just a vindication of O'Connell, but is also a scarcely veiled but tacit attack on the whole Gaelic revivalist ideology associated with O'Faoláin's old mentor, Daniel Corkery, the Gaelic League of Eoin MacNeill and Douglas Hyde, the assertion of a neo-Gaelic Ireland by Patrick Pearse and the values absorbed as youths by both himself and O'Connor during the revolutionary years. This was spotted by several commentators in a *Studies* symposium in 1938.[3] One of the contributors, Michael Tierney, protested against O'Faoláin's apparent consignment of all Irish cultural history before 1690 to the rubbish bin. Tierney granted that O'Faoláin was right to argue that Ireland's modern political culture was derived from English models, but asserted that the Gaelic world, even in a somewhat faked and revived form, had a civilising and humanising influence: 'The real study of Irish history has only begun, that of Irish literature is in its infancy.' Daniel A. Binchy made a similar plea, and expressed scepticism about O'Faoláin's claim to dismiss an Irish history which O'Faoláin himself obviously understood and by which he was really fascinated much as were Binchy and Tierney themselves. Binchy felt that O'Faoláin's strictures on the old Gaelic order were anachronistic, as the common people thought as did their lords, and kept their loyalty to their leaders to the end in 1690. O'Faoláin was to stick to his guns, however, and assert repeatedly in subsequent decades that a century or two of history was quite enough for us Irish, descended as we were from slaves and defeated gentry. Perhaps he protested too much; like most Irish people of that time he was actually obsessed by Irish history and it was indeed a long nightmare from which he was trying mightily to awake; *King of the Beggars* is O'Faoláin's own wake-up call as well as one for the Irish people of the twentieth century.

Almost certainly, the book is as much an attack on Corkery's *The Hidden Ireland* as it is an attack on the neo-Gaelic idea or on insurrectionist republicanism. Certainly, it was a frontal assault on a nostalgic nationalist orthodoxy that was already showing signs of being set in stone for the foreseeable future. It is also evident that, in reality, O'Faoláin was interested all his life in Irish history seen in the *longue durée*, writing essays, for instance, on the intellectual life of early Irish Christianity. Also, he used that history himself as a weapon against his critics. It may be that O'Connor's fascination with what he called 'the backward look' softened O'Faoláin's rejectionism. But then, a few years after writing *King of the Beggars* O'Faoláin published a book on Hugh O'Neill, the sixteenth-century Ulster Gaelic leader, *The Great O'Neill* (1942). Intriguingly, this book argues for O'Neill as a modernising renaissance prince rather than a defender of an archaic social and political order.[4] History was being used again as a weapon in modern Ireland's current political life.

O'Faoláin's O'Connell is a flawed hero. His vituperation, vulgarity, cunning and often unscrupulous style of public argument became recognisable long-term features of Irish democratic life, and not its nobler features at that. Furthermore, despite his extraordinary charisma, O'Connell failed in many of his projects. Even Catholic Emancipation, his greatest success, was passed at the expense of the voting rights of the forty-shilling freeholders, and something close to manhood suffrage was not achieved until the 1880s, fifty years later. He understood that the poorer peasants saw the vote as a burden, as they were afraid to express their political wills freely in an open 'voiced' ballot; it took a certain amount of property to make for political courage in a loud public declaration of preference. Again, he took the side of the more reactionary bishops in the 1840s in the controversy over the Queen's Colleges, meaning that third-level education for Catholics was effectively postponed until the twentieth century. However, the centrality of O'Connellite democracy to Irish political culture has persisted now for nearly two centuries, and various attempts to camouflage that fact have failed. Where he wended his political way, Parnell, de Valera and thousands of others were forced willy-nilly to follow. His name is still on the principal streets of many Irish towns and villages, and as de Beaumont prophesied in 1839, he has never been forgotten by the Irish people. The Irish political party with all of its populism and craftiness was his greatest organisational invention, and it remains central to Irish democracy. *King of the Beggars* documents that fact brilliantly.

Fergus O'Ferrall has pointed out in a penetrating article that O'Connell's central legacy was one of political ideas and practices associated with liberty.[5] Classical liberalism survived in Ireland almost as a folk tradition of tolerance and egalitarianism, despite occasional incomprehension of it by some writers of Catholic provenance:

There exists a traditional lack of understanding of liberalism in Irish Catholic circles. Liberal Catholicism seems a strange, even a contradictory, conjuncture to many. Seamus Deane, for example, in a recent essay on 'Edmund Burke and the Ideology of Irish Liberalism' totally ignores liberal Catholicism, describing 'the dominant liberal tradition in Irish political thought' as stemming from late seventeenth-century writers such as Molyneux, to Burke and the United Irishmen and then, inexplicably, jumping to James Connolly and Liam Mellows.[6]

Despite authoritarianism, censorship and traditions of political secrecy, an essential liberalism has survived in Ireland. O'Connell's politics, which included not only the defence of Catholic rights, but which also included demands for Jewish emancipation and opposition to black slavery has lived on, often not really recognised as such, in modern Ireland. As O'Ferrall argues, O'Faoláin, in a later book *The Irish* (1947 and 1969), addresses the question of Irish attitudes toward liberty, and toward what O'Faoláin acidly termed their 'lovely past'.[7] The Irish did not really turn their backs on that past until a generation or two had elapsed after the revolution of 1913–1923. These younger men and women finally set out to construct a new Ireland that had 'nothing to do with the Past'. In this they were acting squarely in the tradition of O'Connell rather than in that of the Gaelic League. This change from more spectacular forms of revolutionary activity began slowly and tentatively, O'Faoláin argues. It did not really accelerate properly until the sons, in some cases the grandsons and granddaughters, of men and women of the generation of 1916 set out, in earnest, to make liberty viable in terms of the modern commercial and industrial world.[8] The change did not go unchallenged. The gun and the bomb remained on the agenda in the minds of some, as O'Faoláin argued in 1947 and 1969.

... that restless ghost, our Past, still refused to go away. Unplacated, it had tauntingly pursued Fianna Fail for several years after they achieved power, under the shadowy name of the IRA. Haunted like Richard III by the ghosts they had deposed Fianna Fail treated them as they themselves had been treated in their own ghostly days. They imprisoned the ghost, starved it, executed it and apparently crushed it. With the [second world] war the ghost rose bloodily again and sank again. It was again rustling around the pillows of Fianna Fail in the early sixties.[9]

In fact, just at the time O'Faoláin republished *The Irish* in revised form in 1969, the armed struggle myth reasserted itself in Northern Ireland, causing thousands of deaths over the following thirty years. However, the constitutional tradition founded by O'Connell was, in the long term, to prove stronger than the anti-O'Connellite tradition of insurrectionist republicanism, and did so in both parts of Ireland, the North belatedly following the South on to the road of constitutionalism in the 1990s. Ironically, it was in precisely that part of Ireland that O'Connell had had his greatest political failure; he rarely entered Ulster during his political career.

In the seventy five years since the publication of *King of the Beggars*, Irish history has continued to vindicate the essential validity of its central thesis: Daniel O'Connell gave the Irish the democratic political process, and very slowly and very reluctantly that politics has been replacing the older, more primitive culture of incoherent violence that O'Connell despised so much and recognised as the real enemy in its Croppy and Ribbon forms two centuries ago.

TG

Notes

1 Sean O'Faoláin, *King of the Beggars* (London: Nelson, 1938), p.x.

2 Ibid., p,20.

3 Symposium on King of the Beggars. Michael Tierney, 'Daniel O'Connell and the Gaelic Past' with responses by Gerald Murphy, Daniel A. Binchy and Sean O'Faolàin', *Studies*, Vol. 27, No. 107 (September 1938), pp.353–80.

4 Sean O'Faoláin, *The Great O'Neill* [1942] (Cork: Mercier, 1970). First published in London by Longmans, Green.

5 Fergus O'Ferrall, 'Liberty and Catholic Politics, 1790–1990', in Maurice O'Connell, *Daniel O'Connell, Political Pioneer* (Dublin: Institute of Public Administration, 1991), pp.35–56, quote from p.52.

6 Ibid.

7 Sean O'Faoláin, *The Irish* [1947] (Harmondsworth: Penguin, 1969), p.145.

8 Ibid., p.145.

9 Ibid., p.156.

17

Flann O'Brien, *At Swim-two-Birds* (1939)

Brian Nolan, Brian O Nualláin, Myles na gCopaleen, Myles na Gopaleen, Flann O'Brien and several other monickers or *noms de plume* were personae contained in the small body of one extraordinary man, perhaps Ireland's greatest satiric writer since Swift. Flann O'Brien is a reversal of Brian O'Linn, a famous comic figure of nineteenth-century Irish popular culture, and the hero of a well-known comic ballad with dozens of verses almost certainly improvised by many amateur songsters:

> Brian O'Linn had a house with no door,
> The sky for a roof and the bog for a floor.
> A way to jump out and a way to swim in,
> 'Tis a fine habitation,' said Brian O'Linn!

Flann also suggests royal blood, as does the surname O'Brien; the clan supplied the kings of Thomond (north Munster, County Clare) at one time. Flann O'Brien is the self-declared comic King of

Ireland, much as Leopold Bloom in his reveries is the comic King of Dublin where he is to build his New Bloomusalem.

Nolan was not alone in satirising Irish society, politics and political culture. In the early part of the century, satire certainly flourished. Flann/Myles was preceded, of course, by the granddaddy of them all, James Joyce, whose great book *Ulysses* is, among other things, a huge and outrageously funny satire on Dublin life and Irish writing as it was at the beginning of the twentieth century. Again, Myles had a John the Baptist in the form of the now almost forgotten Eimar O'Duffy, whose main output was in the 1920s: *Asses in Clover* and *The Spacious Adventures of the Man in the Street* among others. Again, the playwright Denis Johnston belongs in this honourable crew, particularly for his 1929 masterpiece play, *The Old Lady Says No.*

Johnston is perhaps the most obvious user of a device common to all these writers: the juxtaposition of a romantic and heroic, or romanticised and heroised version of that past with the grubby realities of the present. A ham actor playing Robert Emmet after the failure of the rising of 1803 declares his love to Sarah Curran above in Rathfarnham, when he is accosted by Major Sirr's secret police, and hit over the head with a musket by a soldier. He falls down, and all of the actors fall out of role (Jayzuz I've killed him, etc.). 'Sirr,' the actor calls plaintively to the audience in a 'real' Dublin accent, 'Is there a doctor in the house?' A 'doctor' planted in the audience walks up and tends to the 'injured' actor, replacing his boots with slippers. The curtains close. When they open again, 'Emmet' the actor is still lying at centre stage, but gets up, and starts raving in romantic nationalist Manganesque verse. He walks through the streets of the modern Dublin of 1929, dressed in a green uniform and wearing the slippers of comedy rather than the high boots of tragedy, meeting examples of modern Ireland (young fellows on their way to Irish language classes for the civil service, young flappers talking about jazz and 'fellas', etc.). He encounters a foulmouthed old woman in Moore Street who is, of course, the Shan Van Vocht, and the old sow who eateth her nine farrow etc. but who also is the young girl with the walk of a queen. The same actress appears in both guises. Independent Ireland is seen as a failure, or at least a great disappointment. He has a long conversation with Grattan's statue. Eventually, he sleeps in peace, and the doctor thanks the audience for its patience. The play is a precedent for O'Brien's masterpiece of ten years later.

At Swim-two-Birds was, to put it mildly, tragically unfortunate in its timing, coming out as it did in September 1939.[1] To add insult to injury, most of the Longmans print run was destroyed in the bombing of the London docks by the Luftwaffe. It was not to be reprinted until 1960, when it became a much delayed hit. At Swim-two-Birds perpetrates the usual series of comic collisions between Irish pasts and Irish presents. The title itself is a literal and therefore 'wrong' translation of snámh dhá éin; snámh ('swim') meaning a near-ford or shallow bit of the river, where a man could walk across up to his waist in water while permitting his horse to paddle or swim with him to the other side. The 'frame story' is about the narrator, an unnamed UCD student who apparently spends all his time in bed 'retiring within the kingdom [of his] mind', but who is writing a book about a writer, Orlick Trellis, whose characters seek to revenge themselves on the writer when he is asleep and off his guard. Their mode of attack is to write another book about Trellis within a book within a book, in which he is tortured in various horrible ways by his own characters and a few extra characters invented by his own characters. Trellis, I think, lives above a thinly disguised version of Hartigan's pub on Leeson Street; the address was transferred to Peter Place where there was no pub. Hartigan's was a famous University College Dublin pub of that era where Brian O'Nolan probably spent a good deal of his spare time. Trellis is pithily described as 'a man of average stature but his person was flabby and unattractive, partly a result of his having remained in bed for twenty years'. The characters themselves represent present and past Irish comic archetypes.

The book is about sin and its consequences, and the characters are forced by the tyrannical author to undergo terrible injustices or to commit unnamed terrible injustices which they would, if they had free will, certainly abjure.

In the book, the past is represented by 'Finn Mac Cool ... a legendary hero of old Ireland':

> Though not mentally robust, he was a man of superb physique and development. Each of his thighs was as thick as a horse's belly, narrowing to a calf as thick as the belly of a foal. Three fifties of fosterlings could engage with handball against the wideness of his backside, which was large enough to halt the march of men through a mountain pass.

The past is also represented by the Pooka MacPhellimey, 'a member of the devil class', who ends up as the main torturer of Trellis in the book written by the characters as vengeance against Trellis, himself a creation of the UCD student.

The present is represented by the student, his uncle and the uncle's ridiculous friends, and his own friend Kelly, another impecunious student. Their conversation is in part a parody of Stephen Dedalus and his friend Clancy in *Portrait of the Artist as a Young Man*.

> I was walking through the Stephen's Green on a summer evening with a man called Kelly, then a student, hitherto a member of the farming class and now a private in the armed forces of the King. He was addicted to unclean expressions in ordinary conversation and spat continually, always fouling the flowerbeds on his way through the green with a mucous deposit dislodged with a low grunting from the interior of his windpipe. In some respects he was

151

a coarse man, but he was lacking in malice or ill-humour. He purported to be a medical student but he had failed at least once to satisfy a body of examiners charged with regulating admission to the faculty.

The present is also represented by the vengeful characters in Trellis's book, Furriskey, Shanahan and Lamont, who urge on the fictional writer the most horrible punishments of Trellis. They are caricatures of Dublin working men and clerks, with their love of cliché and admiration for the doggerel works of Jem Casey, the workers' poet, apparently an indirect dig at Seán O'Casey, championing the Irish working class from Great British exile:

When stags appear on the mountain high,
With flanks the colour of bran,
When a badger bold can say goodbye,
A pint of plain is your only man.

When not writing the book about the book about the anti-book, the student and his pal are concerned with literary discourse, alcohol, sure tips on horses, and the pursuit and embracing of young virgins. At all of these activities, they are ineffective in an entertaining way, rather like dogs chasing cars without any idea what to do with them if they were ever to catch one.

An Béal Bocht (Dublin, 1941) is an Irish-language satire on the Gaelic League, and its attempts to revive the Irish language.[2] O'Nolan uses a different pseudonym, ('Myles na gCopaleen') as author. Instead of poor, ragged Irish-speakers begging in bad English for work outside the Gaeltacht, we have rich, posh English speakers speaking bad Irish to the lowest of the low in the Gaeltachtaí. Real Irish speakers in the Gaeltachtaí are completely bewildered by this sudden reversal of traditional roles. The novel begins with a ferocious parody of the actual Englishing of Irish surnames that occurred in the period between 1690 to 1900, resulting in an entire class of bewildered small boys being officially renamed James O'Donnell by a comically brutal schoolmaster. As the novel goes on it becomes increasingly surreal and somewhat frightening. It also begins to show signs of the otherworldly fantasy to be fully realised in the third novel, allegedly lost by O'Nolan after a drunken night in the Dolphin Hotel by being dropped in the Liffey, but actually found whole and entire in his papers after his death, and published posthumously.

The Third Policeman, authored this time by 'Flann O'Brien' is set in a strange and unfamiliar landscape. The narrator is again unnamed, and realises suddenly that he himself does not know his own name. He wishes to commit a murder, and eventually realises that he has already committed it. He has a romantic ride on the most beautiful and loving bicycle in the world. It disappears, and he goes to a police station to inform the police that he has lost his American gold watch. The member in charge asks him would it be about a bicycle, and did his watch have a bell on it.

The police station is sited inside the walls of another house, and you could live in the other house all your life without being aware that it was surrounded, penetrated and even infested by a police station inhabited by supernatural policemen who are in charge of Omnium, the primal substance of the universe. This the policemen use for trivial purposes such as putting butter on bread under the jam when jam has been spread on it absent-mindedly, papering the walls of the station without taking down the bull and dog licence application forms and getting off the dirt from one's unpolished boots after they have been repolished. Eventually the narrator realises that he is dead. The narrative is interspersed with an account of the insane universal theories of an imaginary scientist named de Selby, written in a parody of the learned journal literature of the time. The echoes of *Twenty Years A-Growing* are obvious.

These are three extraordinary books, written in a dozen different styles of English or Irish, and were his reputation to rest on these alone, it would be a very significant one. However, as 'any fule kno', for over quarter of a century he wrote a column in the *Irish Times*, which apparently was occasionally ghosted by Niall Montgomery. He wrote several lesser comic novels in the years after the war. He also wrote thrillers for the British market under a pseudonym. The column *Cruiskeen Lawn* was uneven, but on its good days was brilliant. Characters like the Brother, the Justice and the Defendant became part of Dublin folklore and still live on in exchanges such as:

> You know what it is I'm goin to tell you?
> *I do not.*
> The Brother can't look at an egg.

His wars on pretentious writing and his lampooning of boilerplate journalist's cliché in the 'Myles na Gopaleen Catechism of Cliché' are still remembered. Myles didn't confine himself to English cliché but also attacked their Irish equivalent, sometimes using English phonology to comic effect: *baigh Deaid, Am a raibh Gael in Eirinn beo*. He didn't even leave lordly Latin in peace: *Quid est hoc? Hoc est quid*. Like many another inveterate punster of that era, he could be accused of dogging a fled horse. He disliked intensely Synge's *Playboy of the Western World*, arguing that no Irish person had ever spoken like the characters in the play. It could be argued against him that Synge was well aware of that and that the fake dialect was itself part of the comedy.

Brian O'Nolan was born in 1910 and the family moved when he was a child from Tyrone to Dublin, the father working in the revenue at that time. Brian grew up in Blackrock and attended Blackrock College. He had a brilliant undergraduate and successful postgraduate career in UCD and went on to be an Administrative Officer in the Department of Local Government in the Custom House. There, one of his best pals was John Garvin, who did his best to protect his irrepressible younger friend from official retaliation for his public lampoons of public officials and powerful figures in the Fianna Fáil party.

O'Nolan seems to have had an early emotional crisis.[3] In 1942, there was a fire in an orphanage in County Cavan, and the good nuns had chained the fire doors shut in case the girls would get out into the open in their nighties and get up to all kinds of unimaginable behaviour or otherwise scandalise the locals. The little girls were burned to death. O'Nolan happened to be the Department of Local Government inspector assigned to determine the cause of the tragedy (an overturned space heater, apparently). This seems to have left a permanent mark on him, as his beloved Church seemed to have been criminally negligent. On top of the apparent failure of his books and the frustrations of living in an isolated wartime country, he seems to have retreated to journalism and the pub in rather a big way. He was apparently a terribly disappointed man, the disappointment sharpened by his own intelligence and awareness of evil around him.

His absences without leave became notorious. However, he was also a brilliant civil servant, and his file work which survives is impressive. He bearded a bishop and a bunch of doctors in 1944 when there was an attempt to take over the health service under the cloak of 'vocationalism', pointing out that people's taxes paid for that service, and had to be accounted for democratically. He made gallant attempts to get the Irish state to commit itself to a modern road system in the post-war years, but to little avail. Eventually events caught up with him. In the early 1950s, wearing his Myles na Gopaleen hat, he lampooned repeatedly a well-known political figure, Andy Clarkin, for not fixing his public clock, and Minister Patrick Smith called John Garvin into his office some time in, I think, late 1952. Garvin, Secretary of the department, was ordered to fire O Nualláin. Garvin assented obediently and wondered what to do about his old friend. News got out quickly around the Custom House that the Gop was for the Hop, and the Medical Officer called him up, suggesting that Myles's firing might be postponed for a few months:

> 'I think I can stall it for three months.'
> 'John, the Americans have invented a new illness. If we wait three months, the Gop can retire due to ill-health and keep his pension with *ex misericordiam* consideration. As it is, he goes out destitute.'
> 'Explain: what is this new illness?'
> 'Alcoholism.'
> 'Alcoholism? I always thought that it was an addiction, not a disease.'
> 'That's the beauty of it, John. If it's addictive, it's involuntary and therefore a disease.'

Garvin told the Minister that Myles's specialised knowledge of some building project or other necessitated postponing his dismissal for the requisite period, and got a reluctant nod from the old Cavan gunman. The dismissal letter, reluctantly signed by Garvin, survives in the Irish Archive in the Burns Library in Boston College, together with some letters from Myles to John displaying a moving mixture of resentment and affection. However, the friendship was at an end.[4]

Myles retired on a small pension in early 1953. He had just about enough to live on with his books and his journalism. In 1966 he died of cancer of the oesophagus probably caused by the classic mix of tobacco smoke and whiskey. He was, at the end of his life, clearly a literary success, but probably didn't fully appreciate this himself. That was his real tragedy.

His work lived on triumphantly and a cult of it still flourishes in Ireland and elsewhere. He certainly informed, directly or indirectly, Irish humorous and satirical writers and actors since; Frank Kelly, Eamon Morrissey, Roddy Doyle and Dermot Morgan springing particularly to mind. *At Swim* has inspired a German-language film (*Schwimmen-Zwei-Vögel*), the title itself sounding very much like something out of de Selby. His much-resented ability to lampoon feared power-holders in the state was something of an innovation at the time, and has created many descendants. Myles lives on.

TG

Notes

1   Flann O'Brien, *At Swim-two-Birds* (London: Longmans, 1939).

2   'Myles na gCopaleen', *An Béal Bocht* (Dublin: Three Candles Press, 1945 2nd edition).

3   This is a suggestion of Professor Robert O'Mahony of the Catholic University of America.

4   Personal information (TG).

18

James Kavanagh, *Manual of Social Ethics* (1954)

James Kavanagh's (1914–2002) *Manual of Social Ethics* set out a summary and explanation of Catholic social thought, based on papal encyclicals hugely influenced by the writings of Thomas Aquinas and in turn by those of Aristotle.[1] From the late nineteenth century Thomism provided the intellectual arsenal that accompanied reactionary responses by the Church to modernity, such as the doctrine of papal infallibility. Drawing on Aristotle, Aquinas maintained that natural science abstracted unchanging rules from the study of changing matter and, in doing so, gave human beings knowledge of the material things that existed outside the mind. This included knowledge of human nature. Aquinas understood the natural world to be governed by a natural law which concerned the rational human apprehension of those principles of eternal law that affected human nature and its natural ends. To seek to understand the natural world was to develop an understanding of God. Man had a body and a soul. Material existence was important because it was God's creation. Aquinas took from Aristotle an emphasis on the social nature of mankind and on the necessity of mutual cooperation and government.

The rediscovery of Aquinas provided the basis for specific political and social prescriptions that were at once an expression of interest group politics and an ontological conflict with secular modernity. Neo-Thomism found its first full expression in the 1891 papal encyclical *Rerum Novarum* (the condition of labour)[2]; the proposed Catholic alternatives to liberalism and socialism (but particularly socialism), a third way that strongly influenced European Christian Democrat political parties and Ireland's 1937 Constitution. *Rerum Novarum* strongly attacked socialism as contrary to natural law but defended the just wage, the right of workers to organise, and the need for limited state intervention to help groups in trouble. It harkened back to a time before the Enlightenment when secular individualism did not exist. It idealised the Middle Ages as the form of society that most epitomised the Christian ideal of social solidarity. At one level, Catholic social teaching faced the challenges of twentieth-century modernisation with a static thirteenth-century panacea. At the same time, it offered the industrial age a vision of the good society that drew upon a coherent intellectual legacy stretching back to Aristotle via Aquinas; one that contested both liberalism and Marxism. Liberalism had emerged to contest the fixed *ancien régime* hierarchies and demarcations that were the legacy of the Middle Ages. It emerged alongside capitalism and became seen as the ideology of capitalism. Socialism emerged to contest the inequalities associated with the capitalist modernisation of the West. Neo-Thomism and the new Catholic social thought it inspired were responses to such Enlightenment thought. It sought to reconstruct aspects of the pre-Reformation social order that were considered to be more in accordance with natural law than that which came subsequently. For instance, Catholic corporatists espoused a vocationalist social order along the lines of the mediaeval guilds as an alternative to class conflict.

Catholic social thought as restated in the 1931 encyclical *Quadragesimo Anno* (In the Fortieth Year) proposed a reconstructed social order based on corporatist principles as an alternative to capitalism and socialism. Both encyclicals emphasised the autonomy of 'lesser' social institutions as a bulwark against the state in accordance with the principle of subsidiarity.[3] Simply put, the state should not interfere with family or voluntary cooperation unless there was no other alternative. Catholic social doctrine sought to ameliorate the worst features of capitalism while resisting state interference in civil society. In the Irish case, the principle of subsidiarity was invoked to oppose state influence in the areas of education and health.

The *Manual of Social Ethics* was commissioned by Archbishop John Charles McQuaid, then at the peak of his influence; the foreword of the first edition thanked McQuaid for his 'insistent encouragement'. Its author, James Kavanagh, was one of a number of clerics hand-picked by McQuaid and effectively appointed by him to professorships in University College Dublin. As diocesan priests they were obliged to obey him. These five academic chairs were in the moral and social sciences: Ethics and Politics, Logic and Psychology, Education, Metaphysics and Social Science. Kavanagh was appointed to UCD in 1956 and became Professor of Social Science in 1966. In 1951 he had been selected by McQuaid as the Director of the Dublin Institute of Catholic Sociology. As with the Christus Rex Society founded in 1941, the aim of the Dublin Institute was to apply Catholic social teaching to Irish society. Its model of Catholic social action included courses for trade unionists and youth work. In 1945, to prepare for this role, Kavanagh had been sent by McQuaid to Oxford to study politics and economics.

The Manual of Social Ethics was reprinted in 1955, 1956, 1960, 1964 and 1966. Catholic social thought dominated the teaching of sociology and social work at UCD and intellectually dominated the social sciences elsewhere. Until 1970, the Irish sociology journal *Christus Rex* was published under episcopal imprimatur, meaning that all articles published had to be in accordance with Church doctrine. The Western canon of secular sociology derived from the writings of Karl Marx, Emile Durkheim and Max Weber, was ignored by *Christus Rex*. In this vacuum Kavanagh's *Manual of Social Ethics* summed up the body of permissible ideas. In a characteristic 1972 essay, Kavanagh argued with autocratic certainty that the sociology department he controlled had little time for the 'infantile' and 'arid pessimism' of secular social theorists like Herbert Marcuse. Irish supporters of such 'destructive radicalism' were pithily disparaged as 'sea-green incorruptible Robespierres'.[4] Empirical work was encouraged – bodies such as the Economic and Social Research Institute (ESRI) flourished – but conceptual sociology in Ireland was stunted. For sociological insight, the Irish instead turned to their novelists. For advice, they turned from their clergy to economists, journalists and broadcasters.

The ideas summarised and explained by Kavanagh have had considerable influence on Irish society. For example, in his chapter on the family, he described how natural law understandings of the duty and rights of the family were to be reflected in the 1937 Constitution. Article 41.1 stated that, 'the State recognises the Family as the natural primary and fundamental unit in society and as a moral institution possessing inalienable and imprescriptible rights superior to all positive law'. That such constitutional provisions echoed Catholic social thought was unsurprising, given that Eamon de Valera had allowed these and the foreword of the Constitution to be drafted by the Jesuits. He had also engaged in continuous correspondence with McQuaid while it was being drafted. Chapters in the *Manual of Social Ethics* on education, trade unions, property, capitalism and communism summed up and restated the arguments of the 1891 and 1931 encyclicals. Kavanagh closely followed the argument of the encyclicals against class conflict, emphasising instead the need for systems of arbitration between unions and employers. Here he endorsed an existing state of affairs that had been shaped by Catholic education of the kind offered by the Dublin institute he ran and the Jesuit-run National College of Industrial Relations.

By the time Kavanagh became Professor at UCD his *Manual of Social Ethics* was in its sixth edition, but the era of Catholic hegemony within the Irish social sciences was drawing to a close. For example, in a 1964 article in the Jesuit journal *Studies*, Garret FitzGerald addressed what he saw as the inadequacies of Catholic social teaching in Ireland. The Church viewed the state 'partly for philosophical reasons, but partly also for institutional ones' as a rival claimant on man's allegiance but was in error in doing so. Natural law, he argued, could not be taught as fixed doctrine, and presented as sociology while deliberately excluding efforts to research and understand the social world.[5] In effect, he criticised a conservative unwillingness to study real society in case this might contradict Catholic social thought.

Kavanagh included a short bibliography of suggested readings. These included *Christus Rex*, works by Aristotle, writings on Thomism and *Full Employment in a Free Society* by William Beveridge, the architect of the British welfare state. It also included two works that were widely cited by clerical opponents of the welfare state in Ireland, Hilaire Belloc's *The Servile State* and Friedrich Hayek's *The Road to Serfdom*. In the same 1940s debates where Catholic clergy cited Hayek, Irish economists were wont to cite papal encyclicals.[6] The *Manual of Social Ethics* documented the then status quo as distinct from a vision of a Catholic society that had yet to be achieved. Catholic social thought had a limited influence on the institutional hardware of the Irish state. Corporatist political arrangements were introduced to some extent, most notably in the provisions for election to the Seanad. However, the software of Catholic social ideas exerted huge influence on the constitution and governance of the Irish state; whether with respect to the rights of the family, the right to life of the unborn, demarcations between Church and state defined by the principle of subsidiarity or the system of social partnership that presided over the Celtic

Tiger era. In the *Manual of Social Ethics*, Thomas Aquinas emerges quite literally as one of the most significant architects of modern Ireland.

BF

Notes

1   James Kavanagh, *Manual of Social Ethics* (Dublin: Gill and Sons, 1954).

2   Leo XIII, *Rerum Novarum: On Capital and Labour* (1891). Available from: <http://www.vatican.va>

3   Pius XI, *Quadragesimo Anno: On the Reconstruction of the Social Order* (1931). Available from: <http://www.vatican.va>

4   James Kavanagh, 'Reflections on Sociology', *Studies*, 61 (1972), pp.175–86.

5   Garret FitzGerald, 'Seeking a National Purpose', *Studies*, 53 (1964), pp.337–351.

6   Bryan Fanning, *The Quest for Modern Ireland: The Battle of Ideas 1912–1986* (Dublin: Irish Academic Press, 2008).

19

Paul Blanshard, *The Irish and Catholic Power:*
An American Interpretation (1954)

Decades before the vogue for rhetoric about alleged 'clashes of civilizations' referring to the supposed threat of Muslim minorities wanting to impose Sharia law on liberal democracies, Paul Blanshard depicted Irish Catholics in the United States in a similar light. In his 1954 book *The Irish and Catholic Power*, he described himself as descended from three generations of Protestant clergymen. In 1914 he enrolled in Harvard's Divinity School. Not long after ordination he resigned his ministry because he had lost his faith. He subsequently led investigations on graft and corruption as head of New York City Department of Investigation and Accounts, served as a State Department official during the Second World War and later became an associate editor of *The Nation*, a left-liberal magazine. In 1949, in *American Freedom and Catholic Power*, Blanchard argued that Catholic doctrine was incompatible with liberal democracy, that given suitable circumstances, the *logical* position for the Church to adopt was one that is incompatible with American democracy.[1] Four years later Blanshard's *The Irish and Catholic Power* scrutinised the relationship between Church and State in Ireland. The result was a devastating critique that punched harder than anything published by Irish writers at the time.[2]

The Irish and Catholic Power was the prototype of what became the standard account of clericalism by its opponents although its strident tone alienated even liberal Irish Catholics. John Whyte, in his seminal *Church and State in Modern Ireland: 1923–1970*, dismissed Blanshard as an anti-Catholic writer. He also misrepresented Blanshard in claiming that he had depicted the Republic of Ireland as a theocratic state.[3] Irish sensitivities to outside criticism worked to close the ranks between Catholic conservatives and liberals. During the early 1960s, students such as Tom Garvin who were studying politics at UCD had to obtain written permission from Whyte in order to be allowed to borrow *The Irish and Catholic Power* from the university library.

Blanshard argued that while political democracy in Ireland was genuine, an unofficial Church–State alliance permitted ecclesiastical dictatorship and political democracy to live side by side without any sense of incongruity. The Church's ideal polity, he had argued in his book on Catholic power in America, was for something like the Republic of Ireland, a Catholic society in which the Church had considerable influence upon the State and where the State established through constitution and laws a public morality that accorded with Catholic teaching. In the case of the United States where Catholics were in the minority, the Church nevertheless held on to the ideal of a Church–State relationship that would enshrine Catholic doctrine in law. In *American Freedom and Catholic Power*, Blanshard called this the Catholic plan for America.

In *Studies in Political Morality* (1962), Jeremiah Newman – then a Professor of Sociology at Maynooth, later the Bishop of Limerick – explained that Blanshard's account of the ideal Church–State relationship was essentially correct (though he took issue with Blanshard's disparaging tone).[4] So effective, Newman argued, was anti-Catholic propaganda in the United States, that Senator John F. Kennedy gave assurances that in the event of his becoming President of the United States, there was no question that he would, as a Catholic, undermine the system of separation between Church and State or that he would obey the Pope's instructions in political life. But even in states where Catholics were in the minority, the Church, Newman argued, should never surrender this ideal in theoretical discussions on Church–State relations. Where Catholics were in the majority, special recognition of the Church was legitimate in order to secure their interests. And in the Irish case, where the Church enjoyed a special position, there had, Newman insisted, to be limits to religious tolerance. The rulers in a State comprised almost entirely of Catholics had a duty to influence legislation in accordance with Catholic teaching.

The Catholic Church in America, Blanshard emphasised, was 'virtually an Irish Church, operating under Irish priests and Cardinals', as it did throughout the English-speaking world. Catholic power in America was down to the Irish and its expression, Blanshard concluded, was indelibly Irish:

> All but one of the nine native-born Cardinals of American history have been the sons of Irish immigrant workers. This Irish dominance explains many of the characteristics of American Catholicism. The Irish hierarchy which rules the American Church is a 'becoming' class. It represents the Irish people struggling upwards in a hostile environment, using the Roman system of authoritative power to compensate for an inner sense of insecurity which still seems to survive from the days when the Irish Catholics were a despised immigrant minority. Boston is aggressively Catholic largely because it is aggressively Irish, and it is aggressively Irish because its people have not quite overcome their sense of being strangers in a strange land.[5]

Catholic power in America was essentially Irish Catholic power. Blanshard depicted it as organised so as to promote Irish and Catholic interests simultaneously. Irish Catholicism had become a great political as well as a spiritual phenomenon in Western life. By political he meant 'all those matters of citizenship which are not denominational'; Ireland's priests had no political party in Ireland or elsewhere in the world but they had something very much more important politically: 'a programme for the control of great areas of modern life which belong to democracy, such general areas as education, freedom of thought, domestic-relations law, and medical hygiene', as well as specific political causes such as ending Irish Partition. On such issues Irish bishops and clergy were boldly political in the sense that they carried their moral authority over into the world of citizenship and told their people what they should and should not do.

As part of his research Blanshard spent six months in Ireland between May 1952 and February 1953, during which he interviewed Northern and Southern Catholic and Protestant leaders including Eamon de Valera and Lord Brookeborough, Catholic and Protestant churchmen, Orangemen, veterans of the IRA, labour leaders, newspaper editors and leading writers. He attended debates in the Dáil, Sinn Fein conferences, Orangemen's rallies, anti-Partition mass meetings and gatherings of the right-wing Catholic organisation *Maria Duce*. Many of the men who gave him 'significant information' were Catholics and non-Catholics 'living in an atmosphere approximating genteel terror in which any association with an outspoken critic of the hierarchy's policies might lead to the termination of professional careers'.

Blanshard described the status of Catholicism in the Republic of Ireland as 'triumphantly unique'. Ireland was the only Roman Catholic country in the English speaking world. In practice it was the world's most devoutly Catholic country, not even excepting Portugal and Spain, so confident in its exalted mission in modern society that it sent out to non-Catholic countries, including

Great Britain and the United States, more than three-fourths of all its young priests. Ireland's particular Church–State relations constituted a paradox:

> Although the nation's schools, libraries, newspapers and publishing firms are almost completely dominated by the Catholic outlook, and although that outlook is imposed by a hierarchy chosen in Rome, the majority of Irish people do not resent this domination. They accept it as an organic and established part of Irish life. They permit ecclesiastical dictatorship and political democracy to live side by side without any sense of incongruity. Although they cherish their official political freedom with fierce jealousy, they are more loyal to Rome than the people of any other nation, far more devoted and obedient than the natives of the Vatican's home country.

And in many domains of Irish life they were directly in charge. Blanshard reckoned that almost one-third of professional people in Ireland were in the direct service of the Church, insofar as they worked for the 20,000 or so priests, nuns and brothers that ran the schools, universities, hospitals and some other institutions.

Blanshard's critique of 1950s Ireland focused upon the implications of this domination. *The Irish and Catholic Power* documented the persistence of censorship. Under the Censorship of Publications Act 1946, a five-man Censorship Board could ban indecent or obscene materials and those which advocated 'the unnatural prevention of conception or the procurement of abortion or miscarriage by any method'. All five had to agree in order that a book be banned. In practice, books were often censored following complaints from 'small semi-fanatical Catholic groups' who sent in copies of the offending works with marked passages.

In the twenty-three years between 1930 and 1953, some 4,057

books and 376 periodicals were banned. These included popular books that could be purchased legally in the United States, Great Britain and Northern Ireland. Those listed by Blanshard included Simone de Beauvoir's *The Second Sex*, Havelock Ellis's *The Psychology of Sex*, works by Sigmund Freud, *Married Love* by Marie Stopes and *Threshold of Marriage* published by the Church of England. It included F. Scott Fitzgerald's *Tender is the Night*, J.D. Salinger's *Catcher in the Rye*, John Steinbeck's *Grapes of Wrath*, George Orwell's *Nineteen Eighty-Four* and several novels by Graham Greene. It also included several novels that became successful award-winning movies including Herman Wouk's *The Caine Mutiny* (filmed in 1954), C.S. Forester's *The African Queen* (filmed in 1951), Ernest Hemingway's *For Whom the Bell Tolls* (1943) and James Michener's *Tales From the South Pacific* (filmed as a musical in 1958; it included the songs *There is Nothing like a Dame* and *Happy Talk*). The legion of the banned also included Irish authors such as Walter Macken, Liam O'Flaherty, Sean O'Faoláin and Frank O'Connor.

Ireland was, according to Blanshard, 'an unsuccessful laboratory of love'. Whilst economic factors contributed to low rates of marriage it was also the case, he argued, that Irish priests had exalted virginity to the point where it was almost a national catastrophe. Young women had less chance of marriage than those of the same age in any other country. Priests he interviewed ruefully admitted Ireland's failure to realise Catholic family life for many of its people. Ireland, according to one visiting American priest, was rapidly becoming a nation of bachelors and spinsters. An article in *Christus Rex*, the clerically-dominated Irish journal of sociology, reported that only two out of every five Irishmen between 30 and 34 years of age were married, the lowest proportion in the world. The 1951 census showed that the percentage of unmarried was 'still the highest in the world':

The frequent photographs in the Dublin newspapers of 'young' married couples, with their balding grooms and their ageing brides, look like extracts from the albums of the middle-aged. Whatever may be the cause, it is obvious that marriage in Ireland is surrounded with such anxieties, hesitations, and fears that only the brave, the foolish, and the well-to-do dare to undertake it at the age which is common in other countries.

Blanshard argued that the perception that sex was an impediment to moral excellence pervaded the whole education system. 'The Irish in modern times,' he said, quoting Arland Ussher, 'have no native upper caste except the priesthood, with the consequences that the typical Irishman is a little like a priest.' The celibate lives embraced by clerics had come to be presented as the ideal for all of society. And works of art that poked fun at this ideal like Brian Merriman's *The Midnight Court* (which was translated by Ussher) were banned. Blanshard quoted part of Frank O'Connor's banned 1945 translation of the poem where a woman mocked the influence of priests on Irish manhood:

Has the Catholic Church a glimmer of sense
That the priests won't marry like anyone else?
Is it any wonder the way I am,
Out of my mind for the want of a man,
When there's men by the score with looks and leisure,
Walking the roads and scorning pleasure?
The full of a fair of primest beef,
Warranted to afford relief,
Cherry-red cheeks and bull-like voices,
And bellies dripping with fat in slices.
Backs erect and heavy hind quarters,
Hot-blooded men, the best of partners,
Freshness and charm, youth and good looks
And nothing to ease their mind but books! ...

It passes the wit of mortal man
What Ireland has lost by this stupid ban.

The Irish emigrated in large numbers from a socially dysfunctional society, not just for economic reasons. Emigrant lives could be hard but lives at home were stunted. The suspicion was that Irish young people were leaving their nation 'largely because it is a poor place in which to be happy and free'.

In an analysis that now seems prescient, he charged the Irish clergy and Irish society with moral immaturity. He considered that the writings of the clergy were timid and 'strikingly immature and conformist'. Their sermons tended to be routine and elementary extensions of the catechisms used in schools. The moral world that priests built for their parishioners was 'rather like a house of blocks, neatly arranged in uniform and graded segments'. Morality was taught by rote learning. The result was a 'moral nursery' full of rulings that were incomprehensible to non-Catholics like himself.

By way of example he sought to make sense of Catholic teaching on gambling. A priest was allowed to play the Irish sweepstakes but he was not allowed (under rule number 47 of the Maynooth Statutes) to attend a horse race. Nor was he permitted to place a bet with a bookmaker although bookmaking was a permissible profession for a Catholic. 'Fanatics' like Matt Talbot – a Dublin working man who followed a daily ten-hour schedule of ritual and contrition on top of long working hours and who was found after his death to have mortified his flesh by wearing chains beneath his clothes – were depicted as moral heroes. Immorality was primarily defined as sexual immorality. Yet there was scant emphasis on honesty in business affairs or on the morality of making complete tax returns.

Blanshard's account of Irish 'moral childhood' anticipated arguments that subsequently came to the fore in efforts to understand clerical sexual abuse. These included the thesis that an overt focus on sexual morality coupled with the censorship and the repression of any discussion of sexuality fostered subterfuge amongst priests troubled by their own sexualities and that it also fostered cover-ups of clerical abuse by the hierarchy.[6]

BF

Notes

1   Paul Blanshard, *American Freedom and Catholic Power* (Boston, MA: Beacon Press, 1959).

2   Paul Blanshard, *The Irish and Catholic Power* (Boston, MA: Beacon Press, 1954).

3   John Whyte, *Church and State in Modern Ireland; 1923–1970* (Dublin: Gill and Macmillan, 1971), p.79 & p.369.

4   Jeremiah Newman, *Studies in Political Morality* (Dublin: Scepter, 1962).

5   See Blanshard, *American Freedom and Catholic Power*, p.30.

6   Marie Keenan, *Child Sexual Abuse and the Catholic Church: Gender Power and Organisation* (New York: Oxford University Press, 2012).

20

Michael Sheehy, *Divided We Stand* (1955)

The partition of Ireland in 1920 remained for a long time something that was regarded by many, if not perhaps most people interested in Irish affairs, as something temporary, an improvisation which would eventually be replaced by some kind of all-Ireland settlement. This assumption was shared by many nationalists and unionists and also by many *bien pensant* observers in Britain. In Dublin, during the Second World War, Archbishop John Charles McQuaid looked forward uneasily to this imminent possibility. This assumption of the inevitability of Irish unity was often shared by unionists. This in turn fuelled an acute paranoia among Ulster Unionists, and an aggressive militarism among some nationalists in both North and South. It further encouraged a rhetoric of irredentism that helped de Valera's Fianna Fáil party to win election after election in the South. This anti-partitionist rhetoric in turn copper-fastened the political power in office of a particularly stubborn 'no surrender' strand of Ulster unionism in Stormont. Discrimination against Catholics in electoral politics, government employment and public housing was legitimated by their being perceived as the enemy within. In a milder way, discrimination against Protestants was similarly rationalised in the South. As the Ulster child's rhyme put it quite accurately:

> Lord Craigavon had a cat
> It sat upon the fender.
> Every time it saw a rat
> It shouted 'no surrender!'

> De Valera had a cat.
> It sat upon the grate.
> Every time it saw a rat
> It shouted 'Up Free State!'

In reality, the Second World War had the effect of intensifying the partition of the island. Northern Ireland participated in the conflict, and suffered the consequences in the bombing of Belfast by the Luftwaffe. It also enjoyed the development of the British welfare state after the war; coming to experience a level of popular material well-being which the South could only dream of, the latter's economy being agrarian and stagnant for years after 1945. The two parts of Ireland had very different economies; nationalists claimed that they were complementary, and that independent Ireland had been robbed of its industrial arm. In the coming decades the South was to skip the smokestack phase of industrialisation and go directly to light industry such as electronics, pharmaceuticals, service and information production. On the other hand, the North was to suffer severely from deindustrialisation and political instability.

Back in the 1950s, each part of Ireland pretended that the other part did not exist, or was 'foreign' in some way. Some strange relics of the old unity persisted: Lifeboats were organised on a British Isles basis and Irish lighthouses were organised on an all-island basis. GAA sports and rugby were still organised on an all-Ireland basis, but there were two soccer teams. Weirdly, there were three cycling teams, two of them partitionist and one anti-partitionist. However, the two parts of Ireland were becoming different countries because their collective experiences had become very different. Each became increasingly and almost pathologically ignorant of the internal politics and culture of the other. Nevertheless, the reigning assumption of the inevitability and imminence of reunification lingered on. In 1955, a young man called Michael Sheehy published a little book whose title still reverberates; 'divided we stand' is as true today as it was back then. However, it received very hostile reviews in the Dublin newspapers of the time. It argued the obvious but much-denied point: that Northern Ireland existed in obedience to the collective will of the great majority of its inhabitants. Furthermore, it was not simply a device imposed by a tyrannical or imperialist British Government but was rather the only logical peaceful solution to a perennial Irish problem: the irreconcilable political ambitions of the two sets of inhabitants of the island. Unionists' ideal solution was a continued union of Britain and Ireland, whereas nationalists demanded an independent united Ireland. One ideal excluded the other. A federalised United Kingdom might have provided a compromise, but the Easter Rising of 1916, permitting a revolutionised generation of new nationalist leaders to seize power, led to the ensconcing in power of an aggressive and uncompromising all-Ireland separatism. In effect, the North was militarised in 1912 by the threat of an all-Ireland Home Rule government emerging in Dublin with the blessing of London. This was followed by the militarisation of the South, as both sides ran guns into the island in preparation either for an anticipated all-Ireland civil war or an anti-imperialist rebellion. Sheehy remarks:

> It was in the second decade of the present century that democratic ideas, through the leadership of President Wilson, became a vital force which no liberal power

175

could ignore or flagrantly disregard. By an unfortunate irony it was at this time that the South engaged in an exhausting effort to throw off the English yoke, thereby adopting and asserting an extreme nationalism which had the effect of dividing Ireland. This national effort was in large part unnecessary and the spiritual division it caused a national tragedy. The great difference in scope between the restricted Home Rule Act of 1920 and the dominion status which Britain granted Ireland in 1921 was not, as the South would have us believe, the sole outcome of her own efforts. The powerful tide of democratic ideas was making British policy in Ireland impossible to sustain, even in relation to opinion in Britain. What gave it a semblance of justification in the years after the 1914–18 war, and thus made it politically feasible, was the position of the North which the Republicans wanted to coerce into a united Ireland. This created a contradiction which democratic opinion, in Britain or abroad, was unable to resolve. The Southern demand for self-determination involved an explicit refusal to grant self-determination to the North. The fight for Irish freedom was thus also, paradoxically, a fight for Irish coercion.[1]

Tragically, among the Sinn Fein leaders in 1921, no one was more acutely aware of its essential truth than one Eamon de Valera, who said as much in private during the secret Dáil debates on the Treaty, but not in public. In private he argued that any attempt by nationalists to coerce the North into a united Ireland would open nationalists to the accusation that they were doing to the unionists what they accused the British of doing to themselves: forcing them to join a polity which they did not wish to join. Dev's noisy anti-partitionism was strictly for electoral consumption.

By the mid-1950s, it was evident that a new generation of political leaders was waiting in the wings in the South and the old revolutionaries were outliving their welcome by staying in government. A mild rebellion against the orthodoxies of the Irish revolution took place. Sheehy's book was a harbinger of this shift, which eventually took the form in the late 1950s of a mainly middle-class movement called *Tuairim* (Opinion), which interestingly confined its membership to those under forty years of age. *Tuairim* set itself to analyse various nationalist and religious sacred cows. One of these was to be the critical examination of partition. Almost in anticipation of this, and probably in reaction to the Sheehy book, Frank Gallagher, a well-known veteran of the War of Independence and the Irish Civil War, published in 1957 a denunciation of partition in a well-researched study, *The Indivisible Island.*[2] As David Hogan, Gallagher had previously published a well-known propagandistic account of the revolution in Ireland, *The Four Glorious Years.* During the war years he was de Valera's information officer, unkindly labelled 'Dev's Dr. Goebbels' by British journalists. In the later book, Gallagher gives us a potted history of the English, later British, conquest and governance of the island, emphasising in particular the classic imperial tactic of fomenting conflict among the natives so that London rule of all could be facilitated. The antagonism between Catholic and Protestant could, it was argued, be blamed on the British as could pretty well everything else. Partition was a device to discourage the complete independence of the island in defiance of the wishes of the great majority of its inhabitants.

Certainly there was truth in much of Gallagher's argument, although it could be pointed out that the origins of Irish divisions were rather beside the point: these divisions had long had a life of their own, and it was beyond the power of any British or Irish government to do very much about them other than recognise and accept their enduring reality. Irish disunity was being exacerbated by nationalist hostility and inability to compromise. This was precisely the argument to be made in a long review of

The Indivisible Island written by an up-and-coming young lawyer, Donal Barrington. Barrington was a scion of a well-known Irish family with impeccable nationalist roots in the old Fenian separatist movement of the 1860s. He was *Tuairim's* first President and a founding member of the Irish Council for Civil Liberties. 'Uniting Ireland' was first published in *Studies*, the well-known Jesuit learned journal. It was later reissued as the first of a series of *Tuairim* pamphlets.[3] These pamphlets were to be a major force in changing Irish public opinion about all kinds of topics in the sixties. In 'Uniting Ireland' Barrington remarks cuttingly:

> The weakness of the Nationalists was that they never fully understood the nature or violence of the Unionist opposition to Home Rule, and never believed that the Unionist leaders would go as far as they subsequently did [in 1912]. Redmond saw Home Rule as something to be won from England rather than something to be created in Ireland. He was prepared to give the Unionists guarantees to protect them against victimisation in a United Ireland, but he did not see what more he could do. Home Rule was something to be implemented by means of an Act of the British Parliament, and, if the Orangemen resisted it, the British Army were to coerce them into obedience.
>
> This paradox, that the Irish Nationalists ultimately relied on the British Army to coerce all Irishmen to live together, illustrates the poverty and weakness of the Nationalist position.[4]

Partly influenced by these writings, in the years of Seán Lemass's premiership, official overtures were made to Northern Ireland, and the anti-partitionist official propaganda became muted. Lemass had evidently made up his mind that Northern Ireland was going to be a permanent entity in one legal form or another. At Lemass's insistence, the North was not to be referred to in official documents or in broadcasting as 'the Six County Area' but by its official title of Northern Ireland. This process of political thawing culminated in the Taoiseach's 1965 visit to Terence O'Neill, the Prime Minister of the province. The Dublin *Irish Independent* nominated O'Neill as Man of the Year. Unfortunately, the resulting era of good feelings was to be replaced shortly by a new wave of violence, culminating in a generation-long organised assault on the North's defenders by a new and more ferocious version of the IRA. The enduring determination of the North to defend itself and not to be absorbed into an all-Ireland state became ever more obvious as the violence went on. The necessity for civil rights for the Catholic minority in the North became increasingly pressing. Furthermore, the quiet resistance to IRA propaganda in the South, reflected in the Dublin government's determination not to permit the Republic to be sucked in to a sectarian war of sorts became obvious to everyone. Much of this new understanding was first adumbrated by Conor Cruise O'Brien's *States of Ireland*, published in 1972, a book that shows internal signs of building on the literature examined in this chapter. Eventually, the necessity of a new treaty *between the two Irelands* and facilitated by London, Dublin, Washington and Brussels dawned on pretty well everybody. This in turn led to the Good Friday Agreement of 1998 and what to date seems to be an enduring peace. Sheehy was vindicated by history as a prophet discounted and ignored in his own land. It was a very expensive discounting and ignorance.

TG

Notes

1   Michael Sheehy, *Divided We Stand* (London: Faber and Faber, 1955), p.35.

2   Frank Gallagher, *The Indivisible Island* (London: Gollancz, 1957).

3   Donal Barrington, 'Uniting Ireland', *Studies*, 46, 184 (Winter 1957), pp.379–402.

4   Ibid., p.163.

21

Edna O'Brien, *The Country Girls* (1960)
and John McGahern, *The Dark* (1965)

John McGahern's (1934–2006) first novel *The Barracks* (1963) was critically acclaimed. His second novel *The Dark* was immediately banned in Ireland for its alleged pornographic content.[1] Both were mined from McGahern's own childhood. *The Dark* contained some vivid accounts of teenage masturbation – the use of a sock to ensure that the sheets weren't stained – and describes feelings of guilt ('Five sins already today, filthiness spilling five times') and thoughts on the impracticability of confessing so many sins; thirty-five a week, one hundred and forty impure actions since the protagonist's last confession. It was published two years before Philip Roth's great comic paean to seed spilling, *Portnoy's Complaint*.[2] But there is nothing comic about *The Dark*. Its opening describes a small boy being beaten with a leather strap with one of his sisters present, having first been made to strip naked by his widower father Mahoney. The beating was a punishment for uttering a profane word ('F.U.C.K is what you said, isn't it?'). Alongside descriptions of brutal domestic violence against children, there are inferences of sexual abuse by the unnamed protagonist's father:

> The worst was having to sleep with him the nights he wanted love, strain of waiting for him to come to bed, no hope of sleep in the waiting – counting and losing the count of the thirty-two boards across the ceiling, trying to pick out the darker circles of the knots beneath the varnish.

In his *Memoir* McGahern makes clear that such experiences were autobiographical. There were thirty-two tongue-and-grooved boards on the ceiling in the bedroom he shared with his father after his mother died in 1944 when he was ten years old. His six siblings slept in the other bedroom. McGahern's *Memoir* also described sleepless nights when father would take off all his clothes, massage his son's belly and thighs asserting that this relaxed taut muscles, eased wind and helped bring on sleep:

> In those years, despite my increasing doctrinal knowledge of what was sinful I had only the vaguest knowledge of sex or sexual functions and took him at his word; but as soon as it was safe to do so, I turned away on some pretext or other such as sleepiness. Looking back, and remembering his tone of voice and the rhythmic movement of his hand, I suspected he was masturbating.[3]

The Dark describes a sexualised encounter with Father Gerald, a family friend who was helping him explore whether he had a vocation for the priesthood. During his first night in the priest's house, Father Gerald comes into his room and gets into bed with him ostensibly for a talk about vocations. The priest puts his hand on the boy's shoulder. His roving fingers touched the boy's throat. He questions the boy about feelings for girls and asks him whether he masturbated and how often. A question from the boy as to whether Father Gerald ever had to fight that sin is met with stony silence. In silent anger the boy remembers the nights when his father used to stroke his thighs. No real-life equivalent to Father Gerald was identified in his *Memoir*. But McGahern's real-life vacillations about becoming a priest – his mother had wanted this for him before she died – were similarly focused on the difficulties of celibacy in a society where children, their parents and their priests knew little about sexuality. *The Dark* also describes the sexual harassment of the protagonist's sister by her employer and Father Gerald's concern that this be kept secret in order to avoid scandal. His *Memoir* recounts how he had to rescue his sister Rosaleen from the clutches of a County Cavan draper who made sexual advances from the moment she arrived to work in his shop. The repressive rural Catholic society described in *The Dark* is shown to exert a heavy toll of human misery.

Five years before *The Dark* was published, Edna O'Brien's first novel *The Country Girls* was also banned. Like *The Dark*, *The Country Girls* was a coming of age novel again set in late 1940s rural Ireland. Kate, the narrator of *The Country Girls*, also grows up in a troubled home – her mother drowns at the beginning of the book, her father is a neglectful drunk – and she is damaged by this. How it happened became clearer in the follow-up novels of what became an autobiographical trilogy. O'Brien has elsewhere described her father as a frightening man, a very angry drinker. Although Kate in *The Country Girls* fears her father more than anyone, there have been no beatings and no hints of sexual abuse.

While young Mahoney in *The Dark* rejects the idea of becoming a priest because this would condemn him to a life of loneliness and sexual frustration, Kate never considers whether she has a religious vocation for a second. Although O'Brien describes having been religious as a child, Kate and her friend and rival Baba appear utterly indifferent to religion. Kate exhibits little of the guilt and shame about sexuality that torments the protagonist of *The Dark*. In interviews O'Brien has described a fervid and suffocating religious upbringing. But *The Country Girls* defiantly transcends this. Young

Mahoney's silent rebellion against the priesthood contrasts with Kate's dramatic rejection of the mere boredom of convent school life. Kate and Baba desecrate a holy picture by writing graffiti on it to the effect that Father Tom the chaplain, 'stuck his long thing' into Sister Mary, Kate's favourite nun. The graffiti is left to be found. They do this deliberately to get expelled from school. The girls are not the victims; the priest and the nun are *their* victims. If *The Country Girls* had been set in twenty-first century Ireland, Kate and Baba might well have bullied their teachers on Facebook.

From fourteen years of age Kate innocently yearns to be seduced by Mr Gentleman, a married lawyer, whose real French surname nobody can pronounce. Had the story been told from his point of view, Mr Gentleman might have been a rural Irish counterpart to Humbert Humbert, the narrator of Vladimir Nabokov's *Lolita*. But Kate wants romance and love, her lips, 'poised for the miracle of a kiss. A kiss. Nothing more.' Even four years later, when she is eighteen, her imagination of what she might get up to with Mr Gentleman does not go beyond that. Kate is at no stage a victim. Unlike the protagonists of most coming of age novels by Catholic Irish writers, she appears indifferent to conservative Catholic social mores. Not for her the wrestling with convention and faith that exemplified James Joyce's *A Portrait of An Artist as a Young Man* or its many imitations. *The Country Girls* captured an emerging secular Ireland indifferent to crises of religious faith. This was not an Ireland that interested McGahern.

In *The Lonely Girl*, the sequel to *The Country Girls*, O'Brien works in a reference to another banned work from the same part of East Clare, Brian Merriman's *The Midnight Court*.[4] A dog-eared copy was kept by Jack Holland, a bachelor shopkeeper who had been in love with Kate's mother. He had been caught by her father with his hand on her knee under the table during a game of cards. One line is paraphrased as having been recited by Jack: 'The doggedest divil that tramps the hill, With the grey in his hair and a virgin still.' *The Country Girls* is very much its spiritual descendant.

Merriman's 'perfect crescendo of frustrated sexual passion', as Frank O'Connor put it in the foreword to his banned translation, ridiculed male chastity and clerical celibacy from the perspective of unfulfilled women. In *The Country Girls* Kate's mother lets Jack Holland put his hand on her knee under the table because Jack is kind to her. Baba's mother Mrs Brennan (like the Queen of the Silver Dollar in Shel Silverstein's country and western song of that name) wants only two things from life 'and she got them – drink and admiration'. Most nights she goes down to the Greyhound Hotel, 'dressed in a tight black suit with nothing under the jacket, only a brassiere, and with a chiffon scarf knotted at her throat. Strangers and commercial travellers admired her.' Country and western is still very popular in the pubs of East Clare. Most of the men Kate describes, even putatively predatory ones like Mr Gentlemen, are, to invoke that great Irish insult, harmless.

The Dark was banned in June 1965 by the Censorship Board. McGahern, who had been on a year's leave of absence from his job as a primary school teacher was told by his headmaster, at the behest of Archbishop John Charles McQuaid, that he could not return to the school. McQuaid let it be known that if the Irish National Teachers' Organisation supported McGahern, it would not get any support from the Archbishop in upcoming pay negotiations. His fellow teachers, in effect, sold him out.[5] McGahern's sacking became a *cause célèbre* and the controversy precipitated a review of censorship legislation. A new Act introduced in 1967 imposed a twelve-year time limit on how long books could be proscribed. This immediately removed the ban on several thousand books, though not the ban on *The Dark*.

McGahern, for his part, was unwilling to become a figurehead of liberal, secular Ireland. On Ireland's most watched television programme, *The Late Late Show*, he declared that he could no more attack the Catholic Church than he could his own life. In a 2001 interview he recalled being told that the scandal surrounding the book was marvellous, because it would boost sales. He remembered being quite ashamed because 'we', by which he meant the Irish, 'were making bloody fools out of ourselves'. He had thought that the Censorship Board was something of a joke, that books that were banned could be easily found and quickly passed around, and that there was no fruit that tasted as good as the forbidden fruit. In the same interview he stated that he had nothing but gratitude to the Church, except for its unhealthy attitude to sexuality.[6]

The Country Girls was written in exile in 1958, in a mock Tudor house in the 'outer-outer suburbia' of south west London.[7] Like Kate at the end of *The Country Girls*, O'Brien had moved to Dublin, was working in a shop, wanted to write and was doing her best to have an exciting social life. Like Kate in *The Lonely Girl*, she began an affair with an older man who was a writer. They married and moved to England. She got a job working for a publisher, secured a contract for her novel and wrote it, supposedly, in a matter of weeks. She lost the custody of her two children when she left her husband. He was ostensibly a domineering and controlling man and the breakdown of their marriage seems to have been triggered by his jealousy about the success of her book and the opportunity to live independently that her writing gave her.

It is worth noting that *The Country Girls* was published in the same year as the obscenity trial that followed the publication in Britain of the unexpurgated version of D.H. Lawrence's *Lady Chatterley's Lover*. Prurience about sexuality and the stigmatisation of women who defied social mores was by no means the sole preserve of the Irish. But the *Lady Chatterley* trial marked the end of an era of censorship in England. Each of the four books that O'Brien published before McGahern's *The Dark* appeared, (*The Country Girls*, *The Lonely Girl*, *Girls in their Married Bliss*, *August is a Wicked Month*) were banned in Ireland. So too was her 1966 novel *Casualties of Peace*. *The Country Girls* was burned by her local parish priest. She flouted the censorship of her works and publicly imported copies of these. At a public meeting on censorship in Limerick in 1966 she asked for a show of hands of those who had read her banned books. She was met with a sea of hands and much laughter. Though still banned, *The Country Girls* was serialised in an Irish magazine in 1965.[8] Edna O'Brien did much to reduce the Censorship Board to the joke that McGahern thought it had become.

McGahern's public response to censorship was stoic and dignified and he came to be much admired for this. O'Brien was vilified as a scarlet woman. In response she adopted a flamboyant public persona. She could be reliably counted upon to come up with some scandalous aphorism on Irish or British television. Asked on Robin Day's *Question Time* (the 1970s clip is on YouTube) to describe an ideal evening, she replied, a romantic dinner with a man who gave her champagne without going on about the price or talking about his wife. McGahern went on to be celebrated as the leading Irish novelist of his lifetime. While *The Country Girls* is one of the best and most significant Irish novels of the last century, O'Brien's many subsequent books have not enjoyed the same status. Like Oscar Wilde she poured much of her genius into a public persona that stuck it to those who would vilify her. The façade that she created for herself was, according to one critic, too stage-Irish for the Irish, too Irish for the English and too flighty and romantic for feminists.[9]

Both *The Country Girls* and *The Dark* depicted with respectively frank and brutal accuracy, the sexual and emotional landscape of a rural Catholic society that was by then rapidly unravelling. Subsequent 'revelations' of widespread clerical sexual abuse of children and of ordinary domestic violence were hardly revelations as such. It was all too easy to sweep knowledge of grim realities under the carpet in a country where Catholicism dominated sociology and the social services and where non-fiction books about human sexuality were banned. Literature articulated things that could not be spoken of in official Ireland or dealt with in the so-called non-fictional media.

BF

Notes

1   John McGahern, *The Barracks* (London: Faber and Faber, 1963) and *The Dark* (London: Faber and Faber, 1965).

2   Philip Roth, *Portnoy's Complaint* (New York: Random House, 1969).

3   John McGahern, *Memoir* (London: Faber and Faber, 2005), p.188.

4   Edna O'Brien, *The Lonely Girl* (London: Penguin, 1962).

5   John Cooney, *John Charles McQuaid; Ruler of Catholic Ireland* (Dublin: O'Brien Press, 1999), p.370.

6   Eamon Maher, 'Catholicism and National Identity in the Works of John McGahern', in Bryan Fanning (ed.), *An Irish Century: Studies 1912–2012* (Dublin: UCD Press, 2012), pp.272–9.

7   *Edna O'Brien: Life Stories*, television documentary (RTE, 2012).

8   Donal Ó Drisceoil, '"The best banned in the land": Censorship and Irish Writing since 1950', *The Yearbook of English Studies Vol 35: Irish Writing Since 1950* (2000), pp.146–60.

9   Rebecca Pelan, 'Edna O'Brien's "Stage-Irish" Persona: An "Act" of Resistance', *The Canadian Journal of Irish Studies*, 19,1 (1993) pp.67–78.

22

Cecil Woodham-Smith, *The Great Hunger* (1962)

The Great Famine or the Great Hunger (*An Gorta Mór*) ravaged the island of Ireland between 1845 and 1848, reaching a climax of sorts in the proverbial 'Black '47'. The horror of the event tempted some observers to connect it somehow with alleged sub-human characteristics of the population. An example in point is the use by Charles Kingsley, an Anglican polemicist and popular novelist of the time, of a racialist vocabulary in trying to give himself some emotional distance from the tragedy and the subsequent horrific shambles some years after the event.

> I am haunted by the human chimpanzees I saw along that hundred miles of horrible country [in western Ireland] ... To see white chimpanzees is dreadful; if they were black one would not feel it so much. But their skins were as white as ours.[1]

Something in the region of one million people died of starvation or of hunger-related diseases. The prevalent provision of famine relief was based on the workhouse system, a series of boarding houses where the very poor were housed, fed emergency rations and infected each other. The numbers of needy were so great that even with special exertion, the system was utterly and hopelessly swamped. The memory of this lingered on in the minds of the people for generations after. This hatred of the workhouses led the IRA to burn them out in 1918–21. The basic cause of the Great Famine was the dependence of half the population of nearly nine million on one crop: the potato. Gustave de Beaumont wrote in 1863, 'The economic consequence of this system was that eventually the existence of an entire nation depended completely on one crop.' [2] Besides the dead, a further one million people fled the island over the next few years, mainly to North America, where they were eventually followed by further millions over the following fifty years. The population of the island, uniquely in Europe, more than halved by 1900; in an era of human population explosion, the Irish were simply left out as a nation. The effects on Irish social culture, language usage and political life were permanent and long-lasting. As late as 1950, the British writer Evelyn Waugh felt able to observe, 'The Irish know only two realities: Hell and the United States.'

De Beaumont wrote in 1863 of this strange and terrible 'modernisation' of the Irish:

A psychological revolution had in fact occurred in the minds of Irish people as far as their attitudes toward emigration were concerned. This is a revolution that should be documented. It appears that their appalling misery, in taking from them the only place they knew anything about, had pushed them on to a new path where new horizons were opened to them. Railways and steamships gave them an entire world, which offered itself to them suddenly, and widened their perspectives. A sort of courage that urged them on replaced the fear of emigration that had once filled their souls. Even nowadays [1863] this mood is a reflective and foresighted one. Young Irishmen can be seen, workers or artisans, working furiously to save money which they intend to use to pay expenses of a long voyage and the costs of setting up on foreign soil. Such is the enthusiasm that these ideas ignite in them, that they abstain from every act of debauchery and drunkenness that might, by eating into their savings, delay the moment of their departure. It is a strange kind of social progress (if that is what it is) that is displayed by the Irishman in the form of an eagerness to get out of the country.[3]

This profound effect on the Irish prompted Eamon de Valera, Taoiseach in 1944, to propose an officially-supported academic history of the Famine a century after the event. Cormac Ó Gráda has put together an account of the tangled progress of the project, which involved history being written by committee rather than by a single scholar.[4] The resulting volume, edited by Robert Dudley Edwards and Desmond Williams, appeared in 1956 entitled *The Great Famine*. Because of people dropping out or neglecting to do as they had promised, the published book, at 500 pages, was only half the projected length. It amounted to an administrative history of the famine, according to Ó Gráda, with little narrative structure.[5] The book is rather disjointed, and there is no general account of the events. There is, however, a useful scientific analysis of the disease that destroyed the potato crop and there are good chapters on the history of the great emigrations to America and Australia. The introduction, penned by K.B. Nolan, is eminently sane. As a pioneering book on a difficult and painful subject, it is impressive. In particular, it attempts to avoid the kind of polemical approach to the great tragedy which was so common during the century after the catastrophe. However, this discouraged any attempt to tackle the vital questions of the culpability of the

British government and the Irish landlords as well as the simple criminality of the political negligence that had permitted a huge monocrop-dependent population to grow up in Ireland in the thirty years before the disaster.

Cecil Woodham-Smith was already an established British historian in the 1950s. Before she tackled Ireland she had already published a study of Florence Nightingale and *The Reason Why*, a book on the crazy charge of the Light Brigade up the wrong valley during the Crimean War. Her interest in failures of Victorian social and military policy was already well-developed. Her subsequent Irish Famine project got generous support from the *The Great Famine* academic team. The resulting study, *The Great Hunger*, was published in 1962, caught the public imagination and sold enormously well in Ireland, Britain and the United States. It is in many ways a traditional study, where anecdote is piled on anecdote and thereby eventually achieving an overall picture, and it is none the worse for that.[6] It has been accused of exaggerating the influence of a few major political and bureaucratic figures at the expense, presumably, of structural factors of one kind or other; but in a way the personalities and attitudes of powerful people can be taken as representing deeper forces in culture and society: an inborn contempt for the Irish, an equally deep dislike of Catholicism and an innate sense of the hopelessness of the entire Irish situation spring to mind. These almost pathological beliefs reinforced the innate reluctance of Britain's rulers to do far more than they actually did do to rescue a stricken people. This is not to denigrate the often heroic efforts of the British state and many private individuals and organisations; it is impossible to say how many more might have died were it not for the exertions that were actually made. At one stage during the crisis of 1847, there were over three million people dependent on estate-funded emergency supplies, nearly half the population of the island.

Other cultural problems were addressed in the book. Woodham-Smith argues early on that the Irish regarded only potatoes as food. All other crops represented money, in that they could be sold to pay the rent due to the landlord. Commonly a pig was kept, but he was referred to traditionally as 'the gentleman who pays the rent'. Similarly, corn, game, etc. were seen as answering money needs. When Indian meal from America was introduced by the authorities the peasantry sometimes refused it, and at best had great difficulty in grinding and preparing it for eating, as they had not got the necessary skills or equipment. Incidentally, the eating of Indian meal became traditional later in the century, particularly during the months of scarcity in summertime, as recounted in *The Islandman*. Again, the English seem to have had an almost calculated ignorance about Ireland, and yet again an almost religious devotion to the principle of free trade ruled out what was a common reaction to famine elsewhere in Europe: closing the ports and prohibiting the export of food from the land. It is not always realised that Ireland exported enormous amounts of food during the famine years and, during the worst famine year of all, 1847, there was a bumper harvest of corn and other cereals, while the potato harvest was, of course, pathetically small.

These factors inhibited government action. By the end of 1846, Charles Trevelyan, the permanent head of the Treasury, had, according to Woodham-Smith:

> reached the conclusion that everything that could and should be done for Ireland had been done, and that any further step could only be taken at the expense of the rest of the United Kingdom. 'I deeply regret the primary and appalling evil of the insufficiency of the supplies of food in this country,' he wrote on December 22 [1846], 'but the stores we are able to procure for the western division of Ireland are insufficient even for that purpose, and how can we undertake more?'. In a private letter ... he wrote'...if we were to purchase for Irish use faster than we are now doing, we should

commit a crying injustice to the rest of the country.'[7]

She concludes that the outcome of this attitude was a series of appalling tragedies such as those endured by the district of Skibbereen in west Cork. By early December 1846, Trevelyan had been told that the government's relief scheme in the area was collapsing:

> On December 15 the Commissioners of the Board of Works wrote an official letter drawing the attention of the government to the extreme destitution existing in Skibbereen, upon which, on December 18, Trevelyan wrote a letter to Routh 'with reference to what is now going on in Skibbereen'. He was afraid that Routh would be persuaded to send Government supplies – because a relief committee was not operating in Skibbereen the town was not eligible under the Government plan. Trevelyan reminded Routh that there were 'principles to be kept in view'. The relief committee system must be adhered to, in order to prevent a run on Government supplies and 'to draw out the resources of the country before we make our own issues'. There was, moreover, the unpleasant truth, which Trevelyan admitted by forbidding issues of food, but never stated, that the Government depots did not contain sufficient supplies to meet the demand if an all-out attempt was made to feed the starving.[8]

Furthermore, no supplies from abroad should be ordered, as it might interfere with the everyday business of merchants by upsetting their calculations. The shocking consequences of this allegedly rational but actually inhuman policy were detailed in full by Woodham-Smith. Thousands starved to death in the area. In that year, landlords drew £50,000 in rents from the Skibbereen district. In July 1847, just when the worst part of the famine was to occur, Trevelyan concluded that no more government action was needed. Famously, Trevelyan remarked fatuously 'the famine is stayed'.

Skibbereen was to become a byword in Irish folk culture afterwards, and even now, a hundred and fifty years later, Irish football fans sing a pastiche 'Victorian' ballad (*The Fields of Athenry*) in which a forgotten Trevelyan is genially demonised, much mystifying English football fans. It took a hundred years for forgiveness to come, and the echo of the disaster poisoned relationships between two sister countries in a tragic way that echoed faithfully the greater tragedy of the famine itself. The entire IRA tradition feeds off enduring memories of British indifference to the suffering of their putative ancestors, and many an atrocity has been justified by reference to 'Black '47'. The famine was also a major factor for a century afterwards in damaging British relationships with the United States, because of the existence there of a huge and increasingly powerful Irish diaspora of famine-related origins, in many ways far more embittered by the tragedy than were even the native Irish themselves, the latter becoming more culturally assimilated to British mores than were the Irish-Americans. Furthermore, the native Irish were descended from survivors, whereas the Americans were descended from victims of the event. At least, that is how it felt.

TG

Notes

1   Susan Chitty, *The Beast and the Monk: A Life of Charles Kingsley* (London: Hodder and Stoughton, 1974), p.209.

2   Gustave de Beaumont, *Ireland: Social, Political, Religious* [1839] (Cambridge,

MA: Belknap Press of Harvard University Press, 2006), p.38. This quote is from the 1863 edition, the Preface of which is translated by Tom Garvin.

3   Ibid., p.387.

4   Cormac Ó Gráda, 'Making History in the 1940s and 1950s: the Saga of The Great Famine', in Ciaran Brady, *Interpreting Irish History: The Debate on Historical Revisionism* (Dublin: Irish Academic Press, 1994), p.269–287.

5   Ibid., p.278.

6   Cecil Woodham-Smith, *The Great Hunger* [1962] (New York: Old Town Books, 1989).

7   Ibid., pp.160–61.

8   Ibid., p.161.

23

Conor Cruise O'Brien, *States of Ireland* (1972)

States of Ireland was published just three years after the commencement of the Ulster Troubles, and during the year in which killings by the IRA and the loyalist paramilitaries reached a peak of frightfulness never matched before or since. The killings were to go on for another quarter-century before political initiatives began, slowly and painfully, to put together a series of agreements and institutional reforms that, in an untidy way, went some way to satisfying the various sets of participants. In 1972, even 'Sunningdale', an early failed settlement, was a year away, and an apocalyptic conclusion to the conflict, climaxing in an all-Ireland civil war, did not look impossible. As O'Brien says in his foreword to the book, he saw himself as an Irish patriot and loved Ireland and his people, but when the ancient opposition between Irish Catholic and Ulster Protestant began to become active:

> … one has to take leave of almost everything that is lovable about Ireland: the affection, the peace, the mutual concern, the courtesy which exist in abundance

– if they cannot always be said to prevail – *inside* each community. Instead we must discuss the conditions of a multiple frontier: not just the territorial border, but a very old psychological frontier area, full of suspicion, reserve, fear, boasting, resentment, Messianic illusions, bad history, rancorous commemorations and – today more than ever – murderous violence. This is not Ireland, and it is not peculiar to Ireland: such frontiers, of tribe, colour, religion, language, culture, scar a great part of the surface of the globe. And have cost millions of lives even in this decade... Our frontier is exceptionally old – over three-and-a-half centuries – and now so disturbed that many of us fear we may be approaching the brink of full-scale civil war.[1]

The book is a long and sustained personal meditation on the crisis. O'Brien uses literary evidence for psychological states and social conflict and rarely has much use for the apparatus of the social sciences, despite the avalanche of academic studies that had already begun to descend all over the 'Irish Problem' from universities in Ireland, Britain and the United States. In many ways this absence is a strength. As he tells you in this remarkable book, O'Brien was very much an insider in Ireland. He had been a member of the Irish diplomatic corps for a decade, and at the time of writing *States of Ireland* he was a member of Dáil Éireann in the Labour Party interest.

More importantly, perhaps, he came of a well-known net of Dublin Catholic political families; his uncle, for example, had been a gun-runner in preparation for the 1916 rising and many other close family connections had been conspicuously active in the independence movement. A remote ancestor was a Father Nicholas Sheehy, framed and hanged for Whiteboyism (agrarian agitation) in the late eighteenth century in what amounted to an exercise in judicial murder. Sheehy was seen afterwards as a national and religious martyr in the Irish popular imagination. A great-uncle, Father Eugene Sheehy, taught Eamon de Valera Irish in County Clare, and Dev reminisced fondly about him in Irish, 'It is he who taught me patriotism' (*Eisean a mhúin an tír-ghrá dhom*). His aunt on the Sheehy side of the family, Hanna Sheehy-Skeffington, was a noted feminist. The family was, like many Irish families, divided ideologically and emotionally between different strands of Irish nationalism. Three of his uncles, for example, fought loyally in British uniform for the allies against Germany in the First World War, while other relatives tacitly supported Germany. Both sets expected Irish independence in return for their support of one or other great power. Two famous relatives, Francis Sheehy-Skeffington and Tom Kettle, died in 1916; the first at British hands in Dublin and the other at German hands at the Somme. O'Brien himself was born a year after the Rising, in 1917.

In his youth, he was consequently introduced to various varieties of Irish nationalism and idealist socialism. His father died suddenly when O'Brien was a boy in what were shocking circumstances for a devoted lad; he remarked many years later that this was the only time in his entire life when he feared that he might lose his reason because of his grief. He was reared by his mother and other female relatives. He grew up in the aftermath of the Irish revolution and had, in a sense, a ringside seat to watch the progress of its emotional and cultural aftermath in his childhood and young manhood. As the Irish saying has it, he was reared to it. He says himself that his earliest memory was of a crucial event in the Irish conflict: the beginning of the Irish Civil War of 1922–23, which was to be the forming event of so much of Irish politics for two generations after:

> The first sound I can remember is a series of booming noises which woke me up on Wednesday, June 28, 1922. I was then four-and-a-half years old. That bombardment is generally considered to be

the beginning of the Irish Civil War, which lasted throughout the remainder of my fifth year and into my sixth.[2]

A second feature of his family was its intellectualism. His cousin, Owen Sheehy-Skeffington, son of the man who was murdered in Dublin, was an accomplished lecturer in French at Trinity College Dublin (TCD) and was the young O'Brien's almost fatherly mentor. O'Brien, like many another, admired 'Skeff's' political courage in Irish public affairs. Sheehy-Skeffington correctly predicted the Second World War after a brief visit to Berlin in January 1933 in a long letter to his mother on the emergent Nazi Germany. The young Germans thought they had been cheated out of victory in 1918 by the communists and the Jews. The Germans would start a war in 1938 or 1939 and would be defeated again, the Irish student predicted. In the 1950s and 1960s this extraordinary man was an outspoken member of the Irish Senate, where he attacked many aspects of Irish public policy, particularly the practice of unrestrained physical punishment of small children in schools.[3] He was instrumental in encouraging the writing of Peter Tyrrell, *Founded on Fear*, a personal account of the writer's own experience of Letterfrack industrial school and his tragic subsequent life.

O'Brien did a BA degree in French and Irish, going on afterwards to a Ph.D. on Charles Stewart Parnell, published later in 1956 as *Parnell and His Party*. O'Brien later observed in a revealing phrase that there had been 'something crippled' about Irish politics ever since the fall of Parnell in 1891. The book is brilliant, but contains some odd opinions, in particular the proposition that, in a Home Rule of independent Ireland Parnell might have become some kind of dictator. O'Brien was to have many more odd opinions later on.

A third feature of his family was a sense of being ousted from anticipated power by the events of 1916–23. The old parliamentary nationalists were destroyed by the unionist rebellion against Home Rule in 1912 and the subsequent nationalist revolution and the partition of the island in 1920–22. They were also bypassed in a classic example of Pareto's circulation of elites, by people of (on average) more humble origins, or, to put it more accurately, more *recent* humble origins; people like Michael Collins or Eamon de Valera, both from small-farm backgrounds and typified many of the new leaders who often distrusted or despised the older tradition. There was an element of generational conflict as well, old men of settled opinions and habits being replaced by young, more radical and fiery men. O'Brien's family was not rich however, and he was obliged to go for scholarships to finance his education.

A fourth characteristic of his immediate family was a certain religious marginality. His people were Catholic by faith and tradition, but he was sent as a boy to Sandford Park School in Ranelagh on Dublin's south side, a non-denominational school set up in 1922 in anticipation of a Catholic clerical clampdown on non-denominational education which indeed occurred after independence. Catholics were forbidden by the clergy to send their children to such schools on the grounds that their Catholic faith would be destroyed, and Mrs Cruise O'Brien was seen as being unusually independent-minded in so doing. She did so because her dead husband had wished the boy to have a secular and liberal education. This he certainly got; Sandford Park's religious balance was apparently about one-third each Catholic, Protestant and Jewish. This meant that young Conor got a very different educational experience from the vast majority of young people at that time, herded as they were into single-creed, mainly Catholic schools. It was in this school that he was stunned to be informed by a teacher that Northern Ireland remained in the United Kingdom at the express wish of the vast majority of its inhabitants, an observation that would have been anathema to his family. Furthermore, being handed this seminal and undeniable proposition by an Irish teacher in those times would have been a very unusual experience. On top of all this, he went to the mainly Protestant Trinity College Dublin (TCD) rather than the mainly

Catholic University College Dublin (UCD), a choice which was again seen, as not quite engaging in religious apostasy, but not far off it.

States of Ireland was full of quasi-anecdotal personal information of this kind, which gradually built up into a picture of a society, or set of societies, in the island of Ireland which did not talk to each other and which increasingly perceived each other inaccurately and sometimes grotesquely. In a time of political instability, these stereotypes were liable to become active and could even operate in such a way as to generate violence. O'Brien felt that the period of the early 1970s was easily the most dangerous such time in modern Irish history.

The book unleashed a storm of protest, much of it apparently driven by a perhaps subconscious anger that O'Brien, at least nominally a Catholic, should be arguing that nationalists and unionists in Ireland were really like two peas in a pod, one as bad or as good as the other, especially in Northern Ireland. However, much of its thinking eventually seeped into the official mind and even the popular mind, and arguably was an important progenitor (among many others) of the settlements of thirty years later.

In a strange and disguised follow-up to *States of Ireland*, O'Brien published in *The Siege* in 1986, a history of the State of Israel and its long fight for survival in the Arab–Muslim world around it; an account that has been seen as very sympathetic to the Israeli case. That sympathy has surprised many people outside Ireland who had seen O'Brien as an anti-colonialist because of Ireland's anti-colonial fight for independence and O'Brien's role in the Congolese crisis as a UN officer opposing Katangese secession; an event schemed for by Belgium and Britain. There is, however, a logic and a sociologic about his stance on Israel. First, his 'Protestant side' permitted him to see the other chap's point of view. Certainly, when reading the book soon after publication while living in the United States, I was struck by the way the narrative was actually haunted by Ireland, with the Israelis standing in for the Ulster unionist ('orange') community, and the Arabs for the overwhelmingly large Catholic nationalist ('green') community encircling it on the island. The horrific history of the Jews in Europe made the tragic history of the Irish look trivial; to write about the greater tragedy in terms derived from the lesser one perhaps gave O'Brien some capacity to distance himself from his Irish obsessions. I had some difficulty explaining this to an Iranian colleague (Professor Hormuz Shadadi) in the US. As I fell silent, he looked at me puzzledly and asked finally:

> 'What is the difference between a Catholic and a Protestant?'
> 'Something like that between a Shia and a Sunni Muslim.'
> 'You really have problems in Ireland!'

Ernest Gellner, in one of the few non-Irish commentaries on O'Brien and coming from someone unconnected with Irish affairs, noticed many things. He noticed in particular O'Brien's almost complete disregard for the huge corpus of modern academic writing on nationalism as an ideological and sociological phenomenon in the disciplines of history, sociology and political science. He also noted O'Brien's implicit assumption that the nation state was the logical and appropriate vehicle for political action.[4] As suggested earlier, in a way, O'Brien's use of literary reference rather than sociology was a strength because of his peculiar personal circumstances; he could, as he said himself, use literary criticism as a social science.

During a long and illustrious literary career, O'Brien published many literary and autobiographical studies, as well as many essays on political life. In later life O'Brien also published distinguished studies of Edmund Burke and Thomas Jefferson, but it is for *States of Ireland* he will be remembered longest in Ireland: a book that certainly shook the island.

TG

Notes

1   Conor Cruise O'Brien, *States of Ireland* (London: Hutchinson, 1972; revised version, St Albans: Panther, 1974), p. 13.

2   Conor Cruise O'Brien, *Memoir: My Life and Themes* (Dublin: Poolbeg, 1998), p.5.

3   Andrée Sheehy-Skeffington, *Skeff: the Life of Owen Sheehy-Skeffington, 1909–1970* (Dublin: Lilliput, 1991). See also National Library of Ireland, Sheehy-Skeffington Papers, NLI MS 40, 480/3–11.

4   Ernest Gellner, 'The Sacred and the National', in *Encounters with Nationalism* (Oxford: Blackwell, 1988), pp.59–73.

24

A.T.Q. Stewart, *The Narrow Ground* (1977)

The subtitle of this book is *The Roots of Conflict in Ulster*. The author's own introduction is pithy and explains its structure; it deals with five themes in less than 200 pages: the Plantation of Ulster, the siege of Derry, the United Irishmen, Belfast riots in the nineteenth century, and the partition of Ireland. The title was suggested by a remark of Sir Walter Scott. In 1825 he commented on Ulster that he had never seen a richer land or a finer people, but 'Their factions have been so long envenomed, and they have such narrow ground to do their battle in, that they are like people fighting with daggers in a hogshead.' Stewart, an historian at Queen's University Belfast, writes in the introduction that the book wrote itself almost in defiance of his will, that he suffered from whatever is the opposite of writer's block, and ideas kept tumbling onto the page from his head almost despite himself. On first reading it in the late 1970s, I had a similar sensation, but one of being unable to put it down and a fascination with this description of a view from the other side of the narrow ground, being as I am a Dubliner of nationalist tradition, whereas the author was of Ulster unionist stock. The book made me acutely aware that I only knew Ulster from outside rather than inside. It is certainly even now a book that Irish people from the other provinces of the island should read. Much to the surprise of the author, the book had a quiet, almost underground, success. He remarked himself, 'And in time it became a kind of *vade mecum* for journalists venturing into the Heart of Darkness.'

A central theme of the book is that outsiders to Ulster, in particular the British Government, tend to have certain misconceptions. The first is that the violence in Northern Ireland is rooted in religious intolerance and the other is that all violence there is of the same kind. The conclusion is that the two sides must be reconciled. That means one side or the other must give in, he argues. 'No two communities divided in this way by culture and religion can ever be "reconciled" in the sense that is meant, *they can only be accommodated in a political system.*'[1] Stewart also argues that the deepest divide is not religious difference but rather national allegiance, a characteristic that tends to correlate with religious affiliation, but which is independent of it. There have always been some nationalist Protestants and quite a few unionist Catholics, and also there are many people who recognise the problematic ethnic structure of Northern Ireland and who are normally willing to put up with it.

The book goes on to point out that much Scottish immigration to Ulster long antedated the 'planting' of 1609, and Antrim and Down, the counties of eastern Ulster closest to Scotland, were never planted. Those targeted for plantation were indeed six in number, but only four were in modern Northern Ireland; two (Donegal and Cavan) are now in the Republic of Ireland. The plantations were only very partially successful and most native Irish stayed put, benefitting from the fact that their labour was needed to build the plantation towns and till the fields. The Gaelic aristocrats, deprived of their lands, fled the country or retreated to mountain fastnesses as embittered outlaws or rapparees 'on their keeping'. The bulk of the native population stayed put and remained Catholic. The situation became static and has not changed much in three centuries. Even in towns and cities the original three-way division into Catholic, Protestant and Dissenter tended to be quite literally set in brick and stone with the evolution of segregated streets or quarters for each religious group. It is often forgotten that similar segregations existed elsewhere in Ireland: Dublin had its peripheral communities of Irishtown, Ringsend and The Liberties where Catholics ('the mere Irish') were permitted to live, and the mediaeval small city of Kilkenny has an Irishtown whose vernacular architecture is still distinct from that of the 'English' main town. However, it is only in Ulster that these almost mediaeval distinctions are still alive and kicking. In the other three provinces of Ireland they are forgotten.

Scottish immigration into the North of Ireland in the *late* seventeenth century and the eighteenth, reinforced the pattern by a natural rather than an artificial process, as like tended to associate with like. Ulster became a crossroads, and many of the migrants continued, a generation later, on to the American colonies. The new migrants tended to settle in the east rather than the west of Ulster, and even now the two clusters of Protestant population have different cultural characteristics and political allegiances from each other:

> The upshot of these events was the creation of a permanent community in Ulster that feels itself, accurately or otherwise, to be under siege. Events such as the Catholic rising of 1641 and the Siege of Londonderry in 1689 gave rise to a series of symbols which still resonate over three centuries later. The simple fact that the Protestants of Ulster are a small minority of the population of the entire island gives continuous force to the sense of being surrounded and, perhaps, threatened by the 'native' mainly Catholic majority on the island, usually about four to five

times the demographic weight of the Protestant Ulster minority on the island. It is strange that 'Lillibulero', that song of relief and triumph celebrating the defeat of James II at the Boyne in 1689 should have a chorus in pidgin Gaelic: *An Lile ba léir é, ba linn an lá* (It was clearly the [orange] lily, the day was with us). Brother Teague had to get the message in his own tongue after Aughrim's great disaster of 1690. The narrow ground was institutionalised.[2]

Ireland's geographic position reinforced this stand-off, one probably unwanted by anyone on the island, but imposed structurally on everyone. Ireland was the back door to Britain and therefore vital to the security of a great empire. England was unsympathetic to Catholicism and was menaced by two great Catholic powers in succession, Spain in the seventeenth century and France in the eighteenth. Gradually the nationalist majority on the island developed a Prester John psychology, seeking help from an anti-English great power far away. Spain and France were touted as saviours at first, America in the nineteenth century, and Germany for a while in the twentieth. This mainly rhetorical tradition heightened Unionist paranoia. Each side on the island fed the other psychologically, and the process was particularly immediate and intense in the North. By the 1790s, the revolutionary events in America and France had opened up several incongruous gaps on each side of the narrow ground. Presbyterians in Ulster were sympathetic to their American revolutionary cousins and read Paine's *The Rights of Man* avidly. Down south, Catholics heard of the fall of the Bastille and the execution of a king with excitement and anticipation. In the North, they talked of democracy and annual parliaments. In the south they whispered of agrarian revolution. In the words of a well-known and rather sinister little song of the 1790s:

Oh the French are in the bay,
They'll be here without delay,
And Ireland shall be free,
From the centre to the sea,
Says the Shan Van Vocht.[3]

The *Sean-Bhean Bhocht* is, of course, the Poor Old Woman, or Ireland. In the *Aisling* or 'vision poetry' of the eighteenth century, the country is commonly depicted as a woman who has been forced to marry a bullying neighbour and who longs for gallant foreigners to come to the rescue and restore to her the Four Green Fields that have been stolen from her by Yellow John (*Seán Buí*) or John Bull. The catastrophe of 1798 resulted in a series of badly timed risings in Presbyterian Ulster, Catholic Wexford and Connacht. Perhaps 50,000 people were killed in battle and massacre during the Year of Liberty. A sectarian massacre of Protestants took place in Wexford and had an immediate impact on the Ulster Protestant community. All their paranoid fears seemed to be vindicated. A solidarity between Ulster Protestant and Dissenter was formed which has never been broken since. British rule was re-established quickly and the Irish parliament was abolished, an Act of Union being hurried through it in 1800 in dubious circumstances. Direct Rule from London had arrived in Ireland, and not for the last time.

In a wonderfully entitled chapter ('Landscape with Bandits') Stewart looks at the roots of violence in Ireland. He regards it as of archaic origin, and as endemic, even in times of peace. 'Social historians have been vaguely aware of these patterns for a long time; political historians virtually ignore them.'[4] Travellers' tales and government surveys in the eighteenth and nineteenth centuries confirm this epidemic character at that time. The pattern is that of the secret army, the local public band which commonly had a captain, passwords and a strange title. The tradition, it is argued, stretches from the woodkerne of Elizabethan times to the Provisional IRA, and, although he does not make the point, the orange and loyalist local gangs in Belfast and elsewhere. Stewart draws in particular on the classic 1836 work of George Cornewall Lewis, *On Local Disturbance in Ireland*. Lewis drew in turn on government blue books which studied the phenomenon in 1815 and the 1830s.[5] Stewart does not quite make this point, but the objectives of the violence were quite delimited, and anyone not involved in the quarrel commonly remained unmolested even in areas notorious for their violence. Innocent travellers were commonly treated with extraordinary courtesy and kindness, even though the area might be a murder triangle. There are many instances where local bands actually protected innocent or unknowing travellers. Family feuds and agrarian grievances fuelled much of the fighting and burnings-out. Repetitive patterns of Catholic versus Protestant violence, initiated in Ulster border regions in 1784, became traditional and broke out again and again throughout the nineteenth and twentieth centuries. In the early 1960s, local people in Northern Ireland could accurately forecast the coming of a new 'troubled time' in a few years.[6]

In light of this background, the author asks, how can it be argued that the partition of Ireland is the cause of the violence in Ulster? Partition, he argues, is more a consequence of the violence than its cause. His grim conclusion is: 'partition is preferable to an [all-Ireland] civil war'.[7] Stewart concludes by urging a constitutional settlement in Northern Ireland which recognises these unpleasant realities and their immutability short of genocide. It took time for this message to sink into the often impenetrable minds of both British and Irish governments. But it did eventually sink in.

TG

Notes

1   A.T.Q. Stewart, *The Narrow Ground* [1977] (London: Faber and Faber, 1989), p.10. Emphasis added.

2   The Irish, though pidgin, is superior to the IRA's *Tiochfaidh ár Lá*.

3   See Stewart, *Narrow Ground*, p.106.

4   Ibid., p.115.

5   George Cornewall Lewis, *On Local Disturbance in Ireland* [1836] (Cork: Tower, 1977).

6   Personal observation in Northern Ireland in 1964.

7   See Stewart, *Narrow Ground*, p.157.

25

C.S. Andrews, *Dublin Made Me*, (1979)

The genre of Old IRA autobiography is now just about extinct, for obvious reasons. However, for fifty years after the events of 1913–23, such reminiscences of veterans of the 'War of Independence' and the nasty little Civil War that followed it featured conspicuously in the reading matter of Irish people, and perhaps in particular in the reading matter of hero-worshipping young people. Books such as Dan Breen's *My Fight for Irish Freedom* (1924) or Ernie O'Malley's classic *On Another Man's Wound* (1936) and its more pedestrian sequel *The Singing Flame* (1978) belong to the genre. Logically, however, the oeuvre should be seen to include P.S. O'Hegarty's *Victory of Sinn Fein* (1924) or W. Alison Phillip's *The Revolution in Ireland* (1923), both of them critical, if in very different ways, of the deeds and motivations of the revolutionaries.

Dublin Made Me and its sequel *Man of No Property* (1982) are among the most unvarnished and matter-of-fact memoirs of those years. They are notable for their honesty and directness of opinion, and are quite self-revealing. Unlike many other memoirs, they were written two generations after the events, which makes for memory lapses but also permits calmer reflection. They are in part essays in an undiscovered subject which might be described as the History of Emotions. As Andrews (known to his friends as Todd) puts it himself in the introduction to *Dublin Made Me:*

> Writing in my old age of the happenings of my early years I am conscious that my reactions to these happenings were based mainly on emotionalism and enthusiasm. I rarely thought; I felt. But I am not too critical of what I felt or did. Most of my feelings seem to me in my maturity to have been justified by events.
>
> Despite the tribulations which affected the nation over the years, especially in the years of my youth, I reckon myself lucky to have been one of that fortunate generation which lived to see Irishmen in control of the greater part of the country.[1]

This statement of purpose was typical of Todd's in-your-face approach: unapologetic and 'this is how it seems to me, whatever you might say'. He underestimated, I suspect, the enormous value that emotional history has, as it rapidly becomes difficult, if not impossible, to reconstruct the emotional climate of a time. The past is a foreign country, they do things differently there, as L.P. Hartley famously wrote. I would rather say they feel things differently there, and Irish historians and social scientists badly need, what I can only term rather clumsily as, an historical sociology of the emotions. The two books abound with descriptions of republican mentality and with anecdotes which illustrate such mentality. There are entertaining descriptions of O'Malley, Seán Lemass, de Valera and Liam Mellows among many others, all of them as young people. Ernie O'Malley is seen as a soldier, perhaps misplaced from a professional context into the very amateur warfare of Ireland. Incidentally, Todd was privately convinced that O'Malley's American wife had a hand in creating the 'literary' flourishes in *On Another Man's Wound*. Certainly O'Malley's later writing lacks such flourishes.

There are intriguing illustrations of how individuals who had been on opposite sides in the Civil War sometimes managed to form friendships and sidestep the dreadful bitterness which atrocities committed in that fateful year had generated, often to last for generations as is commonplace in the wake of civil wars. Todd used to say that he would never tolerate the presence of a 'Stater' in his house. It is significant that the conflict was commonly termed *Cogadh na mBráthair* (The War of the Brothers) in Gaelteacht areas for years afterward.

Andrews makes an interesting comment on his own political education. *Gulliver's Travels* was one of his primers on the motivations and viciousness that is often involved in political leadership. He first read the book while on the run from Free State forces in 1922–23, and reread it often over the following decades. His nascent anti-clericalism, fanned into flame by the Catholic bishops' condemnation of the Anti-Treaty forces, was given extra shape by Frank Hugh O'Donnell's wonderful 1902 rant, *The Ruin of Education in Ireland*, which represented the Catholic Church and its control of Irish education as a British government plot to keep the Irish people enslaved mentally.

After the conflict ended, Todd went through the usual cycle of political purism, disappointment and eventual sullen acquiescence:

> The defeat of the Republic had been a matter of great disappointment to me. As the climax of the Civil War was reached I had been close to the events associated with it. I saw all the devotion to the ideal of the republic, supported by bravery, endurance and an indifference to self-interest, crumble through lack of political expertise. The leadership of the IRA (and of course its enthusiastic members like me) had become largely the victims of shibboleths of their

213

own creation. They turned too late to de Valera, the one man who could have led them out of the political morass where they had got bogged down at the time of the 1922 Army Convention. Eventually he did succeed in using the stepping stones embedded in the Treaty settlement to open up the way to re-establish the Republic. But from the time of his release in July 1924 until he came to power in the Twenty-six counties there was a lapse of eight years. It seemed to me and my like an interminable period. Eaten up by bitterness and adherence to 'principle' – that fatuous word so all-pervasive and such a darkener of counsel in story of the Republic – we wasted valuable years giving allegiance to an ineffective, and largely imaginary, underground government and army before de Valera and Seán Lemass broke with Sinn Fein and the Second Dail to form Fianna Fail.[2]

Man of No Property deals with Todd's years in various governmental jobs, where he was close to Seán Lemass and developed a reputation as a 'can-do' man, working in nascent organisations dealing with tourism, the development of peat bogs as sources of fuel, the rail transport network and finally, chairman of the national broadcasting network, RTE. Again, anecdote and character sketches of various historical figures abound. The book is a kind of informal gazetteer of the great and the good in the first generation after the revolution. Jonathan Swift's *Gulliver's Travels* continued to inform Todd in later life in unexpected ways. Many American ambassadors were appointed to Ireland because of their political allegiances or accidental ethnic connection with the Ould Sod.

Some of the [American] political appointees were very wealthy men and had elected to come here for the horses in which they were more interested than in the people. One in particular, whom I met a few times, might well have been high among the Houyhnhnms. To communicate with him satisfactorily one felt it was necessary to whinny or to neigh. For his part he regarded the Irish as yahoos.[3]

The two books make it clear that many of the young men and women who were swept up in the revolutionary movement were pre-political in their mentality. In many cases their noisy allegiance to the Republic was derived from religious affect rather than political conviction. They knew little of liberalism, conservatism or socialism as philosophical systems and used the vocabulary of politics commonly without knowing the real and often arguable meanings of such words and phrases as parliamentary democracy, representative government, the rule of law or responsible government. As Andrews put it, in the fateful year of 1922 democracy had not yet been made into a semi-sacred idea, and Mussolini had yet to make his march on Rome. Bolshevism was a faraway thing, vaguely admired and not understood.

I first met Christopher Andrews when I was an undergraduate at University College Dublin in the early 1960s. He used to call over to our parents' house in Dartry to drink whiskey with our father and reminisce about their youth and their working lives; John Garvin and Todd Andrews were of an age and had both been senior public officials during the first forty years of the Irish state's existence. They also shared a certain bookishness. I was merely the child among them taking notes, so to speak, and was continually struck by the wild and woolly things these respectable older men had been up to in their youth.

Todd was a tall man with a long and weather-beaten face, a large nose and occasionally menacing blue eyes. He had a powerful personality, which he could use as a weapon. He ignored me for about twenty minutes, except for the odd cold-eyed stare, and chatted with John. Then suddenly his manner changed, and

215

he started to cross-examine me on the de Valera Constitution of 1937 which was, even then, beginning to be criticised for its conservatism, anti-feminism and concessions to the Catholic Church. I have no idea how I passed this informal and unexpected oral examination. For the rest of the evening he was a charming and talkative companion, with a curious mixture of attitudes: strong pro-Soviet views, a rather naive admirer of Lenin, very anti-partitionist and rather fond of America and Americans. He was a firm supporter of state action in directing the economy and public information; in this he saw eye to eye with his boss and ideological ally, Seán Lemass.

He seemed to me to be a man of violently-held opinion, rather unused to debate and determined to get his way. A type of decisive and rather authoritarian personality much admired and looked up to in that generation, when Irish social and political culture were rather different than they are now, half a century on. He was also unusual in that he spoke his mind without too much concern for the wounded feelings of others. There was a joke in Bord na Móna that they had a special officer travelling around the country after Todd, heading off the strikes that the boss was provoking by his straight talking. In a rather thin-skinned culture the thick-skinned man could be king.

Andrews was born in Summerhill in Dublin in 1901, but spent most of his youth in Terenure, where his father had a grocery shop. The memoirs sketch a typical Dublin boyhood of the early twentieth century: football in the street, long summer holidays and excursions to the Dodder River nearby. His years at Synge Street Christian Brothers School were, contrary to stereotype, happy and free from clerical violence, although such violence did occur elsewhere in the school. The nickname 'Todd' was derived from a fancied resemblance to a character ('Alonzo Todd') in the *Magnet*, a popular English boys' paper of the time. Dublin schoolboys generally honour very popular or otherwise prominent members of their group with Runyonesque nicknames. In Todd's case, the name stuck, and he seems to have been something of a leader of boys before he was a leader of men.

From conversations with him and from the memoirs, I sensed the anger and frustration that were experienced by many young men and women in the last days of British Ireland and the early years of the new state; also a certain lack of irony and humour, coupled with a wish to appear rather surer of oneself than one really was. Above all, there was a passionate wish to be respected and not to be looked down on, on the basis of religion, caste or social position; a wish often unadmitted, which appears to have lain behind much Irish revolutionary passion.

I once asked Todd, in the late 1970s, why he had closed down the Bray–Harcourt Street railway line in 1959, just when suburban Dublin was about to double in population over the next few years. This had been easily the most continuously criticised decision he ever took as a public figure; de Valera used to remark doubtfully, 'All those nice little railway stations, Todd.' Todd glared at me and growled, 'I got fed up sitting here in Dundrum watching those Freemasons going into Trinity [College] from Foxrock to their meetings at the taxpayer's expense.' There was, of course, more to it than that; Todd was that unusual thing at that time, a believer in the motor car. However, the old emotions were working away there as well.

TG

Notes

1   C.S. Andrews, *Dublin Made Me* (Dublin: Mercier Press, 1979), p.7.

2   Ibid., p.11.

3   Ibid., p.289.

26

Nell McCafferty, *A Woman To Blame:*
The Kerry Babies Case (1985)

On 14 April 1984 the body of a new-born baby was found on a County Kerry beach. The Garda investigation focused on women due to give birth in nearby Cahirciveen and charged Joanne Hayes with its murder. The baby had been stabbed twenty-eight times. Hayes, a twenty-four-year-old single mother, known to have been pregnant, told her friends that she had miscarried in hospital but had in fact given birth to her child in her home and hidden its body on the family farm. It became subsequently clear that this child was not the baby that had been washed up on the beach. But by then the Gardaí had extracted a signed confession from Joanne that she had stabbed her baby and corroborating statements from Joanne's brothers Ned and Mike Hayes that Joanne had given birth to a baby, stabbed it, and that they had thrown its body off a cliff into the sea. Other family members also gave statements along these lines to detectives from the Murder Squad drafted down from Dublin. After being interrogated her family returned to their farm, searched the area where Joanne said she had concealed her miscarried child, found its body and reported this to the Gardaí.

The Gardaí then held a press conference where they claimed that Joanne had given birth to twins.

But the babies were found to have different and incompatible blood groups. They could not have had the same father. The Gardaí stuck to their claim that Joanne was the mother of both and advanced a theory of superfecundation – that she had been impregnated by two men around the same time – something that was theoretically possible but unprovable given the weakness of corroborating technical and forensic evidence. For example, there was no forensic evidence that a baby had been stabbed in Joanne's bed as the confessions obtained by the Gardaí had claimed. Furthermore, there was no evidence that the baby that was buried on the farm was not a stillbirth. The case built up by the Gardaí against Joanne Hayes was riddled with inconsistencies. The Director of Public Prosecutions advised the Garda Superintendent to withdraw the charges at the earliest opportunity. On 10 October 1985 the Hayes family learned in court that all charges against them had been dropped. In response to the controversy generated by the Kerry Babies Case and criticism of the Gardaí, the Minister of Justice convened a tribunal of inquiry into the conduct of the Gardaí and the circumstances in which the charges against Joanne Hayes and her family had come to be made and withdrawn. This was meant to sit in Tralee for three weeks from 7 January 1986 but the inquiry lasted for five months during which 61,000 questions were asked of 109 witnesses.

Much of the inquiry focused on Joanne Hayes rather than upon the conduct of the Gardaí who had extracted dubious confessions and statements. The young woman to blame had entered into a sexual relationship with Jeremiah Locke, a married colleague at the leisure centre in Tralee where she worked as a receptionist. She became pregnant in 1982 but miscarried at work. The following year she became pregnant by him again and gave birth to a daughter who was accepted into her family. Then in 1984 she became pregnant for a third time, gave birth at home in the middle of the night to a baby who died and who she put in a paper bag, wrapped in plastic and placed in a waterlogged ditch near her home.

McCafferty's account of the inquiry used techniques honed during the 1970s in celebrated reports she wrote for the *Irish Times* on cases that came before the district courts.[1] These focused on the treatment of defendants by judges, lawyers and the Gardaí with acerbic humour but always with the serious intent of highlighting, as she put it, the gaps between law and justice. This was often managed by simply recording the remarks of judges ('I just let them open their mouths and put their feet in. I always named the judges, never the guards or the criminals').[2] *A Woman to Blame* challenged the ability of the male participants in the tribunal to understand Joanne Hayes's experiences:

> None of the fifteen legal men, comprising judge, senior and junior barristers and solicitors had ever witnessed childbirth. 'Is it possible', the judge was to ask 'for a woman to give birth standing up?' Women have given birth underwater, in aeroplanes, in comas, lying unnaturally flat on their backs in hospital beds, and even after death, but this man wondered if they could do it standing up. One had even a glancing experience of matters connected with the female reproductive system. Martin Kennedy, senior counsel for the three superintendents, had taken part in the pro-life campaign, canvassing the plush seaside suburb of Dalkey near Dublin.
>
> While Jeremiah Locke was engaging in serial impregnation of two women, Mr Kennedy had been assuring voters, on behalf of a Fianna Fáil party that opposed contraception for single people, that the baby in a woman's womb needed constitutional protection.[3]

McCafferty attacked what she saw as a fear and loathing of, and hypocrisy about, female sexuality that pervaded the inquiry. As put in the opening paragraph of her book:

> In the opening days of the 'Kerry babies' tribunal a married man went to bed in a Tralee hotel with a woman who was not his wife. He was one of the forty-three male officials – judge, fifteen lawyers, three police superintendents and twenty-four policemen – engaged in a public probe of the private life of Joanne Hayes.
>
> When this particular married man was privately confronted with his own behaviour he at first denied it. Then he crumpled into tears and asked not to be exposed. He had so much to lose, he said. 'My wife...my job... my reputation...' He was assured of discretion.
>
> No such discretion was assured to Joanne Hayes, as a succession of professional men, including this married man, came forward to strip her character.[4]

The Kerry Babies controversy occurred in the wake of the politics of the Eighth Amendment to the Constitution on the right to life of the unborn and exemplified the messy and uneven shift towards social liberalism that accompanied the decline of Catholic power. In the aftermath of Pope John Paul's 1980 visit to Ireland Catholic conservative groups pushed for a constitutional prohibition on abortion. McCafferty likened these to the neoconservative movements that had emerged in the United States following the 1973 Roe versus Wade Supreme Court ruling that allowed abortion. What she described as a 'fundamentalist backlash against feminism' occurred in a context where even divorce was still illegal in Ireland. Divorce, McCafferty recalled, had not even featured in the list of reforms sought by Irish feminist groups during the early 1970s. Even though there had been no campaign to legalise abortion in Ireland, Catholic conservatives managed to politicise the issue as a clear and present danger to the moral fabric of Irish society.

In 1983 almost seventy per cent of the electorate who voted in the Referendum approved of the insertion of a new Article 40.3.3 into the Constitution declaring that the State 'acknowledges the right to life of the unborn and, with due regard to the equal right of the mother, guarantees in its laws to respect, and as far as practicable, by its laws defend and vindicate that right'. Even though Catholicism was on the wane – Church attendance and vocations had been falling for two decades by then – a Catholic conservative public morality still prevailed.

The Kerry Babies case exemplified unresolved conflicts between this status quo and the real everyday lives of ordinary Irish people. The 'pro-life' campaign took place in a context where women who became pregnant outside of marriage – got into trouble being the common euphemism – were stigmatised and encouraged by welfare organisations to keep their pregnancies secret, usually by moving away from home until the birth of their child, then to give their babies up for adoption. Many others, an estimated 3,700 in 1983, travelled to England to have abortions. But during 1984 some 103 'illegitimate' births were registered in Kerry, almost two per week. The death of the Kerry babies occurred a few months after fifteen-year-old Ann Lovett gave birth to a baby in a grotto that celebrated the Virgin Birth in Granard, County Longford. Both mother and child died.

McCafferty's 24 February 1984 *Irish Times* essay on their deaths noted that the grotto was one of the most secluded places in Granard. The Convent of Mercy School retained a solicitor to issue a statement that its staff did 'not know' that Ann Lovett was pregnant. McCafferty referred to one dissident teacher who supposedly 'could not stomach' the nice legal distinction between 'knowing' and 'suspecting'. Such denials, she argued, conveniently placed all blame on the Lovett family:

The townspeople cannot or will not help them bear that ordeal. It will be up to the family to explain how could it be that their daughter died unaided and alone. The efforts of the townspeople are directed towards explaining how they, the townspeople, could not come to her aid, though her condition was common knowledge.[5]

Don't ask the State or the Church or the People, she concluded. They did their duty in 1983 by amending the Constitution so as to ensure that all pregnancies would be brought to full term; 'Nowhere in that amendment was provision made for life or lives beyond the point of birth.'

In her autobiography McCafferty recalled strident hostility towards women who campaigned for a right to contraception during the 1970s. The 'singing priest' Father Michael Cleary, a regular on radio and television programmes, was abusive when she leafleted his parish in Ballyfermot in 1977. It subsequently emerged that he had already fathered two children by the housekeeper who lived with him. Senator Mary Robinson, later Ireland's first woman President, received packets of excrement through the post at the time because she had sought to introduce a bill legalising contraception in limited circumstances.[6] Cleary was given a high-profile role in the reception of Pope John Paul in 1980 along with Bishop Eamon Casey who had also secretly fathered a child.

Support for the 'pro-life' referendum in Kerry had been very strong. Fifty of Kerry's leading sportsmen pledged their support for the campaign as did the two main local newspapers, *The Kingdom* and *The Kerryman*. Sermons by the local Catholic bishop pronouncing that artificial methods of contraception were sinful were published verbatim in *The Kerryman*. *The Kingdom* also backed the 'pro-life' campaign. It printed pictures of a foetus on its front page along with descriptions of abortions. Kerry's doctors and pharmacists, according to McCafferty, acted as moral policemen. None of the eight doctors in Tralee openly declared that they were willing to prescribe contraceptives. Some pharmacists were willing to sell the contraceptive pill when it had been prescribed as a cycle regulator. Ten of the twelve pharmacies in Tralee refused to stock condoms as did the sole pharmacy in Cahirciveen. Women seeking contraception advice in closely-knit communities could only do so by becoming conspicuous and by facing down disapproval and stigma. But Irishwomen of Joanne Hayes generation:

> ... had begun to take their place in the paid workforce, were asserting their sexual freedom, and were paying a painful price in the absence of contraceptive protection. The number of children born outside of marriage had risen from 1,709 in 1970 to 3,723 in 1980. The number of women seeking abortion in England had shot up from 1,421 in 1970 to 3,673 in 1983.[7]

The gap between social mores and laws governing sexuality was clearly widening. The Kerry Babies case highlighted the disjuncture between Catholic teaching on sexuality and how some at least Kerry Catholics expressed their sexuality, how the pregnancies of unmarried women were both known about but could not be spoken about in public or amongst families.

A Woman to Blame describes how hundreds of women sent individual yellow roses to Joanne Hayes, organised by a Tralee women's group. The first flower had been ordered with meticulous instructions on 20 January 1985: a single yellow flower, wrapped in cellophane, to be delivered to Joanne Hayes at the building where the tribunal was sitting before the one-thirty national radio news, if possible. As described in *A Woman to Blame* a feminist network 'had fretted into action' and thirty orders for flowers were placed – Joanne emerged from the courthouse later that day clutching them – followed later by hundreds more flowers, letters and mass cards as the campaign caught hold.[8] It would have been wishful thinking, McCafferty wrote, to conclude that there were that many active feminists in Ireland. Expressions of solidarity came from women in all walks of life:

> Joanne Hayes received more than five hundred letters, cards and notes which invoked, on her behalf, the intercession of a loving God who was clearly and certainly seen to be a cut above the human metronomes who clocked up her imperfections. Irish Catholics, wanting genuinely to be good, struggling desperately under a yoke of bewildering rules and regulations, wrote to Joanne Hayes that no man should be allowed to sit in judgement on the human sexual condition.[9]

A Woman to Blame gave prominent emphasis on expressions of solidarity to Joanne Hayes by other women appalled by her treatment. The effect of the Kerry babies controversy, McCafferty argued, was to break the fearful silence about sexuality that had been imposed by the amendment campaign:

> Joanne Hayes's public suffering evoked memories of private ordeals and tribulations, striking chords in a population that had never been able to fully subscribe to the officially sanctioned norm. The letters showed that during her days on the stand people were literally sitting by their radios and televisions, confessing with her, hoping it would never happen to them, grieving that such personal matters should ever see the light of excruciating day.[10]

In her autobiography McCafferty states that she had in fact organised the 'yellow flower' protest. She had been covering the tribunal for *The Irish Press*.[11] She had come to journalism out of the civil rights movement in Derry where she grew up. She was a lesbian in a country where homosexuality was criminalised and a member of women's groups struggling to find acceptance for female heterosexuality. She eschewed feminist theory for a language that spoke of the everyday lives of ordinary women and for the weapons of satire. In a 1983 essay 'Golden Balls', she described how the teenage son of a Fianna Fáil TD had taken to hanging around the Dáil Bar handing out 'pro-life' pins with tiny gold-plated feet. Her modest proposal was that instead, men should be allowed to wear a pair of golden balls on their lapels. These balls would signify that the wearer declines unprotected sexual intercourse with females of child-bearing age. Before they received their golden balls men would have to undergo a simple sex education course where they would be instructed on such matters as sperm count, menstruation, zygotes, implantation, nappy-washing, the four a.m. feed, the length of the Dublin Corporation housing list and the factors influencing the repayment of foreign borrowings which in turn influenced Ireland's ability to feed all newcomers. Any man found without his balls would have to give an account of his movements to a 'ban garda' (policewoman). Any man proposing sexual intercourse with a woman would be required to hand his balls into her safekeeping until such time as her period has arrived or the baby is born; in the latter case, possession of a man's balls by the woman would be proof of paternity.[12]

BF

Notes

1   Collected in Nell McCafferty, *In the Eyes of the Law* (Dublin: Poolbeg Press, 1981).

2   Nell McCafferty, *Nell* (Dublin: Penguin Ireland, 2004), p.295.

3   Nell McCafferty, *A Woman to Blame: The Kerry Babies Case* (Dublin, Attic Press, 1985), p.75.

4   Ibid., p.7.

5   Nell McCafferty, 'The Death of Ann Lovett', *Irish Times*, 24 February 1984.

6   See McCafferty, *Nell*, p.297.

7   Nell McCafferty, *A Woman to Blame: The Kerry Babies Case* (Dublin, Attic Press, 1985) p.33.

8   Ibid., p.115.

9   Ibid., p.117.

10 Ibid., p.117.

11 *Nell*, p.370.

12 Nell McCafferty, *In Dublin*, 3 June 1983.

27

Noel Browne, *Against the Tide* (1986)

In 1948, at the age of thirty-three, Noel Browne became Minister of Health. This occurred on his first day in the Dáil as a TD. Browne's early life had been defined by poverty and tuberculosis. Both his parents died from TB, his father in 1923 when he was eight, his mother when he was ten. When his mother was dying she moved the family to England and placed them in the care of her oldest daughter. Eileen Browne managed to get Noel into a Catholic preparatory school. From there he won a scholarship to Beaumont College. Beaumont was, in the words of its Jesuit Rector, what nearby Eton College once was, 'a Catholic school for the sons of gentlemen'. He spent many of his school holidays as a guest of one or other of his classmates. The Irish family of Lady Eileen Chance, daughter of William Martin Murphy, the newspaper magnate who led the Dublin Lockout against Jim Larkin's trade union in 1913, paid for his medical training at Trinity College Dublin. When Browne contracted TB in 1939 Lady Chance paid for his treatment in one of the best sanatoria in England. His experience as a patient influenced his subsequent medical career.

As one of the two Clann na Poblachta members of the 1948–51 Inter-Party government, the other being party leader Sean MacBride, Browne became embroiled in a controversy over the introduction of free health care for mothers and children, known as the Mother and Child Scheme. This brought down the government in 1951. Browne published the private correspondence between himself and MacBride about the affair. Browne's accounts of events – first at the time of the crisis and retrospectively in his autobiography *Against the Tide* – became an anti-clerical equivalent of Emile Zola's *J'accuse*. The Mother and Child Scheme controversy became one of the most picked-over events in the history of the Irish State and Browne's own account was the standard one. Critics of this account have attributed much of the controversy to Browne's political ineptitude. According to Conor Cruise O'Brien, then a civil servant working for MacBride, Browne was fatally undermined by his own ('anti-socialist') party leader.

Browne's account of his childhood poverty is as striking as the one in Frank McCourt's *Angela's Ashes*. In both cases the narrators who looked back on the chaos, dangers and misery of poverty around the time of Irish independence went on to become educated men; McCourt a teacher in New York, Browne, a doctor. McCourt has been criticised as an unreliable narrator but his childhood circumstances were especially bleak. His father's alcoholism precipitated and exacerbated the wretchedness of his children's lives. Browne described his father as having worked himself to death as an Inspector with the National Society for the Prevention of Cruelty to Children in Athlone. The job was physically arduous; it involved cycling long distances and his father suffered from severe pulmonary tuberculosis. He attributed his mother's early death at 42 years of age to the heavy burden of child-bearing and rearing while being afflicted with the same disease. One of his sisters also died in infancy. After his father's death the family lost their home. He died in the Newcastle sanatorium where his son later worked as a medical officer. In *Against the Tide*, Browne describes reading of the hopelessness of his father's case in his clinical notes:

> Because there was no free tuberculosis service then, hospital care had to be paid for. Since there was no hope that the out-of-work patient could pay as his income had stopped with his work, or was simply inadequate, he would be sent home to die. In the process he would infect one or more of his loved ones. Discharge home from a sanatorium was, in effect, a sentence of death for the patient, and possibly for many members of his family. There were frequent examples of families, in desperate hope of saving the life of a loved husband, wife or child, being compelled to sell off their small farm or business in order to pay for medical expenses or hospital care. Consultants would agree to treat patients only so long as they had money; as soon as the money stopped, the treatment also stopped.

The early sections of Browne's polemical memoir on the relationship between poverty and disease, though written several decades later, recall George Orwell's classic of the same genre, *The Road to Wigan Pier*. In Orwell's case a middle-class narrator inserts himself into the lives of the poor to make the case for socialist social reform. Orwell undoubtedly shaped the facts to best explain his case. Browne sculpted his memoir to explain his commitment to the radical reform of Irish health services. Browne's above-quoted account of the lack of TB services for the poor isn't quite accurate. The Tuberculosis Prevention (Ireland) Act (1908) authorised County Councils to establish sanatoria and dispensaries and take a range of measures believed to impede the spread of TB. Services gradually improved. Browne's father, an ISPCC Inspector, was one of the 700,000 insured persons covered for free medical care under the 1911 Health Insurance Act. The act also provided for free care for those unable to pay.[1] *Against the Tide* does not make this clear in making a broad point about health inequality.

Browne also shared Orwell's personal austerity. In *Against the Tide* enemies are described as gluttons. Browne describes an audience with his namesake Bishop Michael Browne, where the Bishop called 'in his rich round voice' for a glass of champagne, saying, 'I always like champagne in the afternoon' and offered him one of his impeccable hand-made cigarettes. 'These cigarettes', he intoned, 'I had to have made on Bond Street.' Browne's cabinet enemy and Labour Party leader William Norton, is described as wallowing in the sumptuous banquets arranged for visiting foreign dignitaries:

> My wife and I would watch incredulously as he would call for a second helping of his favourite sweet, a spun sugar confection which stood about four inches high and was shaped like a bird's nest. With his table napkin tucked firmly into his straining white collar, his flickering brown monkey's eyes would lovingly follow the waiter and his spoon as he loaded the plate down for the second time. Spoon and fork filled the sugary syrup into his mouth until there remained only the melted warm honey mixture on his plate. This too was greedily scooped into his now slobbering mouth. Like a hungry suckling piglet, frantically probing the fat sow's belly, spoon and fork were followed by his chubby fingers and last of all his thumb, each of them lovingly and lingeringly sucked dry. Fingers licked clean, he would hold a lighted scarlet and gold-labelled Havana in one sticky hand and caress his well-filled brandy glass in the other. Norton, the worker's leader, lived Larkin's 'Nothing is too good for the working classes.' But for the Irish worker the good things of life stopped at Norton.

Browne blamed Norton for undermining his efforts to promote the Mother and Child Scheme within government with the argument that he would not support a free health service for those who could afford to pay – a benefit that the fur-coated ladies of Foxrock would be entitled to – and with various other arguments against universal entitlement that were taken up by MacBride and Fine Gael.

Why the Mother and Child Scheme proposal resulted in such controversy puzzled Browne. It had been contained in the 1947 Health Bill drawn up by the previous Fianna Fáil government. It was more modest than the National Health Service reforms that had been implemented in Northern Ireland with little criticism from the Catholic Church. In the United Kingdom the medical profession successfully resisted collectivisation into NHS clinics, in the Irish case no such threat to the autonomy of privately practiced medicine was envisaged. But opposition from both the Irish medical profession and the Church began to gather steam and found expression in a shrill campaign that warned of the dangers of communism and children being forced to submit to intimate physical inspections by state officials. Browne was, as the title of John Horgan's biography puts it, a passionate outsider who misunderstood and wilfully ignored the rules of Irish politics.[2] He joined a small political party that came to hold the balance of power, having only been briefly an activist in a single-issue group of doctors concerned about TB. He describes shocking fellow members of the 1948–51 Cabinet with his opposition to political appointments for unqualified party hacks and friends of government ministers. He was the product of four Catholic schools but professed not to understand Catholic theology or social thought. As he had received secondary education in England and his medical training in Trinity, he did not experience the typical Irish Catholic formation of his medical peers and fellow politicians.

A letter from the Archbishops and Bishops of Ireland on 10 October 1950 to the Taoiseach, John A. Costello, suggested that the proposed Mother and Child Health Service was contrary to Catholic moral teaching and described it as contrary to Catholic social thought. The proposed service, if adopted into law, was described as constituting 'a readymade instrument for future totalitarian aggression'. Ceding the principle of a state role in the control of health care for families might, it argued, open up the way for birth control and abortion. There was no guarantee that State officials would not give gynaecological care in accordance with Catholic principles.

Browne was outmanoeuvred by the hierarchy. He believed that accommodation was possible. He prepared a memorandum and submitted it to the Taoiseach, intended for transmission to the Hierarchy ('Protocol insisted that a mere Cabinet minister had no direct access to an Archbishop's office') but Browne's effort at compromise was not passed on. This included a commitment 'that whatever guarantees the hierarchy wish in the matter of instruction of mothers would be unreservedly given'. On 10 October 1950 Browne was, in his own words, 'ordered to Archbishop McQuaid's palace by a telephone call from his secretary'. He was informed that there would be three bishops present and was 'bluntly told' that he might not bring his Departmental Secretary. At the meeting on the following day McQuaid read out the letter from the hierarchy to the government and having done so assumed that the meeting was over. Browne argued back, making his case for a free health service for the poor but he also proposed compromises. After the meeting McQuaid depicted Browne as unwilling to compromise his demands for a universal system.

The introduction to *Against the Tide* made it clear that Browne was neither a diarist nor historian and stated that he had kept no records. Later in his book Browne described how, having resigned as Minister of Health, he destroyed all documents in his files 'likely to be used or misused' against him.[3] Details of his narrative have been challenged by other advocates of health reform, notably by James Deeny, the Chief Medical Officer who designed and named the 'Mother and Child Scheme' in 1947. Deeny had been involved in the fight against TB for a number of years before Browne became Minister for Health. His 1989 memoir *To Cure and to Care* describes first meeting Browne when he was an assistant medical officer at (but doing most of the work in) a hospital that had changed little over the previous fifty years, having been himself a TB patient and having been trained in top English sanatoria:

> He had himself been very ill with tuberculosis himself and was lucky to be alive. Because of this, and for other reasons which at the time I did not know, he was very kind indeed to the patients, who adored him. Most of his professional life had been spent in TB institutions of one form or another, large or small, here and in England. Now, just as patients can become institutionalised, so can staff, and life for such people becomes a matter of living in a small world, with limited human experience and equally limited medical experience.

Deeny may have been right about Browne's medical career but not about his earlier life. In *Against the Tide* Browne describes how his childhood was an 'ephemeral, roller-coaster existence of continually appearing and then disappearing people, landmarks, and relationships'. Whilst very young he had to learn how to form instantaneous, superficially warm relationships with total strangers and form a succession of friendships in different families. When he was catapulted from the rank of junior medical officer to the post of Minister of Health it wasn't the first time that he found himself in a new milieu.

He claimed in his memoir that within a short period in office he quickly achieved 2,000 new bed spaces for TB patients. Deeny's memoir described how these had become available after a long period of planning that had begun before Browne entered politics.

Browne claimed responsibility for radical improvements in Irish hospitals that Deeny described in detail as the result of efforts over decades of many doctors and civil servants to improve public health services. A number of influential doctors had worked to improve TB services during the early 1940s, including Robert Collis and Theo Dillon, a brother of Fine Gael's James Dillon, who also took up the issue.[4] Against Browne's 'one man against the world' account of his time in government, Deeny emphasised the importance of scientific innovations in disease control and of improvements in the statistical monitoring of infant mortality. He also gave examples of behind-the-scenes conflicts. For example, he describes how in a home for unmarried mothers outside Cork city, 100 babies out a total of 280 born in a single year were found to have died at birth. On inspection infection was found to be everywhere. The home was closed down, its matron (a nun), and its medical officer sacked.

The Mother and Child Scheme controversy provided a simplistic but very influential account of the workings of Catholic power. In the wider analysis Catholic power was never just a matter of episcopal decree but emanated from a Catholic culture that had become the dominant societal one in the century since Cardinal Cullen's devotional revolution. Catholic politicians saw no need to ask clerics what to do. Catholic doctors like Deeny pursued on-going reform of health services in ways that did not place them in direct conflict with the Church. Catholic control of the education system and health care were seen as strategically necessary for the intergenerational reproduction of this Catholic Ireland. Browne challenged that status quo at a time when most of Ireland's social and political elite were part of it. His political project was never one directed against Catholicism. It was characterised by a socialist perspective that none of his Cabinet colleagues, certainly not those in the Labour Party, shared. Browne depicted himself as the only impediment to joint plans by the hierarchy and the medical consultants to deprive the public of a badly needed health scheme and while this scheme was important, the real challenge being mounted by the hierarchy was their implicit claim to be the effective government of the country. When Browne made public his correspondence with the hierarchy he brought down the government he was part of. His account of these events entered Irish political folklore and became a crucial nail in the coffin of Catholic power in Ireland.

Against the Tide is a political memoir by an arch-iconoclast who resigned from five political parties. After leaving Clann na Poblachta he tried to join the Labour Party but was blocked by Norton. After a spell as an independent TD he joined Fianna Fáil in 1954, recalling years later that he enjoyed the company of the party's rank and file. They were mildly iconoclastic and independent and 'given any chance at all would be first-class material for a properly developed society'. He was a member of the party's executive under the leadership of Eamon de Valera. He depicted de Valera as the architect of a conservative, sectarian Irish republicanism that bore little resemblance to his and Wolfe Tone's liberal secular kind. Again and again *Against the Tide* praises the English for their kindness to him and for their National Health Service. After his expulsion from Fianna Fáil in 1958, he co-founded a new party, the National Progressive Democrats. When this disbanded in 1964 he became a member of the Labour Party. He was elected an independent TD in 1977 and subsequently joined the Socialist Labour Party. He retired from politics in 1982.

BF

Notes

1   James Deeny, 'Towards balancing a distorted record: An Assessment of *Against the Tide* by Noel Browne', *Irish Medical Journal*, 80,8 (August 1987), pp.222–5.

2   John Horgan, *Noel Browne: Passionate Outsider* (Dublin: Gill and Macmillan, 2009).

3   James Deeny, *To Cure and to Care* (Dublin: Glendale Press, 1989), p.161.

4   Ruth Barrington, *Health, Medicine and Politics in Ireland 1900–1970* (Dublin: Institute of Public Administration, 1987), p.161.

28

Fintan O'Toole, *Meanwhile Back at the Ranch:*
The Politics of Irish Beef (1995)

In a 1994 essay, 'Scenes from the Birth of a New Morality', Fintan
O'Toole argued that the twin monoliths of Irish culture, the
Catholic Church and Fianna Fáil, had lost all credibility. It had just
become public knowledge that Cardinal Cahal Daly had known for
many years about Fr Brendan Smyth's sexual abuse of children but
had covered this up and that Bishop Eamon Casey had fathered a
son:

> If anything, Bishop Casey's fall from grace looked by
> the beginning of this week in November 1994 like a
> golden memory from an innocent past. On Monday,
> the three big stories on Irish radio and television news
> were the political repercussions of the Father Brendan
> Smyth case; the death of a Dublin priest in a gay sauna
> (fortunately, two other priests were on hand to give
> him the last rites), and the conviction of a Galway
> priest for the sexual assault on a young man. What was

significant was not that these events had occurred, but that they had come into the public domain.[1]

By a new morality O'Toole meant the replacement of blind trust in authority by expectations of accountability. The initial controversy in the Fr Brendan Smyth case centred on the fact that the Cardinal had not reported him to the police. The old presumption that the Church was somehow beyond and above the power of the State was now under direct assault. But it also emerged that the Irish State had delayed for months in extraditing Smyth to Northern Ireland where he was to stand trial for the sexual abuse of children. The Smyth affair came on top of the findings of a tribunal of inquiry (into the beef processing industry) established by the Oireachtas in May 1991. O'Toole diagnosed similar underlying pathologies in both cases:

> Even in the 1990s, the church had not grasped the fact that most Irish people now find such notions of unaccountable authority intolerable. But then neither had the State, or more precisely the State's vicar on Earth, Fianna Fáil. While Father Brendan Smyth's long career of abusing power and trust was beginning to break the surface of discreet silence, Fianna Fáil's use of power was also coming under scrutiny. The tribunal of inquiry into the beef processing industry was producing tangible, if complicated, evidence of a murky relationship between politics, business and the state.[2]

O'Toole's seminal 1995 book *Meanwhile Back at the Ranch* set the template for a whole genre of books on political corruption and the lack of accountability in Irish public life. The long-running Beef Tribunal for its part set the template for subsequent investigations into payments to politicians and planning corruption. It investigated relationships between the Goodman Group of companies, Ireland's largest beef processing company and the government led by Charles Haughey from 1987 to 1989. *Meanwhile Back at the Ranch* wove together evidence of murky business dealings, tax fraud and scams to defraud EU subsidies with analysis of a reckless government decision to guarantee payment to Goodman International for beef exports to Iraq.

Goodman International had an annual turnover of about £500 million during the 1980s and this accounted for about 4 per cent of Ireland's GDP. Larry Goodman sold 1.3 million head of cattle a year, 'one pound in every twenty generated in the country passed through this man's hands'.[3] Despite this, Goodman International paid only £80,000 corporation tax between 1986 and 1989 whilst drawing large-scale subsidies from the exchequer.[4] It made cash payments to non-existent companies so that employees could be paid off the books. It also made large donations to Fianna Fáil and to other political parties.

In September 1987 Haughey's government agreed to indemnify Goodman for the sum of $134.5 million for a beef sale deal with Iraq that depended on the Irish government providing credit insurance. On one hand the political view was that Goodman's success was in the national interest. Beef stamped as sold outside the EU was worth £150 million per annum to the Irish economy. Yet Goodman International was simultaneously under investigation for several kinds of fraud.

In 1983 a Cork customs officer discovered South African customs stamps en route to an Irish printer that had been ordered by one of Goodman's subsidiaries. The Department of Agriculture called in the Fraud Squad and this led to a three-year investigation of Goodman International. Much of Ireland's beef was sold to the EU beef mountain at subsidised rates. Further EU subsidies applied to beef sold outside Europe. There was much money to be made by surreptitiously relabelling the nature, origins and destinations of produce. Investigations of two of Goodman's plants revealed practices of over-declaring weights of shipments in order to increase the amount of export refunds from the EU, substituting ineligible trimmings and cheap cuts for the more expensive cuts declared on shipping cartons.[5]

For example, in 1991 a Goodman plant at Rathkeale obtained via the Department of Agriculture an EU contract to process and can 1,600 tonnes of frozen intervention beef as food aid to the Soviet Union. Some of the beef paid for by the EU was instead sold on to commercial customers. Low-grade meat, mostly frozen hearts, called 'buffer stock' was used to make up the weight of the cans bound for Russia. According to workers at the plant some of the beef hearts going into this enormous stew were green.[6] 'Anybody', Larry Goodman's counsel told the beef tribunal, 'who thinks that the meat industry is conducted according to the same principle as the activities of Mother Teresa of Calcutta would be mistaken.'[7]

Much of the beef Goodman supplied to Iraq went to feed Saddam Hussein's army, his officials and their dependents. Iraq was at war with Iran and neutral Ireland acquired a vested interest in success for Iraq.[8] The transaction with Iraq was fundamentally political. The deal was represented by Hussein's Ba'athist regime as one with the Irish state. It was in Iraq's geopolitical interest to turn its trade with Ireland into a political deal underwritten by the Irish government. The requirement that the Irish government provide export credit insurance covering the imports accomplished this. Goodman's contract with Iraq was for high-grade halal Irish beef that had been slaughtered no more than 100 days previously. The beef they got was often years old and invariably not halal; much of it was neither high grade nor Irish. In any case, Saddam Hussein never paid for his beef. The eventual losses covered by the Irish State were around €83 million.[9]

The previous government had refused to provide credit insurance for trade with Iraq partly because of the poor reputation Iraq had acquired for making payments and partly because of the Iran–Iraq war. Iraq had acquired the reputation for only servicing debts when ever-increasing amounts of credit were forthcoming. From 1983 the Department of Industry and Commerce had recommended limiting credit exposure to Iraq and in March 1987 Michael Noonan, the then Minister, submitted a memorandum to Cabinet confirming that no cover was being granted for Iraq and that this would remain the case until there was an identifiable improvement in Iraq's repayment record.[10] But within days after Fianna Fáil returned to power in 1987 this policy was reversed by Noonan's successor Albert Reynolds, without a Cabinet decision and with no input from government officials.

Meanwhile Back at the Ranch emphasised how Fianna Fáil's own history and that of the cattle and beef industry had long been intertwined. Fianna Fáil under de Valera had been rhetorically committed to the break-up of the cattle ranches and to the redistribution of the land to land-hungry labourers. In the post-Famine era many Irish nationalists, including John Mitchel, had equated cattle farming with land clearance. In 1687 William Petty, one of the architects of the Cromwellian plantation of Ireland, had notoriously proposed to James II that most of the Irish, one million persons in all, be transplanted to England, leaving Ireland as a thinly-populated agricultural 'factory'. The export of livestock coincided with emigration, often using the same cattle boats. But ideological ambivalence to the ranchers could not be squared with the economic importance of the beef industry.[11] Between 1932 and 1938 de Valera waged and lost an 'economic war' with Britain aimed at breaking Ireland's dependence on the cattle trade:

> Between the end of the economic war and the great shift in Irish political and economic policy in the early 1960s, cattle exports became a steadily more dominant fact of economic life. In 1937–8 cattle and beef exports accounted for just over half of all Irish agricultural exports. By 1960–1 they accounted for over 70 per cent. In the meantime emigration, mostly to Britain, reached

levels of 50,000 a year. William Petty's colonial vision of Ireland as a giant cattle ranch with the bulk of its population resettled in England was being realised.[12]

Goodman as a major political donor and economic player had access to Fianna Fáil's inner circle. Direct access to Reynolds and other government ministers and a very forceful personality enabled Goodman to bypass the proper channels by which applications for credit insurance, subsidies and other considerations would ordinarily be processed by government departments. Reynolds was cut from the same cloth as Goodman. He owed his wealth to a chain of rural dancehalls and later moved into the meat industry, specialising in the export of pet food as distinct from beef. Reynolds had a reputation for shrewdness and competence and famously refused to read any report that was longer than a single page, which turned out to be particularly reckless in the case of the Iraq deal. He took no heed of concerns about Goodman International or about the risks of indemnifying exports to Iraq raised by officials.

The Beef Tribunal found no specific proof of political corruption. O'Toole argued that the problem was not corruption per se, but that the government had abased itself and bent the law in support of Goodman:

> Over a period of five years, certain fundamentals of democratic government – accountability to parliament, the assumption that governments obey the law, the conduct of an independent foreign policy – had been set aside. The government had conducted a secret policy at odds with the stated principle of Irish neutrality, with public agreements between the government and social partners, with the constitutional requirement that the government be answerable to parliament, and, in some instances, of the law of the land. In effect, it had detached itself from the things which made democratic government democratic.[13]

For reasons that still remain unclear the Irish State placed the financial interests of one company above the national interest, a scenario that was arguably replayed on an immensely larger scale when in 2009 another Fianna Fáil-led government recklessly committed the Irish people to guarantee debts run up by a deeply corrupt and irresponsible banking sector.

What responses to revelations of cover-up of child abuse by the Church, of murky business deals by politicians and the State and the Northern Ireland peace process had in common according to O'Toole, was a momentum towards democracy: 'away from all forms of private power', whether it be the brute force of private armies, the subtle hints of senior churchmen, or the discreet intimacies of the Cabinet room. 'A new settlement in Ireland', he argued, would only be possible 'if ideas like democracy, accountability, consent and trust are given real meaning.'[14]

It was the mishandling of the Fr Brendan Smyth affair rather than the Beef Tribunal that brought down Albert Reynolds' government in 1994. Smith had sexually abused children in the United States, the Republic of Ireland, Scotland, Wales and in Northern Ireland over four decades. In 1990 The Royal Ulster Constabulary began an investigation into his abuse of children in the North. In August 1993 nine warrants for his extradition were submitted to the Republic's Attorney General Harry Whelehan, who Reynolds intended to appoint as president of the High Court. The Attorney General came under considerable criticism several months later for being unwilling to process the warrants. He was appointed regardless but resigned a few days later. This immediately triggered Reynolds' resignation as Taoiseach. The Attorney General's role in the Beef Tribunal investigations (acting for the government, O'Toole emphasised rather than in the public interest) had been to shield Reynolds from scrutiny. The Brendan Smyth affair proved the final straw for the Labour Party, Fianna Fáil's coalition partner. Irish society was ready to be outraged at clerical child abuse and the failure of the State to prosecute it but not yet ready for the new public morality O'Toole hoped would also apply to politics and the economy.

BF

Notes

1   Fintan O'Toole, 'Scenes from the Birth of A New Morality' in *The Ex-Isle of Erin* (Dublin: New Island, 1997), pp.197–235.

2   Ibid., p.205.

3   Fintan O'Toole, *Meanwhile Back at the Ranch: The Politics of Irish Beef* (London: Vintage, 1995), p.35.

4   Ibid., p.93.

5   Ibid., p.64.

6   Ibid., p.272.

7   Ibid., p.25.

8   Ibid., p.49.

9   Elaine A. Byrne, *Political Corruption in Ireland 1922–2010* (Manchester: Manchester University Press, 2012), p.125.

10 See O'Toole, *Meanwhile Back at the Ranch*, p.68.

11 Ibid., p.15.

12 Ibid., p.18.

13 Ibid., p.275.

14 Ibid., p.206.

29

Mary Raftery and Eoin O'Sullivan, *Suffer the Little Children: The Inside Story of Ireland's Industrial Schools* (1999)

In May 1999 RTE Television broadcast a three-part documentary series *States of Fear* directed by Mary Raftery. These programmes, together with *Suffer the Little Children,* the tie-in book published later that year, revealed extensive physical and sexual abuse of children in state-funded but clerically-run reformatory and industrial schools. There had been a steady drip feed of criticism in various official reports since the 1960s but damning evidence had been supressed and reports had been sanitised even as the industrial school system was being reformed out of existence. Powerful accounts by victims had emerged in novels such as *Nothing to Say* (1983) by Mannix Flynn and in memoirs such as *The God Squad* by Paddy Doyle (1988).[1] *Suffer the Little Children* was not the first book-length exposé of physical and sexual abuse of children in industrial schools, but it was the first systematic analysis.

In 1999 Eoin O'Sullivan, a social policy academic, gained access to Department of Education files with the support of the then Minister of Education Micheál Martin. When it became clear that civil servants were removing portions of files before allowing him to read them, he again sought the intervention of Martin and secured full access to those not exempt from being made public under the thirty-year rule that generally applied. On 11 May 1999, following the airing of *States of Fear*, Taoiseach Bertie Ahern issued a statement of apology on behalf of the State and all citizens of the State for a collective failure to intervene on behalf of victims of 'childhood abuse'. This apology fell far short of acknowledging the dynamic revealed in *Suffer the Little Children* of decades of complicity by the Irish State in supressing evidence of the physical and sexual abuse of children. This was taking place in Church-run institutions into which children had been placed, a process which was financed and in theory regulated by the State.

Raftery and O'Sullivan describe a 1968 visit by the then Minister of Education Brian Lenihan to Artane Industrial School. When he was leaving a fifteen-year-old boy approached him and begged him to stop the Brothers beating the boys. Lenihan, according to this former inmate, turned to his driver and said, 'Get me out of this fucking place.' This became a catchphrase amongst the boys. A year later, the industrial school at Artane was closed down.[2] Artane featured prominently in subsequent inquiries into institutional sexual abuse. The key questions for these were: who knew what and who failed to act on what they knew? Lenihan certainly knew enough to have written in 1966 to his predecessor Donogh O'Malley, complaining that Department of Education officials were unwilling to establish visiting committees for industrial schools. O'Malley's response was to establish an inquiry chaired by Justice Eileen Kennedy to examine the entire industrial school system. *Suffer the Little Children* closed with a discussion of the Kennedy Report (published in 1970) which was as up-to-date as the book could have been given the thirty-year rule governing the release of state documents. The Kennedy Report severely criticised the industrial school system and its woefully inadequate regulation by the Department of Education and 'sounded the death knell' of a model of institutional child care that had lasted a century.

The industrial school system was introduced to Ireland in 1868. More than 105,000 children were committed to such schools by the courts between 1868 and 1969. 40,000 of these were held in institutions run by the Sisters of Mercy who also ran the Magdalen Laundries in adjoining premises as part of what Raftery and O'Sullivan describe as a massive interlocking system:

> All these institutions were linked together in two key ways. Firstly many of the religious congregations who managed the reformatory and industrial schools also operated Magdalen laundries. Several orders of nuns had constructed large complexes, containing an industrial school, a reformatory and a Magdalen laundry all together on the same site. Secondly, these institutions helped sustain each other – girls from the reformatory and industrial schools often ended up working their entire lives in the Magdalen laundries. Many of the children of unmarried mothers, born in the county homes and Mother and Baby homes, were placed in industrial schools. In some cases the mothers themselves ended up in the Magdalen laundries.[3]

Under the 1908 Children's Act, children could be committed who were found begging, found to be without proper guardianship or visible means of subsistence or due to non-attendance at school or for having committed indictable offences. Most girls – over ninety per cent – were sent to industrial schools under the catch-all category of lack of proper guardianship. This covered children of unmarried mothers not eligible for adoption, children whose parents were incapacitated through illness, those of families unable to take care of them due to poverty and the children of families that had been broken up because of the desertion, imprisonment or death of one parent. About ten per cent were committed for non-attendance at school. The numbers committed for criminal offences were small; eleven per cent of boys and less than one per cent of girls.[4] The use of religious orders to process such children into adulthood was the cheapest option available to the Irish State:

> From the State's perspective, any of the more enlightened approaches that they were aware of would not only have cost more, but would also have been strenuously resisted by the Catholic Church as an erosion of its power.[5]

In 1924 there were more children in Irish industrial schools than in England, Scotland, Wales and Northern Ireland put together. Various reforms in Britain were bringing down the numbers of children committed to these, most notably the removal after 1919 of per capita state funding. The more children Irish industrial schools took in the more funding they received. Religious orders which turned a profit from children they kept or benefited from their labour were often unwilling to release them even when improvements in the circumstances of their families made this feasible. But a 1945 Department of Education memorandum noted that it would be cheaper to support at least one-third of the then-industrial school population by giving some financial support to the families of these children. Government officials believed that much of the funding that was allocated to support the care of such children was not being spent for this purpose by the religious orders. A 1945 memorandum from the Secretary of the Department of Education to the Department of Finance described this as a 'grave situation': children in several industrial schools were severely malnourished.[6]

During the mid-1940s Fr Edward Flanagan, the priest who founded Boys Town in the United States, published several articles in Irish newspapers condemning the use of violence against children in Irish industrial schools and described these as a disgrace to the nation. Spencer Tracy won an Oscar for his portrayal of Flanagan in the 1938 film *Boys Town*. Flanagan's criticism was dismissed by Irish politicians as exaggerated and as a slur on Ireland's reputation. In private correspondence quoted by Raftery and O'Sullivan, Flanagan wrote that he had removed the Christian Brothers from Boys Town ('they left after they found out that they could not punish the children and kick them around'). The Irish, he added, sent missionaries into foreign lands but needed to look at how they had turned their unwanted, unloved, untrained and unfed children at home into slaves. There would be, he believed, a day of reckoning for the Church in Ireland and for others who presided over the mistreatment of children:

> What you need over there is to have someone shake you loose from your smugness and satisfaction and set an example by punishing those who are guilty of cruelty, ignorance and neglect of their duties in high places. We have punished the Nazis for their sins against society. We have punished Fascists for the same reasons... I wonder what God's judgement will be with reference to those who hold the deposit of faith and who fail in their God-given stewardship of little children?[7]

In 1948 Flanagan, who was by then an advisor to President Truman on child welfare, wrote to the Irish government requesting permission to visit a number of penal institutions for adults and children. He died of a heart attack a month before the visit was scheduled to take place. Flanagan's allusions to Nazis and Fascists were not unreasonable. John, who was an inmate of St Joseph's Industrial School in Glin from 1945 to 1952, recalled the following punishment of some boys who had been caught trying to run away:

> I remember they made these fellows stand in the yard in the rain for hours. No one was allowed to talk to

them. It was a bit like a concentration camp – the boys,
with their heads totally shaved, falling on the ground
unconscious, passed out from exhaustion. They were
just left lying where they fell.[8]

One escapee from Glin had come to the attention of Fr Flanagan.
Notes in Fr Flanagan's archive described how fourteen-year-old
Gerald Fogarty had been severely flogged with a cat-o'-nine-
tails. He then ran away to his mother's house in Limerick, 34
miles away. A crowd consisting of the Fogarty family and their
neighbours – almost 100 people – marched to the offices of Martin
McGuire, a well-known Limerick businessman. McGuire was their
local councillor and was no less outraged. He wrote to the Minister
of Education asking if such punishment was legal. The doctor that
examined Gerald Fogarty sent in a medical report on his injuries
to the Department of Education. A reply letter on behalf of the
Minister to McGuire stated that appropriate action had been taken
but gave no details. What appropriate action, asked McGuire in
a follow-up letter. The reply stated that the Minister did not feel
called upon to give details or that McGuire had any right to such
information. On October 1945 Gerald Fogarty's mother received
a letter from the Head Brother at Glin stating that the Minister
of Education had granted a discharge to the boy.[9] In 1946 the
Department of Education had sent a circular to all industrial
schools stating that corporal punishment should be administered
only for grave transgressions and under no circumstances for
mere failure at school lessons and that under such circumstances it
should be limited to slaps on the open hand with a light cane or a
strap. All other forms of punishment were prohibited but none of
these prohibitions were enforced.[10]

In 1950, an employee of Glin wrote to the Minister of Education
Richard Mulcahy and later to the Minister of Justice Sean MacEoin
describing 'awful conditions' and harsh treatment of the boys,
naming specific Brothers who frequently beat boys with leather

straps. The whistle-blower suggested a surprise inspection of the industrial school. MacEoin wrote to the Department of Education demanding an investigation. But the complaint was dismissed and a hand-written annotation on the letter from MacEoin in the Department of Education file stated, 'No action required.'[11]

In 1951 Mulcahy pushed for an inquiry into the running of industrial schools that was successfully resisted by the Association of Reformatory and Industrial School Managers, all of who were clerics. The focus of the proposed inquiry was to have been on how State money was spent, for example, the proportion spent on food for children. A caustic 1955 report by a Department of Education official on St Conleth's Reformatory School in Daingean, Co Offaly, described the boys as less well cared for and worse fed than the farm animals kept by the school and expressed the opinion that very handsome profits were being made by the farm with no evidence of any of these being ploughed back for the benefit of the boys.[12] But no follow-up action was taken by the Department and hundreds of boys suffered miserable conditions over the sixteen years that followed.

Many of the former inmates quoted in *Suffer the Little Children* described experiences of beatings and physical abuse. Terry, one of four siblings sent to an industrial school in 1952 after their mother died (his father, a farm labourer, kept custody of two other children) describes beatings administered daily to children who wet their beds, which many did because of the anxiety they experienced. Similar stories emerged from many other industrial schools. Tom, who entered the industrial school system in 1951 at eighteen months of age, recalled an incident that occurred at Artane where he lived from 1959 to 1965:

> I was about twelve, and I'd grown out of my shoes. When I asked for a new pair the Brother wanted to know why. The old ones looked perfectly okay, he said. I told him they were too small, and he hit me

with a belt across the face. Sent me flying. 'Now tell me the truth', he said. I told him again, 'Because they're too small for me.' He hit me again, and asked me again, and this went on and on, and he kept hitting me. 'You're telling lies', he said at last. 'Your shoes are not too small, you're too big for your shoes.'[13]

In 1962, with the approval of Archbishop John Charles McQuaid, the chaplain at Artane wrote a report that documented extensive physical abuse of boys by Christian Brothers. *Suffer the Little Children* includes an account by 'Barney' who was incarcerated in Artane between 1949 and 1958 with his older brother. Their mother had died when he was seven years old. The boys were so hungry at times that they supplemented their diet with scraps meant for the furnace and food meant for animals kept on the farm. Barney described boys being so badly beaten that they used to suffer from 'head staggers' like punch-drunk boxers. He claimed that boys were chained to trees or had their heads shaved as punishment for misdemeanours. If one boy ran away all the others were punished by having their rations cut. He recalled incidences of suicide by boys who may have been amongst those buried in the unmarked graves found at Artane. Barney also described the sexual abuse of boys conducted in full view of the classroom by Brother Joseph O'Connor who was in charge of the Artane Boy's Band that played in the interval at major GAA matches in Croke Park.

Fr Moore's report was first made public by Archbishop Diarmuid Martin in August 2007, 45 years after it had been first received by Church and State. The supressed report described a culture of excessive physical punishment:

There seems to be no proportion between punishment and offence. In my presence a boy was so severely beaten on the face for an insignificant misdemeanour. Recently, a boy was punished so excessively and for so long a period that he broke away from the Brother and came to my house a mile away for assistance. The time was 10.45p.m., almost two hours after the boys retired to bed. For coming to me in those circumstances he was again punished with equal severity. Some time ago, a hurley stick was used to inflict punishment on one small boy. The offence was negligible.[14]

Fr Moore described the atmosphere at Artane as an 'unnatural situation' – 450 boys and a staff of 40 had no contact with members of the opposite sex – that 'invariably leads to a degree of sexual maladjustment in the boys'. Whether Fr Moore was alluding to sexual abuse is unclear. In Artane, according to Raftery and O'Sullivan, the children referred to this as 'badness', in the absence of a specific vocabulary to describe what many experienced. A former Artane inmate described what happened when a group of boys of which he was one reported a Brother who used to try to sexually abuse them:

> We were kind of afraid, in case the priest would go back and tell the Brother. We were really putting our lives on the line. I remember that when we told the priest, he didn't seem very surprised. Then about a week later, that particular Brother was gone. No explanations – he just wasn't around any more. And that was the last we heard of it.[15]

In 1966 *Tuairim* (in English, 'Opinion') published a pamphlet on the residential care of deprived children in Ireland.[16] One of its authors, Peter Tyrrell, had been committed to Letterfrack in 1924 at the age of eight along with his two elder brothers. Tyrrell wrote a harrowing memoir that was eventually published in 2006 as *Founded on Fear*, thirty-nine years after he burned himself to death on Hampstead Heath, having never recovered from the psychological damage caused by the physical abuse he experienced as a child.[17]

Although the *Tuairim* report was critical of the industrial school system it did not include, to Tyrrell's distress, any descriptions of the kinds of physical abuse he experienced in Letterfrack. In a 1958 letter to Tyrrell, Senator Owen Sheehy-Skeffington, in whose papers Tyrrell's memoir was discovered, argued that vested interests would obstruct efforts to redress the abuse of children in Letterfrack and elsewhere:

> Suppose I write to the Bishop of Galway? He is an arrogant and unscrupulous bully, whose only interest in the matter would be to warn any evil-doers, so that their tracks could be covered. Write to the Minister of Justice? I should be more hopeful there, though these political figures are a bit afraid of a row with anything that looks like a clerical collar. I know what he would tell me, that the matter was being looked in to, that it was all a long time ago, and that suitable action would be taken if required, but it was not the practice to divulge what action, if any, had been taken.[18]

Tyrrell in his memoir described the rations he received in a German prisoner-of-war camp in 1945 as much better than those at Letterfrack. Life in the camp was 'Heaven on earth' compared to that in the industrial school 'where children were brutally beaten and tortured'.[19]

The Kennedy Committee established by the Government in 1967 to examine the industrial and reformatory school system was, unsurprisingly, stonewalled by the Department of Education. In 1968 Justice Kennedy wrote to the Department seeking details of all complaints about such schools over the previous five years and details of how these complaints were dealt with. The Department's response more than a year later referred to just five complaints all of which, it claimed, had no basis.[20] Responses to questions put by doctors on the Kennedy Committee to Fr William McGonagle, then Chairman of the Association of Resident Managers of Industrial and Reformatory Schools, confirmed the frequent practice of getting boys to remove their nightshirts before punishment beatings at Daingean Reformatory School where McGonagle was in charge.[21] But this was the sole instance the Kennedy Committee managed to document of the physical abuse of children in the industrial school system.

A 1991 *Focus Ireland* report on residential care for children and adolescents in Ireland exemplified the desire to move on without acknowledging the pre-1970 abuse by children in industrial schools. In a section on the history of residential care, it described the dominance of religious orders over the industrial school system as the result of the unwillingness of local authorities to provide financial assistance. Just one sentence referred to a number of reservations about the operation of industrial schools, 'mainly concerning the nature of education and training obtained'. There was no mention of physical or sexual abuse. The report stated that criticisms of the system 'primarily in the form of autobiographical or semi-journalistic accounts of the past, do not reflect the present situation', the implication being that these could be discounted.[22]

Suffer the Little Children documented the failure of the State to protect children in its care even though much of the focus was on the culpability of religious orders that directly ran these institutions. Responses to revelations of such abuse cannot be completely disentangled from the anti-clericalism that accompanied secularisation. At the same time, as Nell McCafferty's book on the Kerry babies argued, the moral policemen of Catholic conservatism were not always priests. Officialdom in its various forms was implicated in the suppression of sexuality, the stigmatisation of lone mothers and the secret removal of their 'unwanted' children from families and communities.

In their 2012 book *Coercive Confinement in Ireland: Patients, Prisoners and Penitents*, Eoin O'Sullivan and Ian O'Donnell argue that the preservation of rural Irish society, as it had developed in the post-Famine era, required industrial schools for surplus children and mental hospitals for surplus adults just as much as it required emigration. After the Famine a stem-family system, where just one child would inherit the land and any others were expected to move away, predominated.[23] Memoirs like Peter Tyrrell's suggest that the wider community had a good idea how children were treated in industrial schools and such institutions were part of the local economy. Communal opposition, such as that which occurred with respect to Glin in 1945, was exceedingly rare. Catholic public morality took illegitimate children who threatened rights to property out of the equation. Industrial schools removed children who could not be cared for by their families from circulation. Emigration then removed many of these once they grew up. The State was unwilling or unable to develop the range of welfare services that could have provided alternative care for children wrenched away from their families. Nor did it introduce legislative reform until obliged to do so as a signatory of the UN Convention on the Rights of the Child (1989).

Such institutional failures were by no means unique to the Republic of Ireland even if Catholic public morality shaped the Irish case. Revelations of the experiences of children in Irish institutions mirrored those from Newfoundland and Australia, where similar Catholic institutions had become established. Other countries also have their histories of coercive confinement and institutional neglect. François Truffaut's 1959 film *Les Quatre Cents Coups* (The 400 Blows) depicted how a child became displaced from his family into institutional care in a similar way to some of the cases documented in *Suffer the Little Children.* In the two decades following the Childcare Act of 1991 there have been many further disclosures of on-going institutional failure. For example, the 2012 *Report of the Independent Child Death Review Group* identified 196 young people who died between 2000 and 2010 whilst in contact with social services. As scathingly put by Fintan O'Toole, the State put more time and effort into tracing farm animals than it did into tracing lost children.[24]

BF

Notes

1 Mannix Flynn, *Nothing to Say* (Swords: Ward River Press, 1983) and Paddy Doyle, *The God Squad* (Dublin: Raven Arts Press, 1988).

2 Mary Raftery and Eoin O'Sullivan, *Suffer the Little Children: The Inside Story of Ireland's Industrial Schools* (Dublin: New Island, 1999), p.380.

3 Ibid., p.18.

4 Ibid., p.22.

5 Ibid., p.15.

6 Ibid., pp.95–109.

7 Ibid., p.194.

8 Ibid., p.201.

9 Ibid., pp.212–15.

10 Ibid., p.206.

11 Ibid., p.222.

12 Ibid., p.104.

13 Ibid., p.114.

14 Fr Henry Moore, *Private Report on Artane Industrial School Commissioned by Archbishop John Charles McQuaid, Archbishop of Dublin and Primate of Ireland* (1962) <http://www.paddydoyle.com/category/father-moore-private-report-on-artane-industrial-school/>

15 Ibid., p.120.

16 Tuairim, *Some of our Children: A Report on the Residential Care of the Deprived Child in Ireland* (*Tuairim*: London, 1966).

17 Peter Tyrrell, *Founded on Fear* (Dublin: Irish Academic Press, 2006).

18 Letter cited in Tyrrell, *Founded on Fear*, p.173.

19 See Tyrrell, p.157.

20 See Raftery and O'Sullivan, *Suffer the Little Children*, p.229.

21 Ibid., p.230.

22 Focus Point, *At What Cost: A Research Study on Residential Care for Children and Adolescents in Ireland* (Dublin: *Focus Point*, 1991), p.45.

23 Eoin O'Sullivan and Ian O'Donnell, *Coercive Confinement in Ireland: Patients, Prisoners and Penitents* (Manchester: Manchester University Press, 2012), p.275.

24 Fintan O'Toole, *Irish Times*, 23 June 2012.

30

Elaine Byrne, *Political Corruption in Ireland:
A Crooked Harp?* (2012)

Nationalists usually described British rule in Ireland as being not only tyrannical and anti-national, but also as being inherently corrupt. The passing of the Union, the use of paid informers and the packing of juries to get the 'right' verdict were pointed to. The notorious case of Sadlier and Keogh, two popular leaders who were easily bought off by the Crown in the 1850s and the attempt by *The Times*, with the alleged connivance of the Conservative Party, to frame Parnell for conspiracy to murder were commonly cited. The spectacle of landlords happily pocketing rents in the midst of the Great Famine was continually harped on. It was noisily claimed that Ireland under the Union had been systematically overtaxed. The fact that public employment in Ireland commonly favoured Protestants over Catholics until the end of the nineteenth century was often pointed to as well. Native rule, it was implied tacitly, would be none of these things; it would be patriotic and even-handed, it would give justice without fear or favour and it would usher in a new era of public virtue.

Independent Ireland was a small place, with inherent tendencies toward the formation of monopolies because of that smallness. The ideology of the nationalists claimed that the union with Britain had worked to Ireland's disadvantage, Ireland having no product in which it had a comparative advantage other than cattle. In other words, the union had turned Ireland outside eastern Ulster into England's cattle ranch. Protectionism was touted as the remedy. It should be remembered that protectionism was being practiced by everyone else; there was little untrammelled international free trade in the world in the 1920s.

It seems incredible that the first systematic academic book on political corruption in independent Ireland only appeared in 2012. *Political Corruption in Ireland* is thoroughgoing and informative. It confirms the popular impression that government corruption in Ireland, although present from the beginning in the form of clientelism and preference being given to political allies of the party in power under both William Cosgrave's government of 1923–32 and Eamon de Valera's early governments from 1932 onward, intensified after 1960 or thereabouts. Corruption levels correlate strongly with economic take-off, which occurred about that time and with the retirement from office of the revolutionary generation. These rather puritan old warriors were replaced by men of a very different stripe, more 'modern' in the sense of wanting the country to become rich regardless of any moral decay that might accompany such a change, and wishing for the relaxation of such strictures on private behaviour as film and book censorship, prohibitions on divorce and contraception while supporting the extension of mass education to the general population. Interestingly, the book suggests that political corruption only really took off around 1980, becoming a public scandal only in the 1990s, at a time when both the Catholic Church and the State became objects of general public opprobrium in Ireland for the first time.

It could be argued that corruption literally followed the money; in the early years, there was less corruption because there was little to steal, and it increased as the country slowly became more prosperous. Alternatively, it could be argued that corruption became more fashionable as the culture became less puritan and pious. Certainly, the old men looked on their own successors with some distrust. Paddy Smith, an IRA veteran from Cavan and a Fianna Fáil government minister, remarked of the mohair-suited young men symbolised by Charles Haughey, 'there are worse ways of entering politics than with a rope around your neck'. Gerry Boland, another old IRA gunman, actively despised Haughey and the other young men: ' some of the young men make me actually sick and disgusted. And I feel inclined to kick myself for having helped to build up an organisation to be taken over by these chancers'. He also predicted famously at the same time that Haughey would drag the Fianna Fáil party into corruption and ignominy. However, it can be argued convincingly that de Valera, Lemass and the rest of the veterans did build up a political machine which virtually invited self-enriching behaviour, whether out of *naiveté*, insouciance or, as I strongly suspect, out of a pretty hard-headed conviction that if the country were to get rich it would also have to have crooks.

Among much else, Byrne has an interesting discussion of Irish libel laws. Notoriously, these laws have systematically threatened *pro bono publico* free speech in the country and have been used to protect the reputations of people who deserve no good reputation. As Irish corrupt behaviour increased in the 1980s, comments about it in the public press did not accelerate but remained at a low level until the 1990s, when improper behaviour by many public figures simply became common knowledge and could no longer be ignored by the public press or merely whispered about in pubs. Quite apart from legal considerations, elite control over the media meant that journalists could be threatened or simply refused employment in the country. In the early 1970s, Joe MacAnthony, a journalist, ran an exposé on the Irish Hospitals' Sweepstakes, a long-running sweep which had made millions for its promoters from the 1930s through to the 1960s with tickets being sold illegally in Britain and America through Irish emigrant networks. Only a small proportion of the profits actually went to the hospitals. The rest illegally enriched a small group of people mainly associated with the Fine Gael party. MacAnthony was effectively unemployable in Irish journalism and was forced to emigrate to Canada; he was given an offer he could not refuse.

There were many other similar cases which went unreported for obvious reasons. Ireland's small size in itself encouraged the suppression of free speech through the passive consent or even explicitly expressed will of the people; Tocqueville's tyranny of the majority certainly prospered in Ireland for a long time, and is very certainly not dead yet. Byrne writes:

One of the most striking features of Irish corruption, as revealed by Tribunal inquiries in the 1990s, is that illegal activities were often closely interrelated because of elaborate networks of corrupt exchange. In other words, corruption operated within a *system* rather than the mere aggregation of isolated illegal acts. It had become a market, which, as in the case of every functioning market, has developed internal rules governed by the laws of supply and demand.

There was a limited appreciation [in Ireland] of the corrosive effects of clientelism and patronage. Political will failed to tackle corruption and a self-interested definition of national interest and impunity from consequences for impropriety characterised Irish political culture. The role of clientelism and patronage was understood from within a narrow interpretation of the terms involved.[1]

She argues that the exercise of corruption is anti-democratic because it seeks to give unfair and commonly illegal advantages to a favoured few over the heads of the general population. In this she is quite right, but such disadvantaging is often consented to by the electorate. Known crooks are commonly regarded as local patriots and protectors of the local interest against the intentions of 'those people in Dublin' or even 'those people' in Brussels or New York. The revelations of the Tribunals have severely damaged public trust in Irish government and its leaders. The slippage since 2008 is catastrophic, and Irish governments and politically powerful public figures had better look to themselves and their public image. The old protections of a cautious media, a timid academia and the libel laws have weakened or even disappeared.

However, old corruption is not dead in Ireland and it has staunch supporters. Everybody is against corruption unless it is the practice of 'one of our own'. 'One of our own' is invariably the local hero who gets one up on those folk in Dublin. Irish political history is replete with these local heroes, the prototype again being Charles Haughey, who proctored 'deals' for north side and central Dublin, giving to the poor and politically mobilised while stealing millions from everyone else. In two powerful books, roughly contemporaneous with Byrne's work, Fintan O'Toole documents the extraordinary mixture of greed and anti-intellectualism that wrecked the country and condemned it to an extended period of stagnation and possibly something worse.[2] In 2012, Fintan O'Toole wrote in an afterword of sorts to these polemics:

> Sometimes, you forget how tenuous and fragile a thing is the Irish State, how little it means to so many of its citizens. … The State is a set of institutions – the Government, the Oireachtas, the Civil Service, the law, the courts. It is also a broad but crucial sense of mutual dependence – the idea that there's a collective self that goes beyond the narrow realms of family and locality.
>
> To function at all, we have to make the working assumption that those institutions and that idea are

part of what we are, that, however vehemently we disagree with each other about however many things, there is this common ground on which we stand.

Even when we rail against the institutions (for loyalty is not the same thing as passive obedience), we do so because we identify with them – they are ours to criticise. And even when we are angry at our fellow citizens, we recognise that what affects them affects us too, that there is such a thing as a common good.[3]

O'Toole goes on to point to a large minority in Irish society who have contempt for the law and for the state. There are those who regard non-compliance with the law and even downright criminality as being a form of patriotism rather than it being the exact opposite, a form of betrayal of the Irish people and its public institutions. Some, but very certainly not all, of this is Northern Irish, where the IRA myth of the alleged sell-out of the North by Dublin in 1922 is widely accepted even now among nationalists. This myth is a handy one: it excuses bad and even illegal behaviour on their part in the Republic. It would be interesting to see how many people involved in the recent wave of public scandals have northern or border backgrounds and close or distant IRA connections. Yet again, Haughey furnishes the prototype.

Malachy Mulligan suggests to Stephen Dedalus in the first chapter of *Ulysses* that these young men at the Forty Foot swimming hole would have to 'Hellenise' Ireland in the twentieth century. A century later, Ireland has indeed come to resemble Greece, but not the classical Greece the young men dreamed of, rather the modern one of tax-dodgers and bribery. Both Byrne and O'Toole suggest reforms in the form of new laws and constitutional amendments. Many of these are very good ideas indeed. However, there is one reform that suggests itself above all others to this writer and is not explicitly suggested by either author: the abolition of all libel laws with the possible exception of allegations of capital crimes such as murder, and the substitution for them of an unconditional right of public reply. As it stands at present, the law permits lawyers acting in defence of criminals to do so as is indeed their right, but also to threaten whistle-blowers acting *pro bono publico* with loss of livelihood and financial ruin. The law is possibly unconstitutional, as it is a direct and often-used impediment to freedom of speech. The United States has virtually no libel law, and gets along quite nicely without one. Instead of whispering in pubs, people would have the right to say openly what they thought of anyone else, and the other the unfettered right to answer back. Secrecy is the real bane of Irish public life, and corruption feeds off an apparently widely accepted culture of furtiveness. 'Mind You, I've Said Nothing,' is still an unofficial national motto.

TG

Notes

1   Elaine A. Byrne, *Political Corruption in Ireland: A Crooked Harp?* (Manchester: Manchester University Press, 2012), pp.237–8.

2   Fintan O'Toole, *Ship of Fools* (London: Faber and Faber, 2009); O'Toole, *Enough is Enough; How to Build a New Republic* (London: Faber and Faber, 2010).

3   Fintan O'Toole, *Irish Times*, 7 August 2012.

Publishing References

1. Geoffrey Keating, *The History of Ireland/Foras Feasa ar Éirinn* [1634] (London: The Irish Texts Society, 1902–1914).

2. William Molyneux, *The Case of Ireland's being bound by Acts of Parliament in England, Stated* (Dublin, 1698).

3. Jonathan Swift, *A Modest Proposal* (Dublin, 1729).

4. Andrew Dunleavy, *The Catechism of Christian Doctrine* [Paris, 1742], (third edition Maynooth, 1848).

5. William Theobald Wolfe Tone (ed.), *The Autobiography of Wolfe Tone* (Washington: Gales & Seaton, 1826).

6. John Mitchel, *The Jail Journal* [1861] (Dublin: Gill & Son, 1913).

7. Horace Plunkett, *Ireland in the New Century* [1904] (Port Washington, NY: Kennikat Press, 1970) and Michael O'Riordan, *Catholicity and Progress in Ireland* [1905] (London: Kegan Paul, Trench, Trubner and Co., 1906).

8. James Connolly, *Labour in Irish History* (Dublin: Maunsel, 1910).

9. Canon Patrick A. Sheehan, *The Graves at Kilmorna* [1913] (Dublin: Phoenix, n.d.).

10. Desmond Ryan (ed.), *Collected Works of Padraic H. Pearse: Political Writings and Speeches* (Phoenix: Dublin and Belfast 1917).

11. Daniel Corkery, *The Hidden Ireland: A Study of Gaelic Munster in the Eighteenth Century* [1924] (Dublin: Gill and Macmillan, 1970).

12. P.S. O'Hegarty, *The Victory of Sinn Fein: How it Won It and How it Used It* (Dublin: Talbot Press, 1924).

13. Tomás O Criomhthain, *An tOileánach* (Dublin: Educational Company of Ireland, 1929).

14. Frank O'Connor, *Guests of the Nation* (London: Macmillan, 1931).

15. Sean O'Faoláin, *King of the Beggars* (London: Nelson, 1938).

16. Flann O'Brien, *At Swim-two-Birds* (London: Longmans, 1939).

17. James Kavanagh, *Manual of Social Ethics* (Dublin, Gill and Sons, 1954).

18. Paul Blanshard, *The Irish and Catholic Power: An American Interpretation* (Boston, MA: Beacon Press, 1954).

19. Michael Sheehy, *Divided We Stand* (London: Faber and Faber, 1955).

20. Edna O'Brien, *The Country Girls* (London: Hutchinson, 1960) and John McGahern, *The Dark* (London: Faber and Faber, 1965).

21. Cecil Woodham-Smith, *The Great Hunger* [1962] (New York: Old Town Books, 1989).

22. Conor Cruise O'Brien, *States of Ireland* (London: Hutchinson, 1972); revised version, (St Albans: Panther, 1974).

23. A.T.Q. Stewart, *The Narrow Ground* [1977] (London: Faber and Faber, 1989).

24. C.S. Andrews, *Dublin Made Me* (Dublin: Mercier Press, 1979).

25. Nell McCafferty, *A Woman to Blame: The Kerry Babies Case* (Dublin: Attic Press, 1985).

26. Noel Browne, *Against the Tide* (Dublin: Gill and Macmillan, 1986).

27. Fintan O'Toole, *Meanwhile Back at the Ranch: The Politics of Irish Beef* (London: Vintage, 1995).

28. Mary Raftery and Eoin O'Sullivan, *Suffer the Little Children: The Inside Story of Ireland's Industrial Schools* (Dublin: New Island, 1999).

29. Elaine Byrne, *Political Corruption in Ireland: A Crooked Harp?* (Manchester: Manchester University Press, 2012).

Index

271